Protestant – Catholic – Jew

WILL HERBERG is Graduate Professor of Judaic
Studies and Social Philosophy at Drew University. He is well known as a lecturer and writer
in the areas where religion, philosophy and the
social sciences overlap, and writes regularly for
the better secular and religious journals. He is
the author of *Judaism and Modern Man* (Farrar, Straus, and Young, 1951), *The Writings of
Martin Buber* (Meridian, 1956) and *Four
Existentialist Theologians* (Doubleday Anchor
Books, 1958).

Protestant—Catholic—Jew

AN ESSAY IN AMERICAN
RELIGIOUS SOCIOLOGY

by Will Herberg

A NEW EDITION, COMPLETELY REVISED

Anchor Books
Doubleday & Company, Inc.
Garden City, New York

To the Third Generation
upon whose "return" so much of
the future of religion in America depends

Protestant-Catholic-Jew was originally published by
Doubleday & Company, Inc. in 1955.

Anchor Books revised edition: 1960

COVER BY GEORGE GIUSTI
TYPOGRAPHY BY EDWARD GOREY

Library of Congress Catalog Card Number 60–5931

Foreword

This work is a revision of *Protestant-Catholic-Jew: An Essay in American Religious Sociology*, which first appeared in 1955. It is a thoroughgoing revision in the sense that every part of the book, including the material in the notes, has been carefully re-examined in the light both of the criticisms of the original edition made in published reviews or in personal communications, and of the new material that has come to my attention in the past five years. I am immensely grateful to my many reviewers, as much for their criticisms as for the kindness with which they have received my book; and perhaps even more grateful to those of my readers who have taken the trouble to call to my attention certain aspects of the problem I had overlooked and to certain errors I had committed. I have attempted to take all their criticism and comment into account in this revision, and I hope they will forgive me if I have not always done so with the thoroughness and understanding they had reason to expect. On some points, of course, differences of opinion remain, but I am none the less grateful for the criticisms I could not accept.

The effort has been made to bring the factual and statistical material up to date. Extensive revisions and additions in the notes reflect this effort.

My wife, to whom my indebtedness is so inadequately expressed in the preface of the original edition, collaborated at every stage of the revision. It is an unspeakable grief to me that she is no longer here to receive this revised edition when it appears.

WILL HERBERG

October 1959

Preface

This book is subtitled "An Essay in American Religious Sociology." The phrase implies that what I am attempting is not a comprehensive treatise on the sociology of religion in the United States, but a study of one aspect of the religious situation in this country from a sociological standpoint, in the hope that it may contribute to a better understanding of both religion and society in mid-twentieth century America. The thesis is stated, at least in its essentials, in the earlier chapters, and is developed in a number of directions and in a variety of implications in the rest of the book. The last chapter is devoted to a brief theological appraisal and critique.

My own theological position, which of course helps to define the standpoint from which this study of religion in America was undertaken and carried through, is indicated in the last chapter. A much fuller statement will be found in my earlier work, *Judaism and Modern Man: An Interpretation of Jewish Religion* (Farrar, Straus, and Young, 1951).

The present work is an interpretation of the religious situation; as an interpretation, it is naturally selective in its choice of materials and in its emphases. It is my belief, however, that this selection is not arbitrary, and that the interpretation I advance has come out of a close study of the materials and may be validated in their terms. These materials, I should add, include the data accumulated in the course of years of personal observation of religion in America and concern with its problems.

Since this is an interpretation based on materials largely familiar to students in the field, I have limited my references to sources of quotations and to collateral matter of special interest. As far as possible, I have cited works easily available in English. A list of works cited precedes the index.

My indebtednesses are many and heavy. The writings of H. Richard Niebuhr and Oscar Handlin have, from different directions, deeply influenced my understanding of the present religio-social situation in this country, although they are in no way, of course, to be held responsible for my conclusions. I am indebted also to the sociologists, church historians, and theologians, Protestant, Catholic, and Jewish, with whom I discussed this book while the work was in progress; their encouragement, criticism, and suggestions have proved invaluable. Though I cannot list them by name, they know how profoundly grateful I am for the help they have given me.

I am particularly indebted to my audiences at Union Theological Seminary, Jewish Theological Seminary, and Woodstock College for the insights, challenges, and stimulation that came to me when I lectured at these institutions on "Religion in America," covering the major themes developed in this work.

What I owe to my wife cannot be detailed here, or for that matter, appreciated by anyone but the author himself. She has collaborated with me in every phase and stage of the work, and now that it is over, I realize with deepest gratitude how invaluable her sensitivity and her critical insight have been.

WILL HERBERG

April 29, 1955

CONTENTS

I. Religion in America: The Problem

The religious situation in the United States today confronts us with a perplexing problem. "The fact of a religious revival in America cannot be gainsaid," Barbara Ward noted in her lucid "Report to Europe on America." "We did not need the evidence of polls or church attendance to confirm what we could so easily observe—the walls of new churches rising in town and countryside wherever we went."[1] Miss Ward's impression is fully borne out by the available evidence. Whether we judge by religious identification, church membership, or church attendance, whether we go by the best-seller lists, the mass media, or the writings of intellectuals, the conclusion is the same: there is every sign of a notable "turn to religion" among the American people today.[2]

And yet, writing not much before Miss Ward's visit, a perceptive historian of America noted that at the mid-twentieth century, "the trend toward secularism in ideas was not reversed."[3] Professor Handlin could find as much evidence for his conclusion as Miss Ward for hers, though the secularism to which he referred is not something that can be pointed out as obviously as Miss Ward's evidences of a religious revival. The secularism dominating the American consciousness is not an overt philosophy; it is an underlying, often unconscious, orientation of life and thought. Because it is so pervasive and omnipresent, it is hard to put one's finger on it. Yet perhaps something of what it implies may be suggested by a startling contrast. When Ignazio Silone, the Italian writer and Socialist, was asked what he felt to be the "most important date in universal history," he replied unhesitatingly: "The twenty-fifth of December in the year zero."[4] But when nearly thirty outstanding

Americans were asked not long ago to rate the hundred
most significant events in history, first place was given to
Columbus' discovery of America, while Christ, His birth or
crucifixion, came fourteenth, tied with the discovery of X
rays and the Wright brothers' first plane flight.[5] Silone is
no orthodox Christian, yet it is evident that he takes his
Christianity seriously in a way that the eminent American
historians, educators, and journalists, who forgot all about
Christ in listing significant events in history, obviously do
not. The secularism that pervades the American consciousness is essentially of this kind: it is thinking and living in
terms of a framework of reality and value remote from the
religious beliefs simultaneously professed.

In the five years from 1949 to 1953 the distribution of
Scripture in the United States increased 140 per cent,
reaching an all-time high of 9,726,391 volumes a year.[6]
People were apparently buying and distributing the Bible
at an unprecedented rate. Furthermore, over four fifths of
adult Americans said they believed the Bible to be the "revealed word of God," rather than merely a "great piece of
literature."[7] Yet when these same Americans were asked to
give the "names of the first four books of the New Testament of the Bible, that is, the first four gospels," 53 per
cent could not name even one.[8] The Bible can hardly be
said to enter into the life and thought of Americans quite as
much as their views on its divine inspiration and their eager-
ness to buy and distribute it might suggest.

This is at least part of the picture presented by religion
in contemporary America: Christians flocking to church, yet
forgetting all about Christ when it comes to naming the
most significant events in history; men and women valuing
the Bible as revelation, purchasing and distributing it by
the millions, yet apparently seldom reading it themselves.
Every aspect of contemporary religious life reflects this
paradox—pervasive secularism amid mounting religiosity,
"the strengthening of the religious structure in spite of increasing secularization."[9] The influx of members into the
churches and the increased readiness of Americans to identify themselves in religious terms certainly appear to stand
in contrast to the way Americans seem to think and feel

about matters central to the faiths they profess. America seems to be at once the most religious and the most secular of nations.

The paradox is there, and it would be misleading to try to get rid of it by suppressing one or the other side of the apparent contradiction. It will not do to brush aside the evidences of religious revival by writing off the new religiousness as little more than shallow emotionalism, "escapism," or mere pretense. The people who join the churches, take part in church activities, send their children to church schools, and gladly identify themselves in religious terms are not fools or hypocrites. They are honest, intelligent people who take their religion quite seriously. Of that there cannot be much doubt.

Nor, on the other hand, can there be much doubt that, by and large, the religion which actually prevails among Americans today has lost much of its authentic Christian (or Jewish) content. Even when they are thinking, feeling, or acting religiously, their thinking, feeling, and acting do not bear an unequivocal relation to the faiths they profess. Americans think, feel, and act in terms quite obviously secularist at the very time that they exhibit every sign of a widespread religious revival. It is this secularism of a religious people, this religiousness in a secularist framework, that constitutes the problem posed by the contemporary religious situation in America.

It is the thesis of the present work that both the religiousness and the secularism of the American people derive from very much the same sources, and that both become more intelligible when seen against the background of certain deep-going sociological processes that have transformed the face of American life in the course of the past generation. The distinctive character of American religiosity, so perplexing at first sight in its contradictions and discrepancies, becomes somewhat more intelligible when so interpreted, and the entire religious situation is viewed in its essential relation to the inner development of American society. American religion and American society would seem to be so closely interrelated as to make it virtually impossible to understand either without reference to the other.

And yet, in an inquiry such as this, we must not overlook
that there is something rash and presumptuous in dealing
so confidently with the "religious situation." The religious
situation is indeed in one sense a part of the social and cultural situation and therefore subject to scrutiny and analysis.
But in another sense it is something that transcends the
social and cultural framework in which it is embedded, and
takes on a dimension that relates it to the divine-human
encounter to which it ultimately refers. On this level, objective inquiry, analysis, and forecast become rather dubious if not altogether irrelevant, for man's faith in response
to God's call is not something that can be charted or reduced to plan. When we deal with the religious situation,
we are brought up short before the final mystery in a way
that is even more immediate than in the ordinary affairs of
life. No one who has given any serious thought to the problem of religion can have escaped this sense of depth beyond
depth in dealing with his subject, or have failed to become
conscious of the inherent limitations of objective study. Yet
within these limitations, much of significance may be
achieved by critical inquiry, much too that may contribute
to an understanding of the religion and the sociology of
contemporary America.

FOOTNOTES

1. Barbara Ward, "Report to Europe on America," *The New York Times Magazine,* June 20, 1954.

2. For some of this evidence, see below, chapter iv. Some observers have challenged this conclusion; see Seymour M. Lipset, "Religion in America: What Religious Revival?", *Columbia University Forum,* Winter 1959. For some further comments on the situation and on Lipset's criticisms, see my article, "Is There a Religious 'Revival'?", in a forthcoming issue of *Review of Religious Research.*

3. Oscar Handlin, *The American People in the Twentieth Century* (Harvard, 1954), p. 222.

4. The interview with Silone is reported in *Dissent,* Vol. I, No. 4, Autumn 1954. When asked about the "most important date in recent history," Silone replied: "June 17, 1953, when the East German workers mutinied [against Communist rule]." These two answers, following each other, neatly illustrate the organic

fusion of faith and contemporary social interest in Silone's thinking.

5. See report in *Time*, May 24, 1954. After Columbus' discovery of America in first place, came Gutenberg's development of movable type in the second; eleven events tied for the third place; five events tied for the fourth, among which Jesus' crucifixion was one. Thus the crucifixion was preceded in order of importance by thirteen other events.

6. Report of the American Bible Society at its 138th annual meeting, *Time*, May 24, 1954. The upward trend has continued.

7. "What Do Americans Think of the Bible?", *The Catholic Digest*, May 1954. This article presents the results of a survey by Ben Gaffin and Associates, an independent commercial opinion research agency; it is part of an extensive public opinion survey on religion in America conducted by this agency and published in thirty articles in *The Catholic Digest* from November 1952 to May 1954.

8. *Public Opinion News Service* (Gallup poll), March 31, 1950. The poll showed: naming all four gospels, 35 per cent; naming three, 4 per cent; naming two, 4 per cent; naming one, 1 per cent; naming none, 53 per cent. See also *Public Opinion News Service*, December 20, 1954.

9. Marshall Sklare, *Conservative Judaism: An American Religious Movement* (Free Press, 1955), p. 39.

II. *From the Land of Immigrants to the Triple Melting Pot: Immigration and the Ethnic Group*

"Once I thought to write a history of the immigrants in America. Then I discovered that the immigrants *were* American history." These opening words of Oscar Handlin's moving story of immigration to America[1] point to a profound truth about the American people. Aside from the remnants of Indian tribes, the United States has no autochthonous population; all of its 160,000,000 people are either themselves immigrants or else descendants of more or less recent immigrants. Every aspect of American history, every phase of American life, bears testimony to this fact.

The colonists who came to these shores from the time of the founding of Jamestown in 1607 to the outbreak of the Revolution were mostly of English and Scottish stock, augmented by a considerable number of settlers of Dutch, Swedish, German, and Irish origin. They were predominantly Protestant, and gave a Protestant direction to American religious life from the very beginning. At the time of the Revolution, this British-Protestant element (usually, though inaccurately, known as "Anglo-Saxon") constituted at least 75 per cent of the 3,000,000 whites who made up the new nation. In addition, there were about three quarters of a million Negroes.

The great influx came in the next century. In three huge waves, stretching over something more than a hundred years, over 35,000,000 men and women left Europe to come to continental United States. By the time the great migrations were past, the British-Protestant element had been reduced to less than half the population, and Americans had become linguistically and ethnically the most diverse people on earth.[2]

I

The ultimate source of the movement that brought these millions to the New World was a profound disturbance in the social and economic conditions of the Old. The revolution in industry and agriculture that got under way in the eighteenth century had shattered the old structures of town and country in many parts of Europe and had given rise to large numbers of displaced peasants and artisans who could not hope to repeat the age-old patterns of life that had provided some measure of security for their ancestors. The vast increase in population,[3] linked with the sweeping transformation in technology and productive methods, created a pressure that could only be relieved by emigration, and emigration of course meant emigration to the New World.

By the 1840s the annual number of immigrants was in the hundreds of thousands; indeed, in each of the years between 1847 and 1857 more than 200,000 newcomers reached these shores, the high point being 400,000 in 1854. These immigrants were predominantly from Britain, southwest Germany, and, after the great famine of 1846, from Ireland. The next wave, bridging the years from the conclusion of the Civil War to the opening of the new century, brought millions more—from Britain, Germany, and Ireland, as before, but also Scandinavians and many from eastern Europe. In fifteen of the thirty-five years from 1865 to 1900 the annual influx went beyond 400,000, with some 800,000 entering in 1882 alone. Through the first decade and a half of the new century up to the outbreak of World War I, all previous levels were surpassed: in three of the fifteen years the figure reached a million; in 1907 it topped 1,250,000. This third wave brought many of the older stocks, but also many more from Italy, Poland, Austria, Russia, Greece, and the Balkans. Virtually every European linguistic dialect and ethnic strain was now to be found within the confines of continental United States, together with many more from Africa, Asia Minor, and the Far East.

This "epic story of the great migrations that made the American people"[4] came to an end substantially with World War I and with the restrictive legislation of the 1920s. By that time 35,000,000 Europeans had reached these shores: 4,500,000 from Ireland, 4,000,000 from Great Britain, 6,000,000 from central Europe, 2,000,000 from the Scandinavian lands, 5,000,000 from Italy, 8,000,000 from eastern Europe, and 3,000,000 from the Balkans. This was America.

With some significant exceptions, most of these millions were peasants from the innumerable villages that dotted the map of Europe, and there is no doubt that they hoped to settle on the land and re-establish the old forms of life when they came to the New World. And, especially in the earlier period, many of them did. But the vast majority of the immigrants never went much beyond the ports of debarkation or the great inland railroad centers. Through chance, "old country" connections, and the pressure of demand, they took up unwonted occupations in the expanding American economy. Many of the men became laborers, in the mines, mills, and factories, on the network of railway construction spreading over the continent, in the building trades; others, with some background of craftsmanship perhaps, obtained semiskilled positions in manufacturing, particularly in light industry; still others entered the service trades; a number set themselves up in small-scale business; a still smaller segment was able to make the first step in the professions. As the nineteenth century wore on, a new and significant pattern emerged, testifying to the incredible mobility of American life. Each new group, as it came, pushed upward the level of its predecessors, and was in turn pushed upward by its successors. This process of upward movement took place not without painful friction, not without conflict even; but take place it did, producing a fluidity in our social system virtually unknown at any other place or time. From 1830 to 1930, Irish, Bohemians, Slovaks, Hungarians, and many other peoples followed each other in the service of the pick and shovel, each earlier group, displaced by newcomers, moving upward in the occupational and social scale. "So the Irish who had manned the New England textile mills inexorably gave way to the more recent immigrants; Italians, Portuguese, Armenians, and French Canadians edged in as pickers and sweepers, and soon were everywhere in the plant. . . . The mechanization of coal mining and the replacement of less efficient processes by Bessemer furnaces enabled untrained Poles, Slovaks, and Italians to take the place of experienced Britishers."[5] If successive waves of immigration served as the "push" in this pattern of occupational advancement, education and acculturation to American ways provided the immigrants with the opportunity of making the most of it; the sons of unskilled laborers had the possibility of competing for desirable positions with the sons of people who had already achieved a higher place in the occupational scale. And so in America the sons of families which in Europe had remained fixed in village tradition from generation to generation found themselves caught up in a pattern of social mobility that beckoned them ever upward.

Perhaps most characteristic in this respect were the Jews from central and eastern Europe who began to come in huge numbers in the last quarter of the nineteenth century. In Europe they had been petty merchants, artisans, and laborers—very few wage earners. In this country they settled down in or near the great urban centers. Many of them, particularly of the earlier "German" immigration, went into business, often beginning as itinerant peddlers. Most, however, went into shops and factories, in light industry, or in building and allied trades; they became wage workers and built up a very considerable labor movement. But this process of "proletarianization" was not a lasting one; almost immediately a reverse process of "deproletarianization" set in. The Jewish immigrants came with a traditionally high valuation of education and of "educated" occupations. Some of them very soon left the shop to go into business; others proved able to combine long hours in the sweatshop with after-work study that gained them coveted degrees and licenses in medicine, law, and accountancy. (This "diploma-mania" was much deplored by radical publicists, who themselves were escaping the shops through Yiddish-language journalism.) But it was primarily the sons, and later the daughters, of the newly "proletarianized" Jewish immigrants who were in a position to take advantage of the mobility of American society. Unlike other immigrants, Jewish parents were passionately concerned with giving their children an education,[6] and Jewish young people proved remarkably receptive to Americanization. Equipped with language and knowledge, they quickly passed out of the "proletariat" into white-collar, professional, and academic occupations. The Jewish factory worker, it was a common saying, was "a man of one generation: neither the son nor the father of workers"; his father had been a petty merchant or artisan, his son was to become a businessman or professional.[7]

Warner notes that the "traditionally high evaluation of education" so characteristic of the immigrant Jews fits in very well with the "practical emphasis of education in their new culture."[8] In other words, by being Jewish they were, in a very curious way, becoming more typically American. Basically this was true of most immigrants, but particularly of the Jews, who before long were to reveal themselves as, in a certain sense, paradoxically the most "American" of all the ethnic groups that went into the making of modern America.

But at whatever rate and in whatever way they accommodated themselves to their new environment, America welcomed the immigrants into its economic life, offered them a relatively free course upward, and encouraged them to take advantage of it, though the greater rewards and the higher reaches of achievement were more open to certain ethnic groups than to others. In any case, it did not take long before the immigrants became the mainstay of the American economy.

II

The immigrants themselves were, from the first, naturally preoccupied with economic problems, with making the

transition from work on the land in the "old country" to
labor in the factories, mills, and mines of their new home.
But their big concern was also the preservation of their
wonted way of life; above all, the transplanting of their
churches.[9]

Back home, the church (or synagogue) had been, for
most of them, the meaningful center of life, the repository
of the sacred symbols of community existence. As soon as
they touched land in the New World, they set themselves
to re-establishing it. But here there were difficulties, and in
meeting and overcoming these difficulties they inevitably
transformed the church they thought they were transplanting.

The immigrants were men of their village or region
("province"), and the church they were intent upon transplanting was their village church with all its ways; above
all, with the old village customs and dialect. But how could
they? If they were Catholics—Italian, Hungarian, or even
French Canadian—they were often assigned to already established Catholic churches in their vicinity, usually Irish
or German, that seemed utterly alien to them. Before their
time, the Irish and the Germans had also had this problem.
The Irish who came here early in the nineteenth century
could find no place for themselves among the old-American
Catholics and had to struggle hard before they got churches
they could call their own. The Germans, coming somewhat
later, resented the "Irish-dominated" churches they found
and would not rest till they had churches that spoke the
language and followed the ways of the "old home." But in
order to do so, neither they nor the Irish who preceded
them nor the Italians who followed them could remain vil-
lagers transplanted. A new unity began to emerge, a unity
defined primarily by language, a unity largely unknown in
the Old World but quick to become their very identity
in the New. The immigrant church was the primary expression of this unity.[10]

In the Old World they had, let us remember, been men
of their village or province, and known by that name; until
well into the twentieth century most of them had no conception of national belonging, certainly no understanding

of, or interest in, nationalism as an ideology. They were not Italians, but Apulians or Sicilians. They were not Poles, but Poznaniskers or Mazhevoers; not Germans, but Bavarians or Saxons or Prussians; not Greeks, but Thracians or men from Epirus. And the first societies they formed, as well as the first churches they tried to set up, were along such village and regional lines. But American life was too fluid to permit the indefinite perpetuation of these local identities. Men and women of many villages and regions were thrown together in the same "ghetto," and before long the new conditions of American life confronted the immigrant with a problem he had practically never had to face before, the problem of self-identification and self-location, the problem expressed in the question, "What am I?"

This question is perhaps the most immediate that a man can ask himself in the course of his social life. Everyone finds himself in a social context which he shares with many others, but within this social context, how shall he locate himself? Unless he can so locate himself, he cannot tell himself, and others will not be able to know, who and what he is; he will remain "anonymous," a nobody—which is intolerable. To live, he must "belong"; to "belong," he must be able to locate himself in the larger social whole, to identify himself to himself and to others. There is nothing necessarily deliberate or conscious about all this. The process of self-location and identification is normally a "hidden" social process of which the individual is little aware; only at moments of disintegration and crisis does it emerge to the level of consciousness and require some measure of deliberate decision. Nor is actual social location ever one-dimensional; which aspect of a man's "belonging" becomes operative often depends on the concrete situation. So we can imagine a medieval villager, as long as he remained in his village, thinking of himself, and being thought of by others, in terms of his social caste—peasant, let us say. But once out of his village, the question, "What is he?", corresponding to the inner question, "What am I?", would very likely be answered in terms of his village, as indeed we can see from the structure of so many medieval names. This illustration suggests another significant fact. The way in which one identifies and locates oneself to oneself ("Who, what, am I?") is closely related to how one is identified and located in the larger community ("Who, what, is he?"). Normally they reflect, sustain, and illumine each other; it is only in abnormal situations that they diverge and conflict.

It was in such an abnormal situation of disintegration and crisis that the immigrant found himself as he attempted to rebuild his life in the New World. Who, what, was he? The question had rarely occurred to him in the "old home," but now it arose insistently before him and his children. Perhaps it seemed to him there was no answer; but American reality not only raised the question, it also supplied the answer. "American experience taught these people to disregard the differences in dialect and custom among the various *paesani.* . . . Instead, immigrants found themselves drawn together by a larger affiliation the basis of which was the language that permitted them to communicate with each other. . . . So generally immigrant groups named themselves by their language rather than their place of origin":[11] they became Poles and Russians and Slovaks and Greeks and Swedes and Hungarians, although very often the coverage of these names was not very clear in their own minds or in the minds of others. An emphasis on language gradually outlined the new character of the immigrant groups and answered the aching question of identity. Americans could understand such identification; indeed, they often referred to the immigrants as "foreign-language" groups. To Americans, and to immigrants who gave the matter any thought, language usually meant culture, and very soon nationality as well. The influence of intellectuals and business people, the former often nationalist ideologists and the latter eager to build up a cohesive group of "fellow countrymen" as large as possible, encouraged the emergence of the new and extended form of self-identification, but over and above everything else was the pressure of American reality. When finally identification in terms of "national" group emerged and established itself, it seemed to the immigrants and their children as though

this kind of designation had been there from the very beginning, almost a kind of biological label ("Why, of course,
we were Poles, or Italians, or Germans . . ."). But it had
not been that way; the new form of identification and self-
identification had been the product of *American* reality and
American experience, and represented the first fruits of their
Americanization.[12]

This new form of self-identification and social location is
what we have come to know as the ethnic group. It soon
became self-evident to all Americans, and to almost all the
immigrants and their children, that the newcomers were
falling into ethnic-national, or ethnic-cultural, groups within
the larger American society. All immigrant life—and therefore, in an important way, all American life, since "the immigrants *were* America"—was being rapidly reconstructed
along the new lines. America became the "land of immigrants," and over large parts of it, everyday thinking and
behavior followed "naturally" the patterns of ethnic group
relations. The ethnic group, because it was for so many
millions of Americans the primary context of identification
and social location, entered as a major factor into the economic, social, and political life of the total community, and
into the most intimate personal and social relations of the
"ethnics" themselves. Social-class structure, marriage selection, "availability" of political candidates, church and religious forms, all reflected the profound influence of the
ethnic groups into which American reality had organized
the bewildered immigrants.

The first concern of the immigrants, we may remember,
was with their churches. As the ethnic group began to
emerge, so did the ethnic church, the church that tran-
scended "old country" particularisms and grouped believers
according to the newly relevant ethnic (linguistic, cultural,
"national") lines. Not very surprisingly, great difficulties
arose. Some of the American churches refused to allow
foreign-language subdivisions and so forced the immigrants
to set up their own institutions. Thus, because in the early
days of the nation the Methodist Church rejected foreign-
language branches, two German Methodist bodies, the
United Brethren and the Evangelical Church, had to form

separate establishments.[13] A century later, Warner reports
of "Yankee City," Congregationalist Armenians had to se-
cede from the Congregational Church and establish one of
their own because of language.[14] The Lutherans organized
generally along ethnic lines (German, Swedish, Norwegian,
Finnish, etc.), though the regional element was never fully
overcome, as can be seen from denominational history.[15]
Perhaps the severest trial confronted the Roman Catholic
Church, a universal church made up, in this country, almost entirely of successive immigrant groups. Early in its
history a persistent anti-foreignism manifested itself—against
the French clergy in the late eighteenth century, against
the Irish somewhat later, against the Germans, the Italians,
the Poles, the Slovaks, and so on, each earlier group as it
became secure and adjusted taking over the anti-foreignism
of which it had been victim and directing it against the
newer comers. In reaction, the various ethnic groups among
Catholics in America tended to develop an intense ethnic
nationalism. In the 1890s some German Catholics in this
country demanded the establishment of ethnic dioceses and
the division of the church in America into a number
of quasi-independent organizations along ethnic-language
lines. This movement, known as Cahenslyism after its
spokesman, met with sharp resistance from the American
hierarchy and from Rome, and came to nothing.[16] But
similar movements among Slavic Uniat, Polish, and Lithuanian groups here led to grave defections and to the establishment of dissident ethnic churches. Nevertheless, the
Catholic Church held the loyalty of the vast majority of
Catholic immigrants, and sooner or later came to terms with
their ethnic demands within the framework of ecclesiastical
principles. "More often than not throughout America,"
Warner reports, "the Catholic Church provides an over-all
social structure which organizes, regulates, and helps to
maintain the culture of a particular ethnic group. . . . The
religion of the local parish in the big cities and towns of
America is usually organized on an ethnic basis."[17] In the
transplanting of this church, as of the others, the emerging
ethnic pattern proved a decisive factor. Sometimes, indeed,
ethnic-linguistic solidarity succeeded in overriding religious

barriers, as among the Syrians, where a common language, Arabic, brought together in one self-identified group Melchite or Maronite Catholics, Moslems, Druses, Protestants, and Orthodox.[18]

III

In this new framework of social identities the immigrant and the children born to him in this country had to build their lives and define their roles. The parents at least, however disoriented through migration and resettlement, found in the evolving ethnic group something secure and familiar. They had their societies, where one met people from the "old country" and talked about things still vivid in memory; they had their newspapers, which made one feel close to both the new and the old; they had their churches, and even plays and amusements in the familiar accents of the mother tongue. Aside from the church, they had not known any of these things "back home," but here these innovations seemed to them something of the old life, something that gave an appearance of continuity and security to their existence.

It was for the children, the American-born or -bred *second* generation, that ethnic existence was full of perplexities and conflicts.[19] This second generation was already in part American, but only in part. The children of the immigrants, those born here or brought here very young, almost always spoke English as their first language and thought and felt about things in American ways;[20] yet they also lived in their immigrant families, spoke the old tongue at home, on occasion looked into the foreign-language newspaper, and in general shared the ethnic life of their parents. But they could not share it entirely; they may still have called themselves by the ethnic names, but they could not help but realize that their ethnic status was a deprivation, a limitation, which shut many doors of American advancement in their faces. They were Irish and Poles and Italians, yet not Irish or Poles or Italians; they were Americans, and yet not Americans. They were doubly alienated, marginal men.[21] Them, even more than their fathers, "adjustment to the circumstances of life in the United States brought . . . not nearer to, but more distant from, other Americans."[22]

The second generation responded in various ways to their plight.[23] Some saw in their position "at the boundary" an opportunity to mediate between the two cultures and societies, and built their lives, though obviously not their children's, upon this vocation. Usually intellectuals, professionals, or businessmen, they became the leaders of their ethnic groups, editors of foreign-language newspapers, executives of the many immigrant societies and orders, nationalist agitators, political organizers, intermediaries between their own group and the larger society. They often identified themselves with the ethnic language, culture, and nationality in a manner so passionate that it baffled, even disturbed, their fathers. To the fathers, ethnic "belonging," once it was established, was something to be taken for granted; "the American offspring," however, "turned this group consciousness into nationalism,"[24] something one had to work at and maintain as a commitment.

American politics and ethnic nationalism were the two great preoccupations of this segment of the second generation, and often the two were combined in curious fashion. Many of the immigrants became citizens, and their children were so by birth; they therefore soon came to constitute voting blocs sufficiently important to engage the attention of the political bosses, who were not slow to form connections with the outstanding representatives of the ethnic groups. The Irish were the first to come upon the scene; they were already a political force in New York City in the early days of the Republic. Jews, Italians, Poles, French Canadians followed, shuffling and reshuffling the political lines in many localities and states in bewildering fashion. Patronage, "favors," and community needs played a big part in the political mobilization of the ethnic groups, but ethnic pride and solidarity, as well as nationalist issues, played an even bigger role. Irish grievances against Britain, Italian demands for the repossession of territory under the Austrian "yoke," German concern for the power and prestige of the Fatherland, Polish, Czechish, and Jewish dreams of the reconstitution of their respective "national states" became live issues in American politics and in the community life of the ethnic groups.[25] It was the second generation that supplied much of the leadership and gave articulate form to the passions and loyalties they helped arouse.

But mostly the second generation did not thus identify itself with the ethnic group of its immigrant parents. Some, indeed increasingly many, were anxious to rid themselves of the burden of immigrant foreignness and enter what they felt to be the mainstream of American life so as to be able to take full advantage of the extraordinary mobility of American society. They could not do so as long as they were identified with their parents' communities, and many of them attempted to throw off this identification, which often meant a break with their families. But what, then, were they? They refused to identify themselves any longer in terms of their ethnic background, but no new form of identification had yet emerged. They could pretend they were "just plain Americans," or even (some of the more radical among them) that they were "citizens of the world," but the pretense would not work. In America, as elsewhere, one had to be "something." And so this segment of the second generation found itself in an intolerable position, consumed with ambition, anxiety, and self-hatred.

By and large, however, the response of the second generation was neither of these extremes. Most of the second generation found itself confused, anxious, and discontented, without being really aware of what was troubling it. It went along with the life of the ethnic group without actually understanding or sharing it, feeling vaguely resentful and inferior. "The second generation was [indeed] an unstable element. . . . As it grew in prominence, it created troublesome problems precisely because it had not a fixed place in the society."[26]

Nowhere were the problems more troublesome than in religious life. The church and religion were for the parents the one element of real continuity between the old life and the new. It was for most of them a matter of deepest concern that their children remain true to the faith. In their anxiety, perhaps not only for their children but also for themselves, they tended even to make their pattern of religion more rigid than it had been before the great migration; "what could be taken for granted at home had zealously to be fought for here."[27] Their children, however, could not and did not look upon it the same way. To the first generation, the immigrant generation, church and religion were part of their "natural" immigrant heritage; they were embedded in their very life and culture. To the second generation, including the younger people among the immigrants themselves, church and religion were also that—part of the immigrant heritage—but their attitude toward the immigrant heritage was no longer so unequivocal. Those of the second generation who made a vocation out of ethnic leadership of course continued to go to church and sometimes became pillars of the congregation, but the church to them was only too often just one of the many ethnic institutions that had to be maintained, built up, and given direction in line with what they conceived to be the proper program for their ethnic group. Those who rejected their ethnic identification or felt uncomfortable in it transferred this rejection to the church and religion of their immigrant parents. In revolting against the immigrant heritage, and in the process of establishing their independence and adjusting themselves to their new environment, they tended to cast off their religious identification. To them religion, along with the language of the home, seemed to be part and parcel of the immigrant baggage of foreignness they were so eager to abandon. To the dismay of their parents, and to the distaste of better acculturated Americans, many of the second generation tended to draw away from the religion of their fathers, and from religion altogether. Some, indeed, became consciously, even bitterly, religionless. It was a strange and self-defeating way of accommodating themselves to American life, but they did not know it.

The plight of the second generation posed dramatically the problem of assimilation. Already in the early days of the new nation, America had been hailed as a "melting pot," where "individuals of all nations are melted into a new race of men."[28] The ideologists of the "melting pot" looked forward to a racial and cultural blending of all immigrant strains into a new synthesis, and many older Americans as well as many recent immigrants shared this vision. In sharp opposition, the nationalists agitated for the perpetuation of the ethnic communities as integral parts of American society; they often called it "cultural pluralism," but what they had in mind, whether they knew it or not, was the transplanting of the European multinational, multicultural society to America. Neither the assimilationists of the "melting pot" nor the ethnic champions of "cultural pluralism" gauged aright the dynamics of American life.

The "cultural pluralists" were farthest afield. Although the emergence of the ethnic group under pressure of American experience seemed to sustain their vision of a multicultural society, the realities of American life were actually moving in the other direction. As we shall see in more detail in the next chapter, cultural assimilation began almost as soon as the immigrant touched these shores, but was for a long time masked because of the immense influx of new arrivals. It soon became evident that the ethnic group which America had created, it had created not as a permanent feature of American life but as a transitional and makeshift device. Transitional to what? Only the future would show, but the future was not needed to make evident that the ethnic group itself had no future. The ethnic "pluralists" were backward-looking romantics, or else they were shrewd opportunists intent on exploiting the present without interest in the shape of things to come. In either case they were out of touch with the unfolding American reality.

The enthusiasts of the "melting pot" were right in foreseeing continuous and increasing ethnic fusion among the American people, but this ethnic mixture through intermarriage turned out to be not general and indiscriminate but largely channeled along certain lines. They were wrong also in regard to the cultural aspect of the assimilative process. They looked forward to a genuine blending of cultures, to which every ethnic strain would make its own contribution and out of which would emerge a new cultural synthesis, no more English than German or Italian and yet in some sense transcending and embracing them all. In certain respects this has indeed become the case: our American cuisine includes antipasto and spaghetti, frankfurters and pumpernickel, filet mignon and french fried potatoes, borsht, sour cream, and gefüllte fish, on a perfect equality with fried chicken, ham and eggs, and pork and beans. But it would be a mistake to infer from this that the American's image of himself—and that means the ethnic group member's image of himself as he becomes American—is a composite or synthesis of the ethnic elements that have gone into the making of the American. It is nothing of the kind: the American's image of himself is still the Anglo-American ideal it was at the beginning of our independent existence. The "national type" as ideal has always been, and remains, pretty well fixed. It is the *Mayflower*, John Smith, Davy Crockett, George Washington, and Abraham Lincoln that define the American's self-image, and this is true whether the American in question is a descendant of the Pilgrims or the grandson of an immigrant from southeastern Europe.[29] Anxious ethnic nationalists have repeatedly tried to provide their groups with a kind of putative colonial past—Columbus, Pulaski, Steuben—but these remain exotic figures, either unknown or felt to be irrelevant. Our cultural assimilation has taken place not in a "melting pot," but rather in a "transmuting pot"[30] in which all ingredients have been transformed and assimilated to an idealized "Anglo-Saxon" model.[31] Despite widespread dislike of various aspects of British life, our relation, cultural and spiritual, to our British heritage is vastly different and more intimate than is our relation to the cultural heritages of the later immigrant groups, who with their descendants compose a majority of the American people today. Our cultural assimilation has proceeded in essentially the same way as has our linguistic development—a few foreign words here and there, a few modifications of form, but still thoroughly and unquestionably English. The "Anglo-Saxon" type remains the American ideal to which all other elements are transmuted in order to become American.

Al Capp's Li'l Abner Yokum is certainly the most American of Americans, the very model of the "Anglo-Saxon" type. Yet his name—Yokum—is derived from the German

Joachim:[32] evidently he must have had German ancestors.
But the Germanness of the German ancestors whose name
he bears has left no trace in Li'l Abner; it has been completely transmuted into the "Anglo-Saxon." And this is
equally true of the Brightmans and the Goocheys, who
were once Breitmann and Gauthier, and of countless others:
automatically, as a mere matter of course, they have recast their identities and images of themselves along the
standard American—that is, "Anglo-Saxon"—model.

Mention of Li'l Abner brings to mind the comics. In the
comics we have a remarkable documentation, as yet insuffi-
ciently studied, of the American's image of himself. Aside
from such strips as "Bringing Up Father" and "Mickey
Finn," which are deliberately ethnic in conception, the nuclear characters in the most familiar comics are "Anglo-
Saxons" in appearance and name, white-collar workers or
professionals by occupation, middle-class in outlook and
culture, each family with its little house in Suburbia.[33] And
yet every American, whatever his ethnic background, whatever his occupation or social standing, recognizes himself
in them, not as a picture of his reality perhaps, but as his
image. Very much the same is true of the "soap opera."[34]
In every case the "Anglo-Saxon" prototype proves dominant; it has indeed asserted itself quite decisively in the line
taken by the process of cultural Americanization in the
course of the past century and a half, and it has given the
lie to both the ethnic "pluralist" and the "melting pot"
assimilationist.

This was the reality that the second generation had to
face but could not fully understand, caught as it was between the two worlds. For the third generation, the
American-born children of the American-born or -bred
children of immigrants, American reality has taken on another aspect. To this new generation it seems obvious that
ethnic separateness cannot and should not be perpetuated;
to them the ethnic "pluralism" of the nationalists appears
meaningless and incomprehensible, but they do not therefore fully share the dream of the "melting pot" enthusiasts.
They realize that integration into American life implies as-

similation to the American model in many crucial respects. However important the ethnic group may have been in the adjustment of the immigrant to American society, and however influential it still remains in many aspects of American life, the perpetuation of ethnic differences in any serious way is altogether out of line with the logic of American reality. The newcomer is expected to change many things about him as he becomes American—nationality, language, culture. One thing, however, he is *not* expected to change —and that is his religion. And so it is religion that with the third generation has become the differentiating element and the context of self-identification and social location.

FOOTNOTES

1. Oscar Handlin, *The Uprooted: The Epic Story of the Great Migrations that Made the American People* (Little, Brown, 1951), p. 3; see also Handlin's collection of essays, *Race and Nationality in American Life* (Little, Brown, 1957).

2. These estimates of the British-Protestant element are from George R. Stewart, *American Ways of Life* (Doubleday, 1954), p. 21.

3. "Between 1750 and 1850, the population of the [European] continent leaped from about one hundred and forty million to about two hundred and sixty, and by the time of the First World War, to almost four hundred million. In addition, by 1915, some two hundred and fifty million Europeans and their descendants lived outside the continent" (Handlin, *The Uprooted*, p. 25).

4. This is the subtitle of Handlin's *The Uprooted*.

5. Handlin, *The American People in the Twentieth Century* (Harvard, 1954), p. 88; see also Handlin, *The Uprooted*, pp. 4, 68, 72.

6. "The Greek father [in Yankee City] sees no necessity for his children to be educated or to do anything different from what he has always done. . . . The [Jewish] parents are eager for their children to have as much education as possible. This attitude conforms to their traditionally high evaluation of education and at the same time fits the practical emphasis of education in their new culture" (W. Lloyd Warner, *Structure of American Life* [Edinburgh, 1952], pp. 127, 135).

7. See Will Herberg, "The Jewish Labor Movement in the United States," *American Jewish Year Book*, Vol. 53 (American Jewish Committee, New York, 1952), pp. 28, 29, 53–54.

8. See note 6, above.

9. "The church was the first, the most important, and the most significant institution that the immigrants established" (Marcus L. Hansen, *The Problem of the Third Generation Immigrant* [Augustana Historical Society, Rock Island, Ill., 1938], p. 15).

10. "The only center [of immigrant unity] which was available, as a rule, was religion; the only leaders, with few exceptions, who had braved the difficulties of a new orientation along with the migrating artisans and farmers were the clergy; the only organization which was readily at hand for maintaining the unity of the group was the church" (H. Richard Niebuhr, *The Social Sources of Denominationalism* [Holt, 1929], p. 223).

11. Handlin, *The American People*, pp. 61, 60; *The Uprooted*, p. 187.

12. Here too, in a way, the Jews marked the pattern. In eastern Europe the Jews, like their neighbors, had known themselves by town or region: they were Minsker, Liachovitcher, Berdichever; also by provincial dialect, as Galitsianer or Litvaker. But, because of their tradition and their minority existence in a non-Jewish world, they were also conscious of themselves as Jews. In this country they formed their *lantsmanshaftn* and still referred to themselves by their "old home" designations, but almost from the beginning their self-identification as Jews was dominant, though there was by no means harmony among the various groups of Jews stemming from diverse origins in the Old World, particularly among the "German" and East European groups of the earlier and later immigrations. Jewishness was interpreted as primarily ethnic-cultural, or "national," though some religious element was always felt to inhere. Thus again, the Jews, out of their special Jewish background, early fell into ways that were to become normative for immigrant life in America.

13. See F. E. Mayer, *The Religious Bodies of America* (Concordia, 1954), pp. 305, 340, 341.

14. Warner, *Structure of American Life*, p. 133.

15. See Mayer, *The Religious Bodies of America*, pp. 178–87.

16. For Cahenslyism, see below, chap. viii, pp. 144–45.

17. Warner, *Structure of American Life*, p. 134.

18. Handlin, *The American People*, pp. 66–67.

19. "The assimilative forces which the dominant society exerts upon the ethnic groups are exerted primarily upon the child so that he, rather than the parent, becomes the transmitting agent of social change. . . . In the process, the older and younger generations become isolated and estranged from one another" (Warner, *Structure of American Life*, p. 126).

20. This was true particularly in the large cities, where most of the immigrants settled. In more remote rural districts American-born children of immigrants sometimes continued in the language and ways of their parents for many years—Thorstein Veblen, for example, spoke Norwegian and not English until he left home—and it required another generation to begin the process described above. In a few cases, indeed, such as the "Pennsylvania Dutch" and Swedish groups in the Middle West, the ethnic enclaves were so isolated and self-contained that several generations had to pass before the process of acculturation really got under way.

21. "The sons and daughters of the immigrants were really in a most uncomfortable position. . . . The source of all their woes . . . lay in the strange dualism into which they had been born. . . . Whereas in the schoolroom they were too foreign, at home they were too American. . . . How to inhabit two worlds at the same time was the problem of the second generation" (Hansen, *The Problem of the Third Generation Immigrant*, pp. 6–7).

22. Handlin, *The Uprooted*, p. 142.

23. Cf. the three types of reaction defined by Child: "in-group reaction," "rebel reaction," "apathetic reaction" (Irvin L. Child, *Italian or American?* [Yale, 1943]).

24. Handlin, *The Uprooted*, p. 194.

25. Ethnic nationalism frequently took on chauvinistic and racist forms, but, as Handlin points out, "these sentiments were not rejections of America, but the efforts of confused people to explain their place in it" (*The American People*, p. 198). See also Nathan Glazer, "America's Ethnic Pattern," *Perspectives*, No. 9, Autumn 1954, a perceptive study relevant to many points discussed in this chapter and the next.

26. Handlin, *The Uprooted*, p. 267.

27. Handlin, *The American People*, p. 51; see also Warner, *Structure of American Life*, p. 129.

28. "Here individuals of all nations are melted into a new race of men, whose labors and posterity will one day cause great changes in the world" (J. Hector de Crèvecoeur, *Letters from an American Farmer* [1782, 1904 ed., Fox Duffield], p. 58). The term "melting pot" passed into the common language with Israel Zangwill's immensely popular play of that name written in 1908 and performed in New York, Chicago, and Washington the following year.

29. "Nothing was more Yankee than a Yankeeized person of foreign descent" (Hansen, *The Problem of the Third Generation Immigrant*, p. 8).

30. This valuable distinction in terms is Stewart's (*American Ways of Life*, pp. 23, 28).

31. It should be recalled that "Anglo-Saxon" in this usage is a conventional designation including not only the English but also Welsh, Scots, and some Irish as well. Perhaps "British-American" would be better.

32. Stewart, *American Ways of Life,* p. 207.

33. Nuclear characters engaged in manual occupations are extremely rare in newspaper comic strips: Skeezix and Corkey in "Gasoline Alley" are the best-known exceptions, and even they are not wage workers but small businessmen.

34. Warner, *Structure of American Life,* chapter ix.

III. *From the Land of Immigrants to the Triple Melting Pot: The Third Generation and the Religious Community*

"In language, the transmuting pot has worked with high efficiency; in religion, the conception of the transmuting pot, or even of the melting pot, can scarcely be said to exist . . . [In this country] from the very beginning, we did not really expect a man to change his faith."[1] This fact, to which Stewart here calls attention, is a fact of immense significance for the entire course of American development. It is a fact of the historical and sociological order, not of the theological; the immigrant was not expected to change his faith upon arrival in this country not because Americans were indifferent to religion or were committed to theological views which called for non-interference in religious matters, but because almost from the beginning, the structure of American society presupposed diversity and substantial equality of religious associations.[2]

Of the immigrant who came to this country it was expected that, sooner or later, either in his own person or through his children, he would give up virtually everything he had brought with him from the "old country"—his language, his nationality, his manner of life—and would adopt the ways of his new home. Within broad limits, however, his becoming an American did not involve his abandoning the old religion in favor of some native American substitute. Quite the contrary, not only was he expected to retain his old religion, as he was not expected to retain his old language or nationality, but such was the shape of America that it was largely in and through his religion that he, or rather his children and grandchildren, found an identifiable place in American life.

I

As soon as the immigrant family arrived in the New World it became involved in a far-reaching double process. On the one hand, as we have seen, the conditions of American life made for the emergence of the ethnic group, in terms of which the immigrant identified himself and was located in the larger community. On the other hand, however, the formation of the ethnic group at the center of immigrant life was from the very beginning accompanied by its dissolution at the periphery. The ethnic group emerged to define and express the immigrant's curious combination of foreignness and Americanness; but his children, the moment they entered school, the moment even they were let out on the street to play with children of other tongues and origins, began to escape the ethnic-immigrant life of their parents. Their language, their culture, their system of values, their outlook on life, underwent drastic change, sometimes obviously, sometimes imperceptibly; they were becoming American, assimilated, acculturated, no longer fully at home in the immigrant family and ethnic group, though neither as yet fully at home in the America to which they belonged. Though this double process was operative from the very beginning, the "negative" aspect was not visible so long as large-scale immigration continued; all phases of ethnic life flourished, societies spread and increased in membership, foreign-language publications grew in scope and circulation, cultural institutions prospered. But this prosperity and expansion at the center could not halt the disintegration of ethnic group life that came with the growing Americanization of the second generation.

These conflicting forces drove the second generation into a difficult position and engendered an acute malaise in the sons and daughters of the immigrants. Frequently, though not always, the man of the second generation attempted to resolve his dilemma by forsaking the ethnic group in which he found himself. "He wanted to forget everything," this man of the second generation, "the foreign language . . . the religion [of his immigrant parents] . . . the family customs. . . . The second generation wanted to forget, and even when the ties of family affection were strong, wanted to lose as many of the evidences of foreign origin as they could shuffle off."[3] The great mobility of American society encouraged this process, and was in turn spurred by it. As the second generation prospered economically and culturally, and moved upward in the social scale, assimilation was speeded; the speeding of assimilation stimulated and quickened the upward movement.

First to go was the foreign language and the culture associated with it, for the foreign language was the manifest symbol of foreignness and a great impediment to advancement.[4] Religion too was affected, though not so explicitly. The second generation developed an uneasy relation to the faith of their fathers: sometimes this meant simply indifference; in other cases, relatively few, a shift to denominations regarded as more "American." In most cases, however, the ties with the old religion were never entirely broken.

The immediate reaction of many of the second generation was escape. But enough of this generation always remained in the ethnic group to provide a permanent nucleus around which the incoming masses of immigrants could gather and organize their lives in the New World. Through the nineteenth and well into the twentieth century, the ethnic group throve and flourished.

Then came the stoppage of immigration, first as a consequence of the World War, and later, more definitively, through the legislation of the 1920s. Almost at once the picture changed drastically, for the hitherto hidden effects of the assimilative process became evident. "The total halt to immigration after 1924 severed the last remaining ties [of the immigrants and their children] to the Old World. Without additions from across the ocean, memories of transatlantic antecedents faded. As the second, and in time, the third generation grew to maturity, affiliations based upon some remote immigrant ancestor became ever less meaningful. The old customs grew unfamiliar in the bustle of

American life."[5] The various and multiform activities of
the ethnic group began to shrivel and disappear; the ethnic
group itself, in its older form at least, became less and less
intelligible and relevant to American reality. It was the end
of an era.

But if it was the end, it was also the beginning. The final
drying-up of the steady stream of immigration, which removed the ground from under the ethnic group, coincided,
by a noteworthy historical fact, with the emergence of the
third generation for the great bulk of the immigrant community. The last wave of the "new" immigration had begun in the 1870s; by the 1920s, four or five decades had
passed, grandsons and great-grandsons of the earlier immigrants were becoming increasingly plentiful. During the
years of large-scale immigration, the third generation had
either not yet appeared, or, where it did exist, could hardly
influence the ethnic picture in any important way. With
the cessation of immigration, however, the third generation
became increasingly determinative in outlook and temper,
and a new situation supervened in America's ethnic life.
Not even the momentary upsurge of ethnic nationalism in
the 1930s, and again under the exigencies of the postwar
years, could materially change the new picture.

Marcus Hansen has graphically formulated what he calls
the "principle of third-generation interest" in these terms:
"what the son wishes to forget, the grandson wishes to remember." "After the second generation," Hansen points out,
"comes the third. . . . [The members of the third genera-
tion] have no reason to feel any inferiority when they look
around them. They are American-born. Their speech is the
same as that of those with whom they associate. Their material wealth is the average possession of the typical citizen."[6] The third generation, in short, really managed to get
rid of the immigrant foreignness, the hopelessly double
alienation, of the generation that preceded it; it became
American in a sense that had been, by and large, impossible for the immigrants and their children. That problem,
at least, was solved; but its solution paradoxically rendered
more acute the perennial problem of "belonging" and self-
identification. They were Americans, but what *kind* of

Americans? They could not be simply "shapeless integers of a homogeneous mass. They desired a sense of identity that would explain why they were different from 'One Man's Family.' They wished to belong to a group."⁷ But what group could they belong to? The old-line ethnic group, with its foreign language and culture, was not for them; they were Americans. But the old family religion, the old ethnic religion, could serve where language and culture could not; the religion of the immigrants—with certain necessary modifications, such as the replacement of the ethnic language by English—was accorded a place in the American scheme of things that made it at once both genuinely American and a familiar principle of group identification. The connection with the family religion had never been completely broken, and to religion, therefore, the men and women of the third generation now began to turn to define their place in American society in a way that would sustain their Americanness and yet confirm the tie that bound them to their forebears, whom they now no longer had any reason to reject, whom indeed, for the sake of a "heritage," they now wanted to "remember." Thus "religion became the focal point of ethnic affiliations. . . . Through its institutions, the church supplied a place where children could learn what they were. . . ."⁸ Religious association now became the primary context of self-identification and social location for the third generation, as well as for the bulk of the second generation, of America's immigrants, and that meant, by and large, for the American people.

But in thus becoming the primary context of social location, religious association itself underwent significant change. All of the many churches, sects, and denominations that characterize the American religious scene were still there, and indeed continued to thrive. But "increasingly religious activities fell into a fundamental tripartite division that had begun to take form earlier in the century. Men were Catholics, Protestants, or Jews, categories based less on theological than on social distinctions."⁹ A new and unique social structure was emerging in America, the "religious community."

In the early 1940s, Ruby Jo Kennedy undertook an investigation of intermarriage trends in New Haven from 1870 to 1940. She published her findings in the *American Journal of Sociology* for January 1944 under the significant title, "Single or Triple Melting Pot?"[10] These findings are singularly calculated to illumine the development we have been studying.

Mrs. Kennedy set out to try to find answers to certain central questions. These questions were:

1. To what extent do individuals marry within their own culture [i.e., ethnic] groups? Which groups seem least and which most inclined to in-marriage? Is ethnic endogamy becoming more or less prevalent with the passage of time? What variations appear between the several ethnic groups in this regard . . . ?

2. When out-marriage does occur, is group preference discernible? That is, when individuals of any ethnic group marry out, do they demonstrate pronounced likes and dislikes for specified other groups? What reasons can be discovered for these preferences?

3. How does religious affiliation influence tendencies toward in- or out-marriage?

The years 1870, 1900, 1930, and 1940 were isolated for detailed examination. The ethnic groups that came in for consideration were the British-American, the Irish, the German, the Scandinavian, the Jewish, the Italian, and the Polish. Altogether, records of 9,044 marriages in the four selected years were subjected to classification and analysis, and the relevant facts correlated. This is not the place to give an account of Mrs. Kennedy's procedures; the article is brief and will repay firsthand study. But we do want to present her conclusions.

"The large nationality groups in New Haven," Mrs. Kennedy found, "represent a triple division on religious grounds: Jewish, Protestant (British-American, German, and Scandinavian), and Catholic (Irish, Italian, and Polish) . . ." In its early immigrant days, each of these ethnic groups tended to be endogamous; with the years, however, people began to marry outside the group. Thus, Irish in-marriage was 93.05 per cent in 1870, 74.75 per cent in

1900, 74.25 per cent in 1930, and 45.06 per cent in 1940; German in-marriage was 86.67 per cent in 1870, 55.26 per cent in 1900, 39.84 per cent in 1930, and 27.19 per cent in 1940; for the Italians and the Poles, the comparable figures were 97.71 per cent and 100 per cent respectively in 1900, 86.71 per cent and 68.04 per cent in 1930, and 81.89 per cent and 52.78 per cent in 1940. But "while strict ethnic endogamy is loosening, religious endogamy is persisting . . ." Members of Catholic stocks married Catholics in 95.35 per cent of the cases in 1870, 85.78 per cent in 1900, 82.05 per cent in 1930, and 83.71 per cent in 1940; members of Protestant stocks married Protestants in 99.11 per cent of the cases in 1870, 90.86 per cent in 1900, 78.19 per cent in 1930, and 79.72 per cent in 1940; Jews married Jews in 100 per cent of the cases in 1870, 98.82 per cent in 1900, 97.01 per cent in 1930, and 94.32 per cent in 1940. "Future cleavages," in Mrs. Kennedy's opinion, "will therefore be along religious lines rather than along nationality lines as in the past. . . . Cultural [i.e., ethnic] lines may fade, but religious barriers are holding fast. . . . When marriage crosses religious barriers, as it often does, religion still plays a prominent role, especially among Catholics," in that such marriages are often conditioned upon, and result in, one of the partners being brought into the religious community of the other. "The traditional 'single melting pot' idea must be abandoned, and a new conception, which we term the 'triple melting pot' theory of American assimilation, will take its place, as the true expression of what is happening to the various nationality groups in the United States. . . . The 'triple melting pot' type of assimilation is occurring through intermarriage, with Catholicism, Protestantism, and Judaism serving as the three fundamental bulwarks. . . . The different nationalities are merging, but within three religious compartments rather than indiscriminately. . . .[11] A triple religious cleavage, rather than a multilinear nationality cleavage, therefore seems likely to characterize American society in the future."[12]

Mrs. Kennedy's findings have been subjected to a good deal of scrutiny and criticism. Hollingshead, studying five

factors (race, age, ethnic origin, religion, and class) in the
selection of marriage mates, came to conclusions very much
like hers. He saw religion as dividing the whites into three
"pools"; "persons in the Jewish pool in 97.1 per cent of the
cases married within their own group; the percentage was
93.8 for Catholics, and 74.4 for Protestants."[13] It is not
necessary to insist on these figures, or attribute to them
universal validity, in order to appreciate the significance
of this tripartite division along lines of "religious community." John L. Thomas, in a comprehensive study, disputes
the Kennedy-Hollingshead findings, particularly in the matter of intermarriage among Catholics,[14] but his objections
do not materially alter the basic thesis to the effect that "the
three categories of religion increasingly set the terms
within which many men organize their social life."[15]

Yet though the "religious community"—the term we have
given to what Mrs. Kennedy calls a religious "cleavage" or
"compartment," and Hollingshead a religious "pool"—began
rapidly to emerge as the primary context of self-identification and social location, it would be misleading to conclude
that the old ethnic lines had disappeared or were no longer
significant. The older identifications continued vital, but
their form changed as the third generation began to imprint
its mark upon the ethnic picture. Formerly, religion had
been but an aspect of the ethnic group's culture and activities; it was merely a part, and to some a dispensable part,
of a larger whole; now the religious community was growing increasingly primary, and ethnic interests, loyalties, and
memories were being more and more absorbed in and manifested through this new social structure.[16] The religious
community is fast becoming, if it has not already become,
the over-all medium in terms of which remaining ethnic
concerns are preserved, redefined, and given appropriate
expression.

In politics, half-forgotten, half-buried ethnic allegiances
and prejudices still play a sizable part, as Samuel Lubell
and others have shown.[17] But in politics, too, the party
managers are beginning to think in terms of Catholic,
Protestant, and Jew, subsuming many of the older ethnic
distinctions under this new tripartite pattern.

A revealing illustration of the new tendency to think in terms of these religious categories even where ethnic considerations are central is provided in the way we envisage the problem of "minorities" and "minority" discrimination.[18] It is obvious that such discrimination operates primarily on ethnic or "racial" grounds, not only in the case of Negroes, but also, for example, in the case of Jews who are barred from certain clubs and resorts, and of second- and third-generation Italian-Americans who meet with difficulties in gaining admission to certain colleges and professional schools. There is a vague recognition of this fact in the familiar formula which calls for "no discrimination on grounds of race, religion, or national origin": "race" referring to Negroes, "religion" to Jews and Catholics, "national origin" to ethnic stocks of the "new" immigration (from eastern and southeastern Europe). Yet when a joint committee is set up to fight such discrimination, it is not set up as a committee of representatives of ethnic groups, say Poles, Italians, and French Canadians, along with Negroes and Jews; on the contrary, the committee is almost certain to be composed of Negroes, Jews, *and Catholics,* with Protestants coming in for support and good will. It is assumed that through the Jewish and Catholic communities the various ethnic groups with a grievance will find expression and representation.[19] The Catholic Church in particular is conceived as a kind of over-all institution embracing and representing the major ethnic groups (aside from Jews and Negroes) that still suffer from discrimination. And so it happens that a thoroughly American priest of remote English or Irish ancestry will come forward as spokesman for ethnics of altogether different origin and background. No one thinks it strange; it is accepted as quite natural, since increasingly it is becoming natural to have all ethnic concerns represented through the religious communities. If Handlin is right, as he probably is, in asserting that "the influence of ethnic origin . . . extends also deep into the lives of folk for whom the decisive migration [was] made by ancestors many generations back,"[20] it must be added that characteristically and increasingly this influence comes to expression through the religious community. But then

the religious community itself, as a social institution, tends
to "revolve about an ethnic rather than a dogmatic axis."[21]

II

The religious community we have been describing is a complex structure with aspects both sociological and religious.

Sociologically, as we have seen, the religious community
has emerged under compelling circumstances to serve as a
context of self-identification and social location in contemporary American life. When an American asks of a new
family in town, "What does he do?", he means the occupation or profession of the head of the family, which helps
define its social-class status. But when today he asks, "What
are they?", he means to what religious community they belong, and the answer is in such terms as: "They're Catholic
(or Protestant, or Jewish)." A century or even half a century ago, the question, "What are they?", would have been
answered in terms of ethnic-immigrant origin: "They're
Irish (or Germans, or Italians, or Jews)."[22] And today, it
is still answered in some such terms in certain unusual situations. In New Mexico the question, "What are they?", is
likely to be answered by "They're Americans (or Mexicans)"; in the South, by "They're white (or Negro)"; in
certain parts of New York City, by "They're Puerto Ricans."
In other words, where there are "racial" cleavages, or where
recent large-scale immigration has repeated the pattern so
common in this country until the 1930s, the primary context of social location is still likely to be some term of ethnic
reference, however vague. But, by and large, in the America that has emerged with the third generation, the principle
by which men identify themselves and are identified, locate
themselves and are located, in the social whole is neither
"race" (except for Negroes and those of Oriental origin)
nor ethnic-immigrant background (except for recent arrivals) but religious community. Increasingly the great mass
of Americans understand themselves and their place in society in terms of the religious community with which they
are identified. And "religious community" in this usage refers not so much to the particular denominations,[23] of

which there are scores in this country, but to the three great divisions, Catholics, Protestants, and Jews. America is indeed, in Mrs. Kennedy's terminology, the land of the "triple melting pot," for it is within these three religious communities that the process of ethnic and cultural integration so characteristic of American life takes place. Only, as we have noted, "transmuting pot" would perhaps be more appropriate than "melting pot," since in each of these communities what emerges is a "new man" cast and recast along the same "American" ideal type. It is general conformity to this ideal type that makes us all Americans, just as it is the diversity of religious community that gives us our distinctive place in American society. And in the basic diversity of religious community most other diversities tend to be defined and expressed.

We can restate all this by saying that, while the unity of American life is indeed a unity in multiplicity, the pluralism that this implies is of a very special kind. America recognizes no permanent national or cultural minorities; what Europe knows under this head are in this country regarded as foreign-language or foreign-culture groups whose separateness is merely temporary, the consequence of recent immigration, destined to be overcome with increasing integration into American life. Woodrow Wilson was sociologically wrong when he said that "America does not consist of groups"; of a certain kind of groups it does indeed consist. But he was surely reflecting the American's understanding of himself when he added: "A man who thinks of himself as belonging to a particular *national* group in America has not yet become an American."[24] Self-identification in ethnic terms, while it was a product of the American environment, was also a sign of incomplete integration into American life.

America does indeed know and acknowledge the separateness of so-called minority "races," but such separateness has always been associated with some degree of segregation and consequent relegation to an inferior status in the social hierarchy. To the American mind an ethnic group that becomes permanent and self-perpetuating and resists cultural assimilation—in other words, what the

European would call a "national-cultural" minority—would appear as an alien "race," and would be confronted with the same problems and difficulties as face the Negroes and men and women of Oriental ancestry in this country. The only kind of separateness or diversity that America recognizes as permanent, and yet also as involving no status of inferiority, is the diversity or separateness of religious community.[25] In short, while America knows no national or cultural minorities except as temporary, transitional phenomena, it does know a free variety and plurality of religions; and it is as members of a religious group that the great mass of Americans identify themselves to establish their social location once they have really sloughed off their immigrant foreignness.

For all its wide variety of regional, ethnic, and other differences, America today may be conceived, as it is indeed conceived by most Americans, as one great community divided into three big sub-communities religiously defined, all equally American in their identification with the "American Way of Life." For the third generation, which somehow wishes to "remember" of its background what the second generation was so anxious to "forget," and which is so concerned with finding its place in the larger community but not at the expense of its Americanness, this tripartite structure of American society into religious communities is most welcome and intelligible. And no wonder, since it has been the work largely of this third generation.

Just as sociologically we may describe the emerging social structure of America as one great community divided into three big sub-communities religiously defined, all equally American, so from another angle we might describe Protestantism, Catholicism, and Judaism in America as three great branches or divisions of "American religion." The assumption underlying the view shared by most Americans, at least at moments when they think in "non-sectarian" terms, is not so much that the three religious communities possess an underlying theological unity, which of course they do, but rather that they are three diverse representations of the same "spiritual values," the "spiritual values" American democracy is presumed to stand for (the

fatherhood of God and brotherhood of man, the dignity of
the individual human being, etc.). That is, at bottom, why
no one is expected to change his religion as he becomes
American;[26] since each of the religions is equally and
authentically American, the American is expected to express his religious affirmation in that form which has come
to him with his family and ethnic heritage. Particular denominational affiliations and loyalties within each of the
communities (only Protestantism and Judaism come into
question here, since Catholicism has no inner denominational lines) are not necessarily denied, or even depreciated,
but they are held to be distinctly secondary. With some
important exceptions, it is becoming more and more true
that the American, when he thinks of religion, thinks of it
primarily in terms of the three categories we have designated as religious communities.

All this has far-reaching consequences for the place of
religion in the totality of American life. With the religious
community as the primary context of self-identification and
social location, and with Protestantism, Catholicism, and
Judaism as three culturally diverse representations of the
same "spiritual values," it becomes virtually mandatory for
the American to place himself in one or another of these
groups. It is not external pressure but inner necessity that
compels him. For being a Protestant, a Catholic, or a Jew
is understood as the specific way, and increasingly perhaps
the only way, of being an American and locating oneself in
American society. It is something that does not in itself
necessarily imply actual affiliation with a particular church,
participation in religious activities, or even the affirmation
of any definite creed or belief; it implies merely identification and social location. A convinced atheist, or an eccentric
American who adopts Buddhism or Yoga, may identify
himself to himself and find his stance in life in terms of his
anti-religious ideology or exotic cult, although it is more
than likely that a Yankee turned Buddhist would still be
regarded as a "Protestant," albeit admittedly a queer one.[27]
But such people are few and far between in this country
and are not even remotely significant in determining the

American's understanding of himself. By and large, to be
an American today means to be either a Protestant, a
Catholic, or a Jew, because all other forms of self-identification and social location are either (like regional background) peripheral and obsolescent, or else (like ethnic
diversity) subsumed under the broader head of religious
community. Not to be a Catholic, a Protestant, or a Jew
today is, for increasing numbers of American people, not to
be anything, not to have a *name;* and we are all, as Riesman points out, "afraid of chaotic situations in which [we]
do not know [our] own names, [our] 'brand' names . . ."[28]
To have a name and an identity, one must belong somewhere; and more and more one "belongs" in America by
belonging to a religious community, which tells one *what*
he is. The army sergeant who, when confronted with some
theologically precise recruit (probably a high-church Episcopalian) who insisted he was neither Catholic (that is,
Roman Catholic), nor Protestant, nor Jewish, exclaimed in
exasperation, "Well, if you're not Catholic, or Protestant, or
Hebrew, what in blazes *are* you?", gave voice to the prevailing view of contemporary America.[29] Unless one is
either a Protestant, or a Catholic, or a Jew, one is a "nothing"; to be a "something," to have a name, one must
identify oneself to oneself, and be identified by others, as
belonging to one or another of the three great religious communities in which the American people are divided.

III

A partial answer to the questions raised in the first chapter
may now be ventured. One of the questions, it will be recalled, related to the ambiguous nature of the religious revival under way in this country today: What are the
sources of the religious revival, on the one hand, and of the
"trend toward secularism" (Handlin), on the other? How
does it come about that Americans today are, in one way,
more religious than they have been for a long time and are
becoming increasingly so, and yet, in other ways, are more
remote from the centrality of Jewish-Christian faith than
perhaps they have ever been? On one level at least, the

answer would seem to be that the religious revival under way in this country today—the notable increase in religious identification, affiliation, and membership—is a reflection of the social necessity of "belonging," and today the context of "belonging" is increasingly the religious community. No suggestion of insincerity is here implied, nor does what I have said preclude the operation of other factors lying closer to the heart of faith. Those who identify themselves religiously and join churches as a way of naming and locating themselves socially are not cynical unbelievers shrewdly manipulating false labels; they mean what they say when they call themselves Protestants, or Catholics, or Jews: it is our problem, as I have suggested, to define just what it is they mean. And compounded with this underlying factor of social identification, though not always in harmony with it, there may well be other factors more authentically religious perhaps in the theological sense. In any case, we now find it possible to understand how a religious revival resting on such a basis may be quite compatible with the prevalence, and even growth, of secularism. To bring this problem into clearer focus, we now turn to a more detailed study of the contemporary upswing in religion.

FOOTNOTES

1. George R. Stewart, *American Ways of Life* (Doubleday, 1954), pp. 50, 72. "There were limits within which the realities of American life perpetuated rather than destroyed distinctions. . . . Some differences in the United States had come to be accepted as permanent and not subject to assimilation—among them those of religion" (Oscar Handlin, *Adventure in Freedom: Three Hundred Years of Jewish Life in America* [McGraw-Hill, 1954], p. 164).

2. Cf. Robin M. Williams, *American Society: A Sociological Interpretation* (Knopf, 1951), pp. 320–24; for further discussion, see below, chap. v, pp. 85–87.

3. Marcus L. Hansen, *The Problem of the Third Generation Immigrant* (Augustana Historical Society, Rock Island, Ill., 1938), p. 7.

4. "Ignorance of our language is an important barrier to assimilation. Generally speaking, adherence to a foreign language within a country tends to cocoon an ethnic group and keep it

alien" (W. S. Smith, *Americans in the Making* [Appleton-Century, 1939], pp. 147–48).

5. Oscar Handlin, *The American People in the Twentieth Century* (Harvard, 1954), pp. 190–91.

6. Hansen, *The Problem of the Third Generation Immigrant*, pp. 9–10.

7. Handlin, *The American People*, p. 221.

8. Handlin, *The American People*, p. 222. "Whenever any immigrant group reaches the third generation stage in its development, a spontaneous and almost irresistible impulse arises which forces the thoughts of many people of different professions, different positions in life, and different points of view to interest themselves in that one factor which they have in common: heritage . . ." (Hansen, *The Problem of the Third Generation Immigrant*, p. 12). Speaking of Norwegian immigrants, Warner writes: "As the first and second generation of American-born children . . . have grown up, there is increasing replacement of ethnic symbols by religious symbols" (W. Lloyd Warner, *Structure of American Life* [Edinburgh, 1952], p. 139). "In our society, religion is a socially accepted way of perpetuating group differences" (Marshall Sklare, *Conservative Judaism: An American Religious Movement* [Free Press, 1955], p. 134).

9. Handlin, *The American People*, p. 222.

10. Ruby Jo Reeves Kennedy, "Single or Triple Melting Pot? Intermarriage Trends in New Haven, 1870–1940," *American Journal of Sociology*, Vol. XLIX, No. 4, January 1944.

11. Two major groups stand measurably outside this division of American society into three "melting pots"—the Negroes and the recent Latin-American immigrants (Mexicans in the Southwest, Puerto Ricans in New York and other eastern centers). Ethnic amalgamation within the religious community does not yet include them to any appreciable extent; their primary context of self-identification and social location remains their ethnic or "racial" group. (See C. Wright Mills, Clarence Senior, and Rose Kohn Goldsen, *The Puerto Rican Journey* [Harper, 1950]; John R. Scotford, *Within These Borders: Spanish-Speaking Peoples in the U.S.A.* [Friendship Press, 1953]; and Christopher Rand, *The Puerto Ricans* [Oxford, 1957].) There is reason to believe that with the cessation of large-scale Puerto Rican immigration and the emergence of an American third generation, this group will tend to break up into two distinct sections, one "white," the other "colored" (defined by a complex of "racial" and socio-cultural factors), with each section moving toward absorption into the major divisions of the general community. The future of the Negroes in the United States constitutes a much more difficult problem, about which very little may be said with any assurance today.

12. The very meaning of the word "intermarriage" (as applied to whites) has undergone a significant change in line with the changing structure of American society. A generation ago, it still meant *ethnic* intermarriage (*Abie's Irish Rose*); today, it regularly means *religious* intermarriage (Protestant-Catholic-Jewish), and is so commonly used.

13. August B. Hollingshead, "Cultural Factors in the Selection of Marriage Mates," *American Sociological Review*, Vol. XVI, No. 1, October 1950. "Increasingly in the United States, marriages for all groups fell into the religious divisions: Catholic, Protestant, Jewish" (Handlin, *Adventure in Freedom*, p. 165).

14. John L. Thomas, "The Factor of Religion in the Selection of Marriage Mates," *American Sociological Review*, Vol. XVI, No. 4, August 1951.

15. Handlin, *The American People*, p. 223. The extraordinary cohesiveness of these religious communities as contexts of "belonging" is strikingly evidenced by the fact that in 1955 only 4 per cent of adult Americans had shifted their adherence from the community of their birth; 96 per cent still belonged to the community—Protestant, Catholic, Jewish—into which they had been born (see report of the survey [Gallup poll] conducted by the American Institute of Public Opinion, *Public Opinion News Service*, March 20, 1955). The same survey indicates that most of those who had left the religious community of their birth because of intermarriage or other reasons did not remain unattached, but joined, or identified themselves with, another of the three communities.

16. "American ethnic groups are tending to change their outward appearance. They can preserve themselves as religious groups" (Sklare, *Conservative Judaism: An American Religious Movement*, p. 37). I would, however, suggest that it is more than "outward appearance" that is being changed.

17. Samuel Lubell, *The Future of American Politics* (Harper, 1951).

18. The term, "minorities," is singularly inappropriate to American reality. It was borrowed from the vocabulary of European nationalism during World War I, and has virtually no meaning in a country where, on the one hand, everyone belongs to a minority of some sort, and, on the other, no permanent and self-perpetuating national minorities of any size are known.

19. Thus, in summarizing a report to the New York Board of Regents on discriminatory practices in medical school admissions, in which it is made clear that the grounds of discrimination are primarily ethnic origin and recency of immigration, Warren Weaver, Jr., writes: "A student who wants to study medicine in New York State stands a better chance of getting

admitted to one of the nine professional schools if he is Protestant rather than Catholic, or Catholic rather than Jewish, a report to the Board of Regents indicated today" (*The New York Times,* July 10, 1953). Here, quite as a matter of course, the religious communities are made to do service for the ethnic groups they are assumed to include and represent.

20. Handlin, *The American People,* p. 48. "It is the general consensus of informed observers that these three groups constitute social environments for their members: that is, the overwhelming majority of Protestants, Catholics, and Jews associate with their fellow religious-group members. This community pattern is probably related more to the persistence of ethnic communities and to social discrimination than it is to religious faith." (Seymour Martin Lipset, *et al., Union Democracy* [Free Press, 1956], pp. 114–15).

21. Handlin, "Group Life Within the American Pattern," *Commentary,* Vol. VIII, No. 5, November 1949.

22. Note that today "Jew" refers to a religious community, whereas in the earlier context it signified primarily an ethnic-immigrant group; for further discussion of this point see below, chap. viii, pp. 186–87.

23. In some parts of the country, perhaps, where very few Catholics and Jews are to be found, social location may take place in terms of the major Protestant denominations.

24. Quoted by Handlin, *The American People,* p. 121.

25. "While ethnic separation is not very highly valued in our culture, religious distinctiveness is allowable—even esteemed in a way, because it is American" (Sklare, *Conservative Judaism: An American Religious Movement,* pp. 36–37).

26. That does not mean that *every* religion is so regarded. All religions, of course, are entitled to, and receive, equal freedom and protection under the Constitution, but not all are felt to be really American and therefore to be retained with Americanization. The Buddhism of Chinese and Japanese immigrants, for example, is definitely felt to be something foreign in a way that Lutheranism, or even Catholicism, never was; the Americanization of the Chinese or Japanese immigrant is usually felt by the immigrant himself, as well as by the surrounding American community, to involve dropping the non-American faith and becoming a Catholic or a Protestant, usually the latter.

27. I know a distinguished professor in a New England college who is at once a Unitarian and a Buddhist (he was indeed initiated into one of the Buddhist sects); this is regarded by his friends as rather odd, but as in no way impugning his Protestantism. And his is not the only case of this kind that has come to my attention.

28. David Riesman, *Individualism Reconsidered* (Free Press, 1954), p. 178.

29. Thus Fred Lewis, described as an "American of Russian extraction" and a spokesman of Eastern Orthodoxy in the United States, quite understandably laments: "We [Eastern] Orthodox Catholics are indignant each time we hear about the Three Great Faiths. We know it should be Four, and individually we have tried to convince our fellow-Americans of this. But we have gotten nowhere" ("Concerning a National Orthodox Council of America," *St. Vladimir's Seminary Quarterly*, Vol. II, No. 4, Summer 1954). It would be interesting to discover how Mr. Lewis knows "it should be four"; obviously, he takes the American scheme of the "three great faiths" for granted, and merely wants to add his own as a fourth.

IV. *The Contemporary Upswing in Religion*

I

No one who attempts to see the contemporary religious situation in the United States in perspective can fail to be struck by the extraordinary pervasiveness of religious identification among present-day Americans. Almost everybody in the United States today locates himself in one or another of the three great religious communities. Asked to identify themselves in terms of religious "preference,"[1] 95 per cent of the American people, according to a recent public opinion survey, declared themselves to be either Protestants, Catholics, or Jews (68 per cent Protestants, 23 per cent Catholics, 4 per cent Jews); only 5 per cent admitted to no "preference."[2] Some differences, one or two perhaps of real significance, are indicated when these figures are broken down according to race, age, sex, education, occupation, income, region, and degree of urbanization; but, by and large, the conclusion seems to be that virtually the entire body of the American people, in every part of the country and in every section of society, regard themselves as belonging to some religious community. The results of the survey are fully borne out by the reports of informed observers of the American scene.

Such information as that which this survey provides is unfortunately not available for earlier times, and so direct comparison is impossible. But it seems safe to assume that these figures, reflecting the situation in the early 1950s, represent an all-time high in religious identification. Through the nineteenth century and well into the twentieth America knew the militant secularist, the atheist or "freethinker," as a familiar figure in cultural life, along with

considerably larger numbers of "agnostics" who would
have nothing to do with churches and refused to identify
themselves religiously. These still exist, of course, but their
ranks are dwindling and they are becoming more and more
inconspicuous, taking the American people as a whole.[3]
The "village atheist" is a vanishing figure; Clarence Darrow
and Brann the Iconoclast, who once commanded large and
excited audiences, have left no successors. Indeed, their
kind of anti-religion is virtually meaningless to most Americans today, who simply cannot understand how one can be
"against religion" and for whom some sort of religious
identification is more or less a matter of course. This was
not always the case; that it is the case today there can be
no reasonable doubt. The pervasiveness of religious identification may safely be put down as a significant feature of
the America that has emerged in the past quarter of a
century.

The figures for church membership tell the same story
but in greater detail. Religious statistics in this country are
notoriously inaccurate,[4] but the trend is so well marked
that it overrides all margins of error. In the quarter of a
century between 1926 and 1950 the population of continental United States increased 28.6 per cent; membership of religious bodies increased 59.8 per cent: in other
words, church membership grew more than twice as fast as
population. Protestants increased 63.7 per cent, Catholics
53.9 per cent, Jews 22.5 per cent. Among Protestants, however, the increase varied considerably as between denominations: Baptist increase was well over 100 per cent, some
"holiness" sects grew even more rapidly, while the figure
for the Episcopal Church was only 36.7 per cent, for the
Methodist Church 32.2 per cent, for the Northern Presbyterians 22.4 per cent, and for the Congregationalists 21.1
per cent.[5] In general, it may be said that "practically all
major types of American religion have staged what is
popularly called a 'comeback.'"[6]

In 1950 total church membership was reckoned at
85,319,000, or about 57 per cent of the total population.
In 1958 it was 109,557,741, or about 63 per cent, marking
an all-time high in the nation's history.[7] Indeed, all avail-

able information tends to show that the proportion of the
American people religiously affiliated as church members
has been consistently growing from the early days of the
republic. In his address to the Evanston Assembly of the
World Council of Churches, President Eisenhower pointed
out that: "Contrary to what many people think, the percentage of our population belonging to churches steadily
increases. In a hundred years, that percentage has multiplied more than three times."[8]

President Eisenhower was here probably understating
the case. Comparisons are difficult, and figures even approximately accurate are not available for earlier times, but
it seems to be generally agreed that church membership
in the United States at the opening of the nineteenth century was not much more than 10 or 15 per cent of the
population;[9] through the century it grew at a varying rate,
reflecting many factors, but above all the success of the
evangelical movement in bringing religion to the frontier
and the vast influx of Roman Catholic immigrants with a
high proportion of church membership. At the opening of
the present century, church membership stood at something like 36 per cent of the population; in 1926, when the
Census of Religious Bodies established a new basis of calculation, it was about 46 per cent; in 1958, 63 per cent.[10]
The trend is obvious, despite the lack of precision of the
particular figures.

It is not easy to understand just what these figures reveal beyond a steady increase through a century and a
half. Church membership does not mean the same today as
it meant in the eighteenth or early nineteenth century,
when something of the older sense of personal conversion
and commitment still remained. Further, such factors as
recent population trends and the increased mobility con-
ferred by the automobile cannot be ignored in any serious
effort to estimate the reasons for the growing proportion of
Americans in the churches. There is also the significant
fact that considerably more Americans regard themselves
as church members than the statistics of church affiliation
would indicate. Asked, "Do you happen at the present
time to be an active member of a church or of a religious

group?", 73 per cent of Americans over 18 answered in the affirmative: of those identifying themselves as Catholics, 87 per cent said "yes"; of those identifying themselves as Protestants, 75 per cent; and of those identifying themselves as Jews, 50 per cent.[11] The over-all total of 73 per cent is considerably higher than the percentage indicated in church membership statistics: 57 per cent in 1950 and 63 per cent in 1958. It would seem that many more people in the United States regard themselves as members, even "active" members, of a church than are listed on the actual membership rolls of the churches. The fact of the matter seems to be that: "In America, there is no sharp division between those within the religious fold and those outside, as there tends to be in Europe. It is extremely difficult, in fact, to determine just how many members the churches have, since no clear boundary marks off members from those who participate without formal membership."[12]

About 70 to 75 per cent of the American people, it may be safely estimated, regard themselves as members of churches;[13] another 20 or 25 per cent locate themselves in one or another religious community without a consciousness of actual church membership—they constitute a "fringe of sympathetic bystanders,"[14] so to speak. Only about 5 per cent of the American people consider themselves outside the religious fold altogether.

Church attendance constitutes another, and more restrictive, measure of religious "belonging." The survey we have been using also included the question, "Did you happen to attend any Sunday or Sabbath church services during the last twelve weeks?" To this, 68 per cent answered in the affirmative—82 per cent of the Catholics, 68 per cent of the Protestants, and 44 per cent of the Jews.[15] In 1944 an American Institute of Public Opinion (Gallup) poll revealed that 58 per cent of adult Americans stated that they had attended a religious service in the past four weeks;[16] according to more recent surveys church attendance grew considerably between 1952 and 1957.[17] Church attendance in America, while not always very regular, is fairly substantial and is certainly increasing.[18]

The picture no doubt differs considerably in different

parts of the country, among various classes and ethnographic groups, but for our purposes, at this point at least, the common features are more important: the pervasiveness of religious "belonging," the relatively high percentage of membership, and the substantial attendance characteristic of American churches.[19]

Along with membership and attendance, Sunday school enrollment has shown a marked rise in recent years. Reports for 241 religious bodies in the United States indicate that the rate of increase in enrollment from 1947 to 1949 "surpassed the rate of increase both of church membership and of general population . . . for the first time in a number of years."[20] In these two years Sunday school enrollment gained 7.3 per cent, total church membership increased 5.8 per cent, while population rose 3.6 per cent. From 1952 to 1953 the increase in enrollment was even greater: 8.1 per cent as against an increase in church membership of 2.8 per cent. Reported Sunday school enrollment in 1953 stood at 35,389,000; in 1958, it stood at 41,197,313.[21]

Virtually all surveys indicate also a very considerable expansion in church construction in the course of the past decade, particularly in the suburbs of the big cities. The value of new "religious buildings" jumped from $76,000,-000 in 1946, to $409,000,000 in 1950, to $868,000,000 in 1957.[22] In 1952 it was reported that "since World War II, the Catholics have been opening 150 to 200 churches a year, often averaging nearly four a week."[23] The same report also indicates that increasing numbers of synagogues were going up all over the country.[24] A good deal of this expansion of church building no doubt reflected the increasing prosperity of large sections of the American people; it was also, however, undeniable testimony to the high valuation Americans placed on religious institutions in the scale of priority of community expenditures. Very much the same conclusion may be drawn from a study of other aspects of church financing in America in the past fifteen or twenty years.[25] Churches rate high in the community picture in every part of the United States.

On the whole, the jubilant declaration of the Methodist

Council of Bishops in the spring of 1954 that there was a "great upsurge in church life" under way in the United States was not without its justification. "Our people," the Methodist bishops noted in their message, "are attending public worship in larger numbers than we have ever known. . . . New churches are being enterprised in every area of America. . . . Giving has reached an all-time high. . . . A new spirit has fallen upon our people."[26] With regard to religion, a new spirit was indeed abroad in the land.

The enhanced standing of churches and religion among the American people is strikingly indicated by the enhanced status of religious leaders. According to surveys conducted by Elmo Roper, Americans, in answering the question, "Which one of these groups do you feel is doing the most good for the country at the present time?", placed religious leaders third, after government leaders and business leaders, in 1942, but first in 1947. In the former year (1942), 17.5 per cent thought religious leaders were "doing the most good," as against 27.7 per cent who put more trust in government leaders, and 18.7 per cent in business leaders (6.2 per cent trusted most in labor leaders and another 6.2 per cent in Congress). Five years later, however, in 1947, 32.6 per cent of the people chose religious leaders as those who were "doing most good"; 18.8 per cent chose business leaders; 15.4 per cent, government leaders; 10.6 per cent, labor leaders; and 6.7 per cent, Congress.[27] A similar survey, conducted by Mr. Roper in 1957, found that 46 per cent of the American people picked religious leaders as the group "doing the most good" and most to be trusted. "No other group—whether government, Congressional, business, or labor—came anywhere near matching the prestige and pulling power of the men who are the ministers of God."[28] The picture of the clergyman that Americans have may not be without its ambiguous aspects, but there can be little doubt that the "minister of God" ranks high, and is rising rapidly, in the American scale of prestige. This rise of public confidence in clergymen no doubt reflects the rising status of religion and the church in American social life.

Much the same may be said about the high and growing repute of religion in the American public mind. "Religion is given continued public and political approval. . . . 'Godless' is a powerful epithet. . . . At least nominal public acceptance of religion tends to be a prerequisite to political success . . ."[29] It was not always so; there was a time when an atheist or agnostic like Robert G. Ingersoll, who went around the country defying God and making antireligious speeches, could nevertheless occupy a respected and influential position in American politics.[30] Today that would be quite inconceivable; a professed "unbeliever" would be anathema to either of the big parties and would have no chance whatever in political life. The contrast between the days of Ingersoll and our day, when every candidate for public office is virtually required to testify to his high esteem for religion, measures the position that religion as a "value" or institution has acquired in the American public mind. Of the 528 members of the two houses of the 85th Congress, only 4 gave no religious affiliation; 416 registered as Protestants, 95 as Roman Catholics, 12 as Jews, and one as a Sikh.[31]

That public opinion is markedly more favorable to religion today than it has been for a long time is recognized by all observers. "A hostile attitude toward religion as such," Schneider notes, "gets less of a hearing today than a century ago, or even half a century ago."[32] Foreign visitors are almost without exception amazed at the extreme deference paid to religion, religious leaders, and religious institutions in present-day America.[33] It is probably true that "in no other modern industrial state does organized religion play a greater role" than it does in the United States.[34]

With institutional growth and enhanced public status has come a notable increase in the self-assurance of the spokesmen of religion, who no longer feel themselves defending a losing cause against a hostile world. "It [has become] clear that, contrary to what many . . . leading historians and sociologists asserted early in the century, religion has not declined in America since 1900";[35] very much to the contrary. Spokesmen of religion are now beginning to speak with the confidence of those who feel that things are going their way and that they are assured of a respectful hearing. Indeed, there have lately arisen voices among the "irreligious" minority who profess to see their "freedom *from* religion" threatened by the increasingly pro-religious climate of our culture and the new aggressiveness of the churches.[36] It is a far cry indeed from the 1920s, when religion and the churches were in retreat, faith was taken as a sign of intellectual backwardness or imbecility, and the initiative had passed to the "emancipated" debunkers of the superstitions of the "Babbitts" and the "Bible Belt." That age has disappeared almost without a trace, and the generation that has arisen since finds it well-nigh impossible to imagine what those days were like, so remote from our consciousness have they become.

Particularly significant as reflecting a reversal of trend is the new intellectual prestige of religion on all levels of cultural life. On one level, this means the extraordinarily high proportion of so-called "religious books" on the best-seller lists;[37] on another, the remarkable vogue in intellectual circles of the more sophisticated religious and theological writing of our time. Kierkegaard (rediscovered in this generation), Tillich, Maritain, Reinhold Niebuhr, Buber, Berdyaev, Simone Weil: these writers have standing and prestige with the intellectual elite of today in a way that no religious writers have had for many decades. Religious ideas, concepts, and teachings have become familiar in the pages of the "vanguard" journals of literature, politics, and art. "It is certainly true," a recent English survey of religion in America concludes, "that the intellectual climate for religious thinking and the social climate for religious living are much more congenial than they were in the twenties and thirties."[38]

Indeed, the intellectual rehabilitation of religion has become so pronounced that even observers like Reinhold Niebuhr, who are exceedingly cautious in weighing the claims of a contemporary "revival" of religion, acknowledge the signs in this area to be quite unmistakable. "There is evidence," Dr. Niebuhr writes, "that in the world of culture, there is at least a receptivity toward the message of the historic faiths which is in marked contrast to the indifference or hostility of past decades." He himself feels that the "increase of interest in religious problems in the academic communities of the nation, in which, for obvious reasons, the 'secular' spirit of the age was . . . pronounced," is particularly noteworthy. He calls attention to the fact that "there is scarcely a college or university which has not recently either created a department of religion or substantially enlarged existing departments," and he stresses the difference in quality and temper that distinguishes so much of current academic teaching in the field of religion from that of earlier decades. "Until very recently, religious studies in our colleges were very much on the defensive. . . . This defensive attitude has been replaced by a type of teaching which avails itself of all the instruments of modern historical scholarship, but is guided by a conviction of the importance and relevance of the 'message' of the Bible, as distinguished from the message of, say, Plato, on the one hand, or Herbert Spencer, on the other."[39]

The renewed interest in religion in the academic community, and among intellectuals generally, is indeed a noteworthy sign of the times. The extraordinary expansion of departments of religion and programs of religious instruction is only one aspect; perhaps even more important is the widening interest that transcends the academic and goes beyond instructional programs. There is, many observers have noted in recent years, a genuine "stirring" on the campuses of the nation,[40] particularly among the intellectual elite. "Ten or fifteen years ago," Professor H. Stuart Hughes recently remarked in a review of a book by John Hallowell, "no self-respecting 'enlightened' intellectual would have been caught dead with a religious interpretation of anything. Only the Catholics thought in these terms —plus a scattering of Protestants, whom we dismissed as harmless eccentrics. We were either 'idealistic' socialist-radicals or sceptical, hard-boiled Freudian-Paretans. Any other attitude would have been considered a betrayal of the avant-garde. Now Mr. Hallowell confirms the suspicions that have gradually been drifting up to us from the students we confront. The avant-garde is becoming old-fashioned; religion is now the latest thing."[41]

Professor Hughes has here put his finger on the ambiguous character of the recent intellectual prestige of religion; there is undoubtedly an element of vogue or fashion in it, as there is also a deeper concern and interest. However that may be, the new intellectual climate is certainly of symptomatic significance; even if much of the interest in religion is vogue or fashion, the fact that vogue or fashion now runs in favor of religion rather than against it is surely itself a fact of considerable importance for our understanding of the time.

Even the old-line, hard-boiled secularist intellectuals seem to be affected. In four successive issues, February through May 1950, *Partisan Review* ran a symposium on "Religion and the Intellectuals," in which twenty-nine writers, most of them of radical background, took part.[42] Of the twenty-nine participants, about half were still hostile, five presented explicit statements of faith, and the rest, some ten, took an uncommitted but friendly position. "The startling thing about the collection," a reviewer at the time noted, "is the size of the middle group, the fellow-travelers of faith . . ."[43] These "fellow-travelers of faith," mixing and merging with those for whom faith has a much deeper meaning, are increasingly giving the tone to the more advanced intellectual life of the nation.

Though we are obliged to note the qualifications and ambiguities of the current turn to religion, among the intellectuals as among other sections of the population, it would be a gross error to ignore or deny the genuine personal faith and commitment to be found in American religion at all levels. "It is probably true," Schneider concludes, "that . . . Americans take religion more personally than other peoples do." He mentions "an Anglican visitor to the United States recently [who] reported that there prevails a 'shocking personal religiosity among Americans.'"[44] This "personal religiosity" has many sides, which we shall attempt to examine later in the discussion, but its existence cannot be denied, nor its importance in subtly transmuting

much of the externalism of the religious institutions and
activities to which we have devoted our attention so far.

I I

That there has in recent years been an upswing of religion
in the United States can hardly be doubted; the evidence
is diverse, converging, and unequivocal beyond all possibilities of error. It is another matter, however, when we
come to assess the factors that have made, and are making,
for this notable shift in the social attitudes and cultural
climate of our time. When we try to isolate these factors or
reveal their mode of operation, we begin to sense the in-
adequacy of all sociological "explanation" of phenomena
that in their very nature transcend the sociological. Nevertheless, it seems to me that certain significant things may
be said about the present religious situation which might
contribute to an understanding of the current turn to religion in America.

We may proceed with our analysis on various levels.
Most generally and comprehensively, the rise in religious
identification, membership, and attendance would seem to
be closely related to the change in social structure of the
American community we have described in earlier chapters. America, it was there pointed out, has changed from
the "land of immigrants," with its thriving ethnic groups,
to the "triple melting pot," in which people tend more and
more to identify and locate themselves socially in terms of
three great sub-communities—Protestant, Catholic, Jewish
—defined in religious terms. To find a place in American
society increasingly means to place oneself in one or another of these religious communities. And although this
process of self-identification and social location is not in
itself intrinsically religious, the mere fact that in order to
be "something" one must be either a Protestant, a Catholic,
or a Jew means that one begins to think of oneself as religiously identified and affiliated. *Naming* oneself a Protestant, a Catholic, or a Jew carries with it a distinctive
attitude to "one's" church, an attitude that is definitely favorable. Since one "is" a Protestant, a Catholic, or a Jew,

and recognizes oneself as such, one tends to think of oneself as somehow part of a church and involved in its activities and concerns. Whether one actually joins or not, the inclination is to think of oneself as a member: hence the significant fact that many more people report themselves as members of churches than are on church rolls.[45] And increasingly one does actually become a member and join in the activities of the church; increasingly too the children are sent to church and church school—for many reasons, not least, however, because "the church supplies a place where children come to learn what they are."[46] There does not seem to be any real question that the restructuring of American society that emerges with the third generation has been a major factor in the turn to religion so characteristic of our time. Religion has become a primary symbol of "heritage," and church membership the most appropriate form of "belonging" under contemporary American conditions.

Another factor of prime sociological importance has worked toward the same end, and that is the basic change in character structure that seems to be under way among certain sections of the American people. The reference here is to the shift from inner-direction to other-direction, which David Riesman has analyzed and documented so impressively.[47] Riesman, it will be recalled, distinguishes three types of character structure—tradition-directed, inner-directed, and other-directed—which he finds predominating at different times in different societies yet also entering in different degrees into contemporary American life. Tradition-direction, in which each generation receives from its predecessor and internalizes for itself a fairly fixed pattern of folkways, is characteristic of primitive and stable peasant societies; it has never really been part of the ongoing life of a dynamic society such as ours, although the collapse of tradition-direction upon the peasant immigrant's first encounter with the New World has had repercussions into our own time. American society has hitherto been, and still is, predominantly inner-directed; each succeeding generation internalizes not a traditional pattern of folkways but a set of "goals" or "principles," to which the individual is

kept true by a powerful inner drive. Borrowing a figure
from Gardner Murphy, Riesman pictures the inner-directed
man as operating with a kind of built-in gyroscope which
holds him steadily, sometimes ruthlessly, to his course,
driving ahead for the fulfillment of his purposes. The inner-
directed man is work-conscious, intent upon achievement,
not afraid to stand on his own feet and if necessary against
the crowd, interested in "results" not in "personalities." It
is the inner-directed man who has been characteristic of
American life and achievement so far.

Lately, however, for reasons that are still obscure
though we are beginning to get some inkling of them, there
has been emerging on certain levels another character type,
described as other-directed. Instead of possessing a built-in
gyroscope to keep him true to his course, the other-directed
man operates with a kind of built-in radar apparatus which
is ceaselessly at work receiving signals from the person's
"peer group" and adjusting him to the situation indicated
by these signals. The other-directed man is a man who is
concerned with adjustment rather than with achievement;
he is personality-conscious rather than work-conscious,
bland, tolerant, co-operative, "civilized"—but dreadfully
afraid of being too "different," of getting too much out of
line with his "peer group." Indeed, the greatest horror of
the other-directed man, that which renders him so acutely
uncomfortable, is to feel "unadjusted" and "unsociable"
("anti-social"); whereas the inner-directed man, as we have
seen, is always ready to stand up against his environment
and indeed seems to get a kind of grim satisfaction out of
doing so. The "morality" of the inner-directed type becomes "morale" for the other-directed; "character" becomes "personality"; moral indignation and intolerance
give way to a kind of all-embracing tolerance—tolerance of
everything and everybody except the "unadjusted" and the
"anti-social." The operative law of life of the other-directed
man is conformity and adjustment; the built-in radar that
characterizes other-direction sees to it that such adjustment
to a fluctuating environment is generally achieved quite
unconsciously and is therefore invested with the emotional
power of unconscious motivation.

In America today, though inner-direction remains dominant, other-direction has already become prevalent in the new suburban middle-class society consisting of professionals and junior executives, and seems bound to spread upward and downward in the social hierarchy. The emergence of this type, and its growing prominence in the community, brings with it a number of far-reaching consequences for the social and cultural life of our time.

In particular, it is not difficult to see the current turn to religion and the church as, in part at least, a reflection of the growing other-directedness of our middle-class culture. The people in the suburbs want to feel psychologically secure, adjusted, at home in their environment; the very character structure that makes this so urgent a necessity for them also operates to meet the need. Being religious and joining a church is, under contemporary American conditions, a fundamental way of "adjusting" and "belonging"; through the built-in radar apparatus of other-direction it becomes almost automatic as an obvious social requirement, like entertaining or culture. The vogue of Van Gogh and Renoir reproductions in the suburban home and the rising church affiliation of the suburban community may not be totally unconnected; both may, without disparagement, be interpreted, in part at least, as the consequence of the craving for adjustment and conformity involved in other-direction. The right kind of art reproductions testifies to one's being adjusted to the culture of one's "peer group"; belonging to the church is experienced as the most satisfactory form of social "belonging." The trend toward religious identification and church affiliation may thus to an extent be a reflection of the growing need for conformity and sociability that the drift to other-direction brings with it.[48]

The operations of other-direction fall in rather neatly with the over-all effects of the restructuring of American society in terms of religious community. To identify and locate oneself in the social context is a requirement under all conditions; it becomes particularly pressing and urgent under conditions of other-direction, since other-direction craves conformity and adjustment as a veritable necessity of life. On the other hand, the other-directed need for "belonging" finds its most direct and appropriate expression in present-day America in identifying oneself with a religious community and joining a church. Whether we approach it from one direction or the other the result seems to be the same: a marked trend toward religious identification and church affiliation.

These more obviously sociological factors ought not, however, to obscure other, perhaps less definable, forces operating at other levels of human life. The contemporary crisis of Western civilization, which has brought a sense of total insecurity to men everywhere, is surely one of the most significant of these. The utter predicament of human existence is no longer simply a philosophical or theological proposition; it is the most patent of everyday facts. The hydrogen bomb, on which our survival depends, yet which threatens us with destruction, is the sinister symbol of our plight. Confronted with the demonic threat of Communist totalitarianism, we are driven to look beyond the routine ideas and attitudes that may have served in easier times. On every side insecurity assails us, and yet security is becoming more and more the urgent need of our time. In the midst of our prosperity, we need, desperately need, reassurance and the promise of peace.

In this situation of pervasive crisis, religion appeals to many as "synonymous with peace," indeed as offering the "best hope of peace in the world today"[49]—"peace of mind" for the individual amid the anxieties and confusions of contemporary existence, peace for the nation in the life-and-death struggle with Communism. Particularly in this latter conflict religion commends itself as our greatest resource and most powerful "secret weapon." In the week in which I first wrote these words three outstanding clerical leaders of the three religious communities of the nation made eloquent pleas for religion on this ground: one called religion the "shield of the nation"; the other proclaimed it as "more powerful than the H-bomb"; the third recommended it as "America's strongest weapon against atheistic Communism." Even erstwhile secularists are beginning to see things in a new light; the *Zeitgeist* has not been without effect among them, nor the urgencies of the present world situation. They are beginning to show a growing appreciation of the social utility of religion for Western culture, especially in fighting Communism. Quite a few old-time secularists are no longer so sure that religion is on its way out; nor for that matter are they so sure that they would be happy to see religion go, for when religion goes (many secularists now ruefully admit), it is only too often replaced not by "reason" and "enlightenment" but by one or another of the wild superstitions and demonic cults that the modern age has spawned. Religion has suddenly emerged as a major power in the "hundred years of Cold War" that appears to confront mankind.

On another, more personal, or rather more private, level, too, religion has been found to serve the need for security. On this level the turn to religion is to be linked, many think, with the sensational reversal of long-time population trends and the sudden rise of birth rates among college graduates and professional people in the United States. Since 1946 these rates have been increasing every year, and in 1954 married graduates of the class of 1944, ten years out of college, already averaged more children than the class of 1921 when it had been out twenty-five years in 1946, the year the study we are citing was initiated.[50] This demographical fact would seem to confirm the impression many observers have had in recent years that, amid the mounting insecurities of our time, increasing numbers of younger people are turning to the security to be found in the enduring, elemental ways and institutions of mankind; in the family, they feel, they can find the permanence and stability, the meaning and value they crave amid a world falling into chaos. Religion, like the family, is one of the enduring, elemental institutions of mankind; indeed, the two have been closely linked from the very earliest times. The turn to the private life, reflecting the attempt to find meaning and security in what is basic and unchanging, rather than in the fluctuating fortunes of social or political activity, is one of the major factors in the upswing of religion among the American people today.

It is perhaps not without significance that the Oak Ridge community in Tennessee, consisting largely of atomic scientists and technicians with their families, for long showed little interest in the political status of the community but very early displayed an intense concern for building religious institutions. In 1953 the Oak Ridgers, by a big majority, turned down a proposal for local autonomy and voted to let the AEC continue operation of their municipal services. But, as the report points out, that was not because they were apathetic or regarded themselves as transients at Oak Ridge; rather it was because they saw the "key" of their family and community development in the development of their churches. The first meeting to establish a church was held in 1943, within a few weeks after the launching of the Oak Ridge project; in 1953, ten years later, Oak Ridge, with a population of 31,000, had thirty-seven different congregations holding regular services and performing the multiform functions of the American church. Building activity was still going on, in many cases church members performing part of the work with their own hands. For Oak Ridge, though a prosperous community, had no rich people to endow churches or make huge contributions; everything had to be done by the people themselves. "While residents here feel that Oak Ridge still has some years to go before it can completely cut its municipal ties with the federal government," the report concludes, "most of them agree that in the religious growth here, the community's roots are very definitely showing."[51] In the Oak Ridge scheme of priorities religion and the church obviously ranked at the top, along with the home and the school. It is surely of considerable import that this age-old trinity of American life—the home, the church, and the school—should find so impressive a rebirth in this most modern of communities of the atomic age.

Personal need enters into the present religious situation in still another way. Confronted with the depersonalizing pressures of contemporary life, modern man experiences a profound exigency to preserve some remnant of personality and inwardness against the erosions of a mass culture. Increasingly, he turns to religion to provide him an inexpugnable citadel for the self in a world in which personal authenticity is threatened on every side; indeed, the quest for personal authenticity is itself substantially a religious quest. Reflecting, as it does, the crisis of our time, it also points to its deeper meaning. For ultimately, the crisis of our time is a crisis of faith. The secular faiths of our culture have ignominiously collapsed under the shattering impact of the events of our time. Many of the "truths" by which "modern-minded" men lived in earlier decades have revealed themselves to be little more than vain and fatuous illusions. We can no longer look to science, to "progress," to economics, or to politics for salvation; we recognize that these things have their value, but we also know that they are not gods bringing redemption from the confusions and perils of existence. An age intoxicated with utopian dreams about the boundless possibilities of "scientific progress" and "social reconstruction" has been succeeded by an age more sober, more realistic—some would say too much so. But one cannot live by sober, limited, pragmatic programs for restricted ends; these soon lose whatever meaning they have unless they are embedded in a transcendent, actuality-defying vision. Man needs faith, a total, all-embracing faith, for living. The faiths by which men live in a secular age "base the meaning of existence upon some assumed stability of human virtue or reason [or power], some pattern of history or societal security";[52] when these are swept away by the great upheavals of history, the way is opened for a better appreciation of the power and relevance of the historic faiths. How far turning to these faiths at a time of crisis represents "escapism" in the bad sense of the term, and how far it reflects a deeper searching for the realities of existence, no one can tell for another, perhaps not even for himself; we may safely assume that something of each is present, compounded with the other. But that it is not simply irresponsibility or a "failure of nerve," that it may indeed help to nerve one for greater endurance and unyielding resistance to evil and unreason, is surely sufficiently attested by the events of our time. At its deepest level the turn to religion we are witnessing owes much of its force to the search for a new and more viable "philosophy" of existence amid the spiritual chaos of our age.[53]

This analysis is neither complete nor exhaustive; no analysis of this kind can be. But it is felt that all of the factors brought to notice are genuinely relevant to the situation and that together they serve to cast some light on the problem. It is perhaps not necessary to stress the point that these factors are by no means clearly defined or independent of each other. They are all fused and compounded in a single social-cultural-spiritual complex in which we in America today live and have our being. Taken in this way, the considerations here brought forward may help us understand something of what is involved in the current upswing of religion in the United States. But it is well to repeat that religion, touching as it does man's ultimate relation, in the end escapes all explanatory categories.

FOOTNOTES

1. The use of the term "preference" to indicate religious identification is itself of considerable significance; it reflects the feeling of Americans that somehow they *choose* ("religious preference") their *status* ("religious community"). Actually, no more than 4 per cent of Americans leave the religious community (Protestant, Catholic, Jewish) of their birth (see above, chap. iii, note 15).

2. "Who Belongs to What Church?", *The Catholic Digest*, January 1953. This is a report of a survey conducted by Ben Gaffin and Associates. (Only adults over 18 are considered. It is also worth noting that the category "other religions" proved too small for analysis and is included under "no preference.") As will appear in the sequel, the results of this survey agree remarkably well with the conclusions of other recent surveys on religion at points where comparison is possible. A survey of churches in 23 metropolitan districts, made by the Committee for Cooperative Field Research some years ago, indicated that "in none of them did more than 7 per cent of the people fail to give themselves a religious classification, not merely by faith but generally by denominations" (*Information Service* [National Council of Churches of Christ], January 21, 1950). See also the Gallup poll of the "religious preference" of adult Americans

made early in 1955, according to which 96.9 per cent were found to identify themselves religiously (70.8 per cent Protestants, 22.9 per cent Catholics, 3.1 per cent Jews) and only 3.1 per cent gave answers that placed them in the "other, none" category (see *Public Opinion News Service*, March 20, 1955). According to a survey made by the U.S. Census Bureau in 1957, involving a nationwide sample of about 35,000 households, 66.2 per cent of Americans identify themselves as Protestants, 25.9 per cent as Catholics, and 3.2 per cent as Jews; only 4 per cent are included in the category of "other or none" (1.3 per cent "other", 2.7 per cent "none"; 0.7 per cent "not reported"); see *Current Population Reports*, Series P–20, No. 79, February 2, 1958.

3. Herbert W. Schneider speaks of the "dwindling band of radical secularists" and the "few remaining militant atheists and freethinkers" (Herbert Wallace Schneider, *Religion in 20th Century America* [Harvard, 1952], pp. 32, 31).

4. There are many reasons for the confusion in religious statistics. Not all churches calculate membership on the same basis: Roman Catholics, Greek Orthodox, and latterly some Lutheran and Episcopal groups include all baptized persons, infants as well as adults; Protestant groups generally report only those over 13 years of age; "Jewish congregations" usually take in all Jews in communities having synagogues or temples. Then there are also the vague and imprecise ways of reporting at every level. To this must be added the fact that statistics after 1926 are strictly not comparable with those before that date, since a new basis of calculation was introduced with the 1926 Census of Religious Bodies. See *Yearbook of American Churches*, 1953 edition, ed. by Benson Y. Landis (National Council of Churches of Christ, 1953), sec. 3. Williams believes that "the total number of church members is underreported by the United States Census" (Robin M. Williams, *American Society: A Sociological Interpretation* [Knopf, 1951], p. 322 note).

5. *Information Service*, March 8, 1952. The trend continues. In the thirty-two years between 1926 and 1957, the population of continental United States increased about 45 per cent while the membership of religious bodies increased nearly 92 per cent, more than twice as fast (*Yearbook of American Churches*, edition for 1959, p. 294).

6. Schneider, *Religion in 20th Century America*, p. 16.

7. *Yearbook of American Churches*, edition for 1960, pp. 258, 279. The report for 1957 shows a slight percentage decline (104,189,000, but only 61 per cent). The decline seems to be due to the fact that for some reason three fewer religious bodies reported for 1957 than for 1956, and does not reflect a trend (*Yearbook of American Churches*, edition for 1959, pp. iv, 266–

67, 293–94). The increase in the past fifteen years is especially
noteworthy. "It is apparent that the gains officially reported
were at a more rapid rate from 1940 on than during the preceding two decades. There is statistical evidence that the people
turned to the churches in 1940–57 to a greater extent than during the '20s or the '30s" (*Yearbook of American Churches*, edition for 1959, p. 293). Valuable information on religion in America will be found in Donald J. Bogue, *The Population of the
United States* (Free Press, 1959), Chap. 23, Religious Affiliation,
pp. 688–709.

8. *The New York Times*, August 20, 1954.

9. "In 1800, less than 10 per cent of the people of the United
States were members of any church" (Winfred E. Garrison,
"Characteristics of American Organized Religion," *The Annals
of the American Academy of Political and Social Science*, Vol.
256, March 1948, p. 20). See also Schneider, *Religion in 20th
Century America*, p. 16. According to Jerald C. Brauer, in the
middle of the eighteenth century, "America had fewer church
members than did any other so-called Christian nation" (Jerald
C. Brauer, *Protestantism in America* [Westminster, 1953], p.
59).

10. *Yearbook of American Churches*, edition for 1955, pp.
288–89; edition for 1960, pp. 278–79.

11. "Who Belongs to What Church?", *The Catholic Digest*,
January 1953. A Gallup poll in 1954 found 79 per cent of
American adults answering the question, "Are you a member of
a church?" in the affirmative (*Public Opinion News Service*,
July 21, 1954).

12. Williams, *American Society*, p. 325. See also Willard L.
Sperry, *Religion in America* (Macmillan, 1946), pp. 19–21.

13. See Brauer, *Protestantism in America*, p. 286; according
to a survey conducted for the *Ladies' Home Journal* in 1948,
some 76 per cent of Americans described themselves as church
members (Lincoln Barnett, "God and the American People,"
Ladies' Home Journal, November 1948).

14. Williams, *American Society*, p. 325.

15. "Who Belongs to What Church?", *The Catholic Digest*,
January 1953. See also "Do Americans Go to Church?", *The
Catholic Digest*, December 1952, where figures on attendance
are given in greater detail. A Gallup poll made public on January 1, 1956 revealed that during an "average week of the past
year" just about one half of adult Americans had attended
church (in 1940 slightly more than one third had gone to church
the week surveyed). Catholics led with 74 per cent; Protestants
came next with 42 per cent; and Jews came last with 27 per
cent (*Public Opinion News Service*, January 1, 1956).

16. See *Public Opinion News Service*, June 11, 1944.

17. See *Yearbook of American Churches,* edition for 1959, p. 297.

18. A Gallup poll made public on January 1, 1956 announced: "Year 1955 Sets All-Time High in Church Attendance" (*Public Opinion News Service,* January 1, 1956).

19. "The reviewed evidence shows that militant anti-clericalism is lacking, that church membership is large, and that in some areas fervent sects are continually arising . . ." (Williams, *American Society,* p. 326).

20. *Religious Education Statistics for Religious Bodies in Continental United States, 1949,* published by the Division of Christian Education of the National Council of Churches; see also *Information Service,* January 13, 1951, and *Yearbook of American Churches,* edition for 1959, p. 274.

21. See *Yearbook of American Churches,* edition for 1955, pp. 260–65; edition for 1960, pp. 265, 280.

22. See *Yearbook of American Churches,* edition for 1959, p. 300. Estimating the 1954 figure as $675,000,000, Arch A. Mercey adds: "Population pressures have increased need for new religious edifices, but even that has not been as great a factor as the tremendous rise in church attendance" ("Church-Building Boom Sets a Record for U.S.," *New York Herald Tribune,* May 29, 1955).

23. *New York Herald Tribune,* December 14, 1952; see also *Information Service,* December 20, 1952.

24. See Will Herberg, "The Postwar Revival of the Synagogue," *Commentary,* Vol. IX, No. 4, April 1950.

25. See comparative figures in *Yearbook of American Churches,* edition for 1959, pp. 289–90; every category of giving showed an increase considerably higher than the corresponding increase in church membership. "In 14 Protestant bodies, total contributions reported for benevolences between 1939 and 1952 increased about 130 per cent, in terms of 1939 dollars, and the annual per capita contribution increased about 80 per cent. For current expenses, the total amount reported increased, in 1939 dollars, 88 per cent, and the annual per capita about 50 per cent, during the same period" (*Information Service,* October 2, 1954). These fourteen Protestant bodies accounted for about half the total contributions received by all religious bodies in the United States and for about 70 per cent of the total reported by all Protestant groups.

26. *General News Service of the Methodist Church* (Commission on Public Relations and Methodist Information), release of May 1, 1954. See also the summary account of the current upsurge of religion in Paul Hutchinson, "Have We a 'New' Religion?", *Life,* April 11, 1955, pp. 138–40.

27. See Elmo Roper, "What People Are Thinking," *New York Herald Tribune,* July 3, 1947. It is interesting that in 1942 more people (7.4 per cent) thought religious leaders were "doing the *least* good" than business leaders (5.9 per cent) or government leaders (3.3 per cent); in 1947, only 3.9 per cent thought religious leaders were "doing the least good," far less than the figures for the other groups.

28. Roper, NBC "Newsweek Documentaries," December 27, 1953; see also *Information Service,* April 3, 1954. The 1957 figures are from Mr. Roper's *The Public Pulse,* December 21, 1957.

29. Williams, *American Society,* pp. 326, 336.

30. Robert Graves Ingersoll (1833–99), Civil War colonel, was known in his day as "the great agnostic." His anti-Christian lectures and writings were notorious. Yet he was an influential Republican leader, and at the national Republican convention in 1876 was designated to nominate James G. Blaine for the Presidency.

31. Report of the Legislative Reference Service of the Library of Congress, released April 6, 1957.

32. Schneider, *Religion in 20th Century America,* p. 32.

33. *The Catholic Digest* notes a marked trend "for the better" in the public relations enjoyed by religion in the past twenty years: "Two decades ago, almost any editor would have dropped dead if someone had predicted what is happening today: newspapers publishing Fulton Oursler's books on page one; magazines practically never coming out without an article on religion; book companies searching for religious titles; four or five of the ten best sellers on religion; Bishop Sheen leading the TV pack; Conrad Hilton putting copies of *Guideposts* in every one of his hotel rooms; chapels being built in industrial plants and in airports, and such like" ("The Religious Press," *The Catholic Digest,* February 1954). And, according to *Time,* "praying dolls" have now joined walking dolls, talking dolls, and dolls who drink their bottles and wet their diapers: "In response to 'the resurgence of religious feeling and practise in America today,' the Ideal Toy Co. is putting on sale a knee-jointed doll that can be made to 'kneel in a praying position'" (*Time,* September 20, 1954). Note also religion's "capture of the juke box" (Hutchinson, "Have We a 'New' Religion?", *Life,* April 11, 1955, pp. 138–40).

34. Williams, *American Society,* p. 304.

35. Schneider, *Religion in 20th Century America,* p. 16.

36. See, e.g., Schneider, *Religion in 20th Century America,* p. 33.

37. See *Publishers' Weekly,* January 23, 1954: "The theme

of religion dominates the non-fiction best sellers in 1953, as it has in many of the preceding years." Discussing religious book publishing in America in 1953, a writer in *The Times Literary Supplement* states: "As a classification, they [religious books] stood third, ranking below fiction and juvenile, and just above biography. . . . Of the ten best-selling fiction titles, the two most in demand were books with religious themes. . . . In the non-fiction category, seven out of the ten best-selling titles were religious titles" (*The Times Literary Supplement*, No. 2746, September 17, 1954, Supplement, p. lxiv). It is, perhaps, also of some significance that "Christmas cards with a religious motive have 'more than doubled' during the past five years, according to the National Association of Greeting Card Publishers. One in every five cards sold last year had a spiritual theme as against one in ten about five years ago" (*Christopher News Notes*, No. 62, November 1954).

38. *The Times Literary Supplement*, No. 2746, September 17, 1954, Supplement, p. lxiv.

39. Reinhold Niebuhr, "Is There a Revival of Religion?", *The New York Times Magazine*, November 19, 1950.

40. See Herberg, "The Religious Stirring on the Campus," *Commentary*, Vol. XIII, No. 2, March 1952. Commenting on his observations in various parts of the country, Dr. Henry Knox Sherrill, presiding bishop of the Protestant Episcopal Church, noted "a new interest in religion, especially in the colleges and universities" (*New York Times*, August 25, 1953). See also, Charles W. Gilkey, "Religion in Our College Generations," *Christianity and Crisis*, Vol. IX, No. 19, November 14, 1949. "There is a widespread and deep interest in religion among college and university undergraduates today. This is in marked contrast to twenty years ago": such is the opening sentence of the *New York Times* account of the survey of religion on the campus made by the Rev. James L. Stoner, director of the University Christian Mission of the National Council of Churches (*New York Times*, October 22 and 24, 1955). "Religiousness is widespread among the contemporary American student generation . . . some recent surveys report a clear upswing in religious interest among college students" (Philip E. Jacob, *Changing Values in College* [Harper, 1957], pp. 20, 56).

41. H. Stuart Hughes, "On Social Salvation," *Saturday Review of Literature*, March 3, 1951, p. 14. For an impressive statement of the advanced student mind on religion, see *Religion at Harvard: A Harvard Student Council Committee Report*, Cambridge, Mass., February 1956. Revealing, too, is a study by Irving E. Bender of the religious attitudes of 112 Dartmouth men at the time they were seniors in 1940 and fifteen years later, in 1956. A "significant increase in the religious

value scores" was found after the fifteen-year interval. More-over, Dartmouth undergraduates in 1956 showed the same higher "religious value scores" in comparison with their counterparts fifteen years before. Bender concludes: "Apparently the same need for religion exists now among the young as among the older" ("Changes in Religious Interest: A Retest after 15 Years," *The Journal of Abnormal and Social Psychology*, Vol. 57, No. 1, July 1958).

42. The symposium was reprinted as a brochure: James Agee and others, *Religion and the Intellectuals: A Symposium (Partisan Review*, 1950). That *Partisan Review* should have come around to running such a symposium, in which the attitude of intellectuals to religion is regarded as something susceptible of more than one kind of answer, is itself of real significance; some years earlier *Partisan Review* had featured another symposium, but that had been entitled "The Failure of Nerve," and was devoted exclusively to the lamentations and explanations of anti-religious intellectuals confronted by the rising tide of religious interest among the cultural elite. The second symposium was introduced with the following editorial comment: "One of the most significant tendencies of our time has been the turn to religion among intellectuals and the growing disfavor with which secular attitudes and perspectives are now regarded in not a few circles that lay claim to the leadership of culture."

43. Asher Brynes, "Religion More or Less," *The Freeman*, October 30, 1950.

44. Schneider, *Religion in 20th Century America*, p. 166.

45. See above, pp. 48–49.

46. Oscar Handlin, *The American People in the Twentieth Century* (Harvard, 1954), p. 222; the tenses have been changed to the present.

47. See David Riesman, *The Lonely Crowd* (Yale, 1950); *Faces in the Crowd* (Yale, 1952); *Individualism Reconsidered* (Free Press, 1954).

48. Curiously, in his own account of the present-day rise in religious identification and church membership in the United States, David Riesman does not make use of his valuable insights into the changing character structure of the American people; see *Individualism Reconsidered*, chap. xxiv.

49. Roper, in NBC "Newsweek Documentaries," December 27, 1953; see report in *Information Service*, April 3, 1954.

50. See report of the Population Reference Bureau, *Boston Daily Globe*, June 10, 1954. The trend has continued, though with some fluctuation.

51. *The New York Times*, April 19, 1953. The report includes the following interesting paragraph: "One of Oak Ridge's top

scientists credits the inspiration of helping to build a parish from scratch in this twentieth century pioneer community with converting him from a nominal churchgoer into an ordained minister. He is Dr. William G. Pollard, executive director of the Oak Ridge Institute of Nuclear Studies. He was ordained an Episcopal minister here in December, after two years of preparatory study." See the "profile" of Dr. Pollard in the *New Yorker*, February 6, 1954.

52. Reinhold Niebuhr, "Is There a Revival of Religion?", *The New York Times Magazine*, November 19, 1950.

53. "Present-day youth has to rest its large-scale security on deeper foundations and this is probably the source of much of its religious interest. . . . Some of it is finding no greater security than an Epicurean philosophy of chance offers; but much of it is getting down to bedrock and finding a foundation on which life can rest unmoved, if not unshaken, in these stormy times. There is a venturesomeness in this quest, but it is a hidden thing and not apparent to those who think of risk only in terms of risked capital or risked lives. In this respect, once more, youth today, so far as it participates in this movement of the human spirit toward a less vulnerable faith in life than that which has been tested and found wanting, is more representative of a period of history than merely of itself" (H. Richard Niebuhr, "On Our Conservative Youth," *Seventy-Five* [Yale Daily News, 1953], p. 90).

V. *The Religion of Americans and American Religion*

What do Americans believe? Most emphatically, they "believe in God": 97 per cent according to one survey, 96 per cent according to another, 95 per cent according to a third.[1] About 75 per cent of them, as we have seen, regard themselves as members of churches, and a sizable proportion attend divine services with some frequency and regularity.[2] They believe in prayer: about 90 per cent say they pray on various occasions.[3] They believe in life after death, even in heaven and hell.[4] They think well of the church and of ministers.[5] They hold the Bible to be an inspired book, the "word of God."[6] By a large majority, they think children should be given religious instruction and raised as church members.[7] By a large majority, too, they hold religion to be of very great importance.[8] In all of these respects their attitudes are as religious as those of any people today, or, for that matter, as those of any Western people in recent history.

Yet these indications are after all relatively superficial; they tell us what Americans say (and no doubt believe) about themselves and their religious views; they do not tell us what in actuality these religious views are. Nowhere are surface appearances more deceptive, nowhere is it more necessary to try to penetrate beyond mere assertions of belief than in such ultimate matters as religion.

We do penetrate a little deeper, it would seem, when we take note of certain curious discrepancies the surveys reveal in the responses people make to questions about their religion. Thus, according to one trustworthy source, 73 per cent said they believed in an afterlife, with God as judge, but "only 5 per cent [had] any fear, not to say expectation, of going [to hell]."[9] Indeed, about 80 per cent, according to another source, admitted that what they were "most serious about" was not the life after death in which they said they believed, but in trying to live as comfortably in this life as possible.[10] And in their opinion they were not doing so badly even from the point of view of the divine judgment: 91 per cent felt that they could honestly say that they were trying to lead a good life, and 78 per cent felt no hesitation in saying that they more than half measured up to their own standards of goodness, over 50 per cent asserting that they were in fact following the rule of loving one's neighbor as oneself "all the way"![11] This amazingly high valuation that most Americans appear to place on their own virtue would seem to offer a better insight into the basic religion of the American people than any figures as to their formal beliefs can provide, however important in themselves these figures may be.

But perhaps the most significant discrepancy in the assertions Americans make about their religious views is to be found in another area. When asked, "Would you say your religious beliefs have any effect on your ideas of politics and business?", a majority of the same Americans who had testified that they regarded religion as something "very important" answered that their religious beliefs had no real effect on their ideas or conduct in these decisive areas of everyday life; specifically, 54 per cent said no, 39 per cent said yes, and 7 per cent refused to reply or didn't know.[12] This disconcerting confession of the irrelevance of religion to business and politics was attributed by those who appraised the results of the survey as pointing to a calamitous divorce between the "private" and the "public" realms in the religious thinking of Americans.[13] There is certainly a great deal of truth in this opinion, and we shall have occasion to explore it in a different context, but in the present connection it would seem that another aspect of the matter is more immediately pertinent. *Some* ideas and standards undeniably govern the conduct of Americans in their affairs of business and politics; if they are not ideas and standards associated with the teachings of religion, what are they? It will not do to say that people just act "selfishly" without reference to moral standards of any kind. All people act "selfishly," of course; but it is no less true of all people, Americans included, that their "selfishness" is controlled, mitigated, or, at worst, justified by some sort of moral commitment, by some sort of belief in a system of values beyond immediate self-interest. The fact that more than half the people openly admit that their religious beliefs have no effect on their ideas of politics and business would seem to indicate very strongly that, over and above conventional religion, there is to be found among Americans some sort of faith or belief or set of convictions, not generally designated as religion but definitely operative as such in their lives in the sense of providing them with some fundamental context of normativity and meaning. What this unacknowledged "religion" of the American people is, and how it manages to coexist with their formal religious affirmations and affiliations, it is now our task to investigate.

II

"Every functioning society," Robin M. Williams, Jr. points out, "has to an important degree a *common* religion. The possession of a common set of ideas, rituals, and symbols can supply an overarching sense of unity even in a society riddled with conflicts."[14] What is this "common religion" of American society, the "common set of ideas, rituals, and symbols" that give it its "overarching sense of unity"? Williams provides us with a further clue when he suggests that "men are always likely to be intolerant of opposition to their central ultimate values."[15] What are these "central ultimate values" about which Americans are "intolerant"? No one who knows anything about the religious situation in this country would be likely to suggest that the things Americans are "intolerant" about are the beliefs, standards, or teachings of the religions they "officially" acknowledge as theirs. Americans are proud of their tolerance in matters of religion: one is expected to "believe in God," but otherwise religion is not supposed to be a ground of "discrimination." This is, no doubt, admirable, but is it not "at least in part, a sign that the crucial values of the system are no longer couched in a religious framework"?[16]

What, then, is the "framework" in which they *are* couched? What, to return to our original question, is the "common religion" of the American people, as it may be inferred not only from their words but also from their behavior?

It seems to me that a realistic appraisal of the values, ideas, and behavior of the American people leads to the conclusion that Americans, by and large, do have their "common religion" and that that "religion" is the system familiarly known as the American Way of Life. It is the American Way of Life that supplies American society with an "overarching sense of unity" amid conflict. It is the American Way of Life about which Americans are admittedly and unashamedly "intolerant." It is the American Way of Life that provides the framework in terms of which the crucial values of American existence are couched. By every realistic criterion the American Way of Life is the operative faith of the American people.

It would be the crudest kind of misunderstanding to dismiss the American Way of Life as no more than a political formula or propagandist slogan, or to regard it as simply an expression of the "materialistic" impulses of the American people. Americans are "materialistic," no doubt, but surely not more so than other people, than the French peasant or petty bourgeois, for example. All such labels are irrelevant, if not meaningless. The American Way of Life is, at bottom, a spiritual structure, a structure of ideas and ideals, of aspirations and values, of beliefs and standards; it synthesizes all that commends itself to the American as the right, the good, and the true in actual life. It embraces such seemingly incongruous elements as sanitary plumbing and freedom of opportunity, Coca-Cola and an intense faith in education—all felt as moral questions relating to the proper way of life.[17] The very expression "way of life" points to its religious essence, for one's ultimate, over-all way of life is one's religion.

The American Way of Life is, of course, conceived as

the corporate "way" of the American people, but it has its implications for the American as an individual as well. It is something really operative in his actual life. When in the *Ladies' Home Journal* poll, Americans were asked "to look within [themselves] and state honestly whether [they] thought [they] really obeyed the law of love under certain special conditions," 90 per cent said yes and 5 per cent no when the one to be "loved" was a person belonging to a different religion; 80 per cent said yes and 12 per cent no when it was the case of a member of a different race; 78 per cent said yes and 10 per cent no when it concerned a business competitor—but only 27 per cent said yes and 57 per cent no in the case of "a member of a political party that you think is dangerous," while 25 per cent said yes and 63 per cent said no when it concerned an enemy of the nation.[18] These figures are most illuminating, first because of the incredible self-assurance they reveal with which the average American believes he fulfills the "impossible" law of love, but also because of the light they cast on the differential impact of the violation of this law on the American conscience. For it is obvious that the figures reflect not so much the actual behavior of the American people—no people on earth ever loved their neighbors as themselves as much as the American people say they do—as how seriously Americans take transgressions against the law of love in various cases. Americans feel they *ought* to love their fellow men despite differences of race or creed or business interest; that is what the American Way of Life emphatically prescribes.[19] But the American Way of Life almost explicitly sanctions hating a member of a "dangerous" political party (Communists and fascists are obviously meant here) or an enemy of one's country, and therefore an overwhelming majority avow their hate. In both situations, while the Jewish-Christian law of love is formally acknowledged, the truly operative factor is the value system embodied in the American Way of Life. Where the American Way of Life approves of love of one's fellow man, most Americans confidently assert that they practice such love; where the American Way of Life disapproves, the great mass of Americans do not hesitate to confess that they do not practice it, and apparently feel very little guilt for their failure. No better pragmatic test as to what the operative religion of the American people actually is could be desired.[20]

It is not suggested here that the ideals Americans feel to be indicated in the American Way of Life are scrupulously observed in the practice of Americans; they are in fact constantly violated, often grossly. But violated or not, they are felt to be normative and relevant to "business and politics" in a way that the formal tenets of "official" religion are not. That is what makes the American Way of Life the "common religion" of American society in the sense here intended.

It should be clear that what is being designated under the American Way of Life is not the so-called "common denominator" religion; it is not a synthetic system composed of beliefs to be found in all or in a group of religions. It is an organic structure of ideas, values, and beliefs that constitutes a faith common to Americans and genuinely operative in their lives, a faith that markedly influences, and is influenced by, the "official" religions of American society. Sociologically, anthropologically, if one pleases, it is the characteristic American religion, undergirding American life and overarching American society despite all indubitable differences of region, section, culture, and class.

Yet qualifications are immediately in order. Not for all Americans is this American religion, this "common religion" of American society, equally operative; some indeed explicitly repudiate it as religion. By and large, it would seem that what is resistive in contemporary American society to the American Way of Life as religion may be understood under three heads. First, there are the churches of immigrant-ethnic background that still cherish their traditional creeds and confessions as a sign of their distinctive origin and are unwilling to let these be dissolved into an over-all "American religion"; certain Lutheran and Reformed churches in this country[21] as well as sections of the Catholic Church would fall into this classification. Then there are groups, not large but increasing, that have an explicit and conscious theological concern, whether it be "orthodox," "neo-orthodox," or "liberal"; in varying degrees, they find their theologies at odds with the implied "theology" of the American Way of Life. Finally, there are the ill-defined, though by all accounts numerous and influential, "religions of the disinherited," the many "holiness," pentecostal, and millenarian sects of the socially and culturally submerged segments of our society;[22] for them, their "peculiar" religion is frequently still too vital and all-absorbing to be easily subordinated to some "common faith." All of these cases, it will be noted, constitute "hold outs" against the sweep of religious Americanism; in each case there is an element of alienation which generates a certain amount of tension in social life.

What is this American Way of Life that we have said constitutes the "common religion" of American society? An adequate description and analysis of what is implied in this phrase still remains to be attempted, and certainly it will not be ventured here; but some indications may not be out of place.

The American Way of Life is the symbol by which Americans define themselves and establish their unity. German unity, it would seem, is felt to be largely racial-folkish, French unity largely cultural; but neither of these ways is open to the American people, the most diverse in racial and cultural origins of any in the world. As American unity has emerged, it has emerged more and more clearly as a unity embodied in, and symbolized by, the complex structure known as the American Way of Life.

If the American Way of Life had to be defined in one word, "democracy" would undoubtedly be the word, but democracy in a peculiarly American sense. On its political side it means the Constitution; on its economic side, "free enterprise"; on its social side, an equalitarianism which is not only compatible with but indeed actually implies vigorous economic competition and high mobility. Spiritually, the American Way of Life is best expressed in a certain kind of "idealism" which has come to be recognized as characteristically American. It is a faith that has its symbols and its rituals, its holidays and its liturgy, its saints and its

sancta;[23] and it is a faith that every American, to the degree
that he is an American, knows and understands.

The American Way of Life is individualistic, dynamic,
pragmatic. It affirms the supreme value and dignity of the
individual; it stresses incessant activity on his part, for he is
never to rest but is always to be striving to "get ahead";
it defines an ethic of self-reliance, merit, and character, and
judges by achievement: "deeds, not creeds" are what count.
The American Way of Life is humanitarian, "forward looking," optimistic. Americans are easily the most generous
and philanthropic people in the world, in terms of their
ready and unstinting response to suffering anywhere on
the globe. The American believes in progress, in self-
improvement, and quite fanatically in education. But above
all, the American is idealistic. Americans cannot go on making money or achieving worldly success simply on its own
merits; such "materialistic" things must, in the American
mind, be justified in "higher" terms, in terms of "service" or
"stewardship" or "general welfare." Because Americans are
so idealistic, they tend to confuse espousing an ideal with
fulfilling it and are always tempted to regard themselves
as good as the ideals they entertain: hence the amazingly
high valuation most Americans quite sincerely place on
their own virtue. And because they are so idealistic, Americans tend to be moralistic: they are inclined to see all issues
as plain and simple, black and white, issues of morality.
Every struggle in which they are seriously engaged becomes a "crusade." To Mr. Eisenhower, who in many ways
exemplifies American religion in a particularly representative way, the second world war was a "crusade" (as was
the first to Woodrow Wilson); so was his campaign for the
presidency ("I am engaged in a crusade . . . to substitute
good government for what we most earnestly believe has
been bad government"); and so is his administration—a
"battle for the republic" against "godless Communism"
abroad and against "corruption and materialism" at home.
It was Woodrow Wilson who once said, "Sometimes people
call me an idealist. Well, that is the way I know I'm an
American: America is the most idealistic nation in the
world"; Eisenhower was but saying the same thing when

he solemnly affirmed: "The things that make us proud to
be Americans are of the soul and of the spirit."[24]

The American Way of Life is, of course, anchored in the
American's vision of America. The Puritan's dream of a new
"Israel" and a new "Promised Land" in the New World,
the *"novus ordo seclorum"* on the Great Seal of the United
States reflect the perennial American conviction that in the
New World a new beginning has been made, a new order
of things established, vastly different from and superior to
the decadent institutions of the Old World. This conviction,
emerging out of the earliest reality of American history, was
continuously nourished through the many decades of immigration into the present century by the residual hopes
and expectations of the immigrants, for whom the New
World had to be really something new if it was to be anything at all. And this conviction still remains pervasive in
American life, hardly shaken by the new shape of the world
and the challenge of the "new orders" of the twentieth century, Nazism and Communism. It is the secret of what outsiders must take to be the incredible self-righteousness of
the American people, who tend to see the world divided
into an innocent, virtuous America confronted with a corrupt, devious, and guileful Europe and Asia. The self-
righteousness, however, if self-righteousness it be, is by no
means simple, if only because virtually all Americans are
themselves derived from the foreign parts they so distrust.
In any case, this feeling about America as really and truly
the "new order" of things at last established is the heart
of the outlook defined by the American Way of Life.[25]

In her *Vermont Tradition,* Dorothy Canfield Fisher lists
as that tradition's principal ingredients: individual freedom,
personal independence, human dignity, community responsibility, social and political democracy, sincerity, restraint in
outward conduct, and thrift.[26] With some amplification—
particularly emphasis on the uniqueness of the American
"order" and the great importance assigned to religion—this
may be taken as a pretty fair summary of some of the
"values" embodied in the American Way of Life. It will not
escape the reader that this account is essentially an idealized description of the middle-class ethos. And, indeed, that

is just what it is. The American Way of Life is a middle-class way, just as the American people in their entire outlook and feeling are a middle-class people.[27] But the American Way of Life as it has come down to us is not merely middle-class; it is emphatically inner-directed. Indeed, it is probably one of the best expressions of inner-direction in history. As such, it now seems to be undergoing some degree of modification—perhaps at certain points disintegration—under the impact of the spread of other-direction in our society. For the foreseeable future, however, we may with some confidence expect the continuance in strength of the American Way of Life as both the tradition and the "common faith" of the American people.[28]

III

The American Way of Life as the "common faith" of American society has coexisted for some centuries with the historic faiths of the American people, and the two have influenced each other in many profound and subtle ways. The influence has been complex and reciprocal, to the point where causal priority becomes impossible to assign if indeed it does not become altogether meaningless. From the very beginning the American Way of Life was shaped by the contours of American Protestantism; it may, indeed, best be understood as a kind of secularized Puritanism, a Puritanism without transcendence, without sense of sin or judgment. The Puritan's vision of a new "Promised Land" in the wilderness of the New World has become, as we have suggested, the American's deep sense of the newness and uniqueness of things in the Western Hemisphere. The Puritan's sense of vocation and "inner-worldly asceticism" can still be detected in the American's gospel of action and service, and his consciousness of high responsibility before God in the American's "idealism." The Puritan's abiding awareness of the ambiguity of all human motivations and his insight into the corruptions of inordinate power have left their mark not only on the basic structure of our constitutional system but also on the entire social philosophy of the American people.[29] Nor have other strands of early Ameri-

can Protestantism been without their effect. There can be
little doubt that Pietism co-operated with frontier revivalism in breaking down the earlier concern with dogma and
doctrine, so that the slogan, "deeds, not creeds," soon became the hallmark both of American religion and of the
American Way of Life.[30] These are but aspects of an influence that is often easier to see than to define.

The reciprocal action of the American Way of Life in
shaping and reshaping the historic faiths of Christianity and
Judaism on American soil is perhaps more readily discerned.
By and large, we may say that these historic religions have
all tended to become "Americanized" under the pervasive
influence of the American environment. This "Americanization" has been the product not so much of conscious direction as of a "diffuse convergence" operating spontaneously
in the context of the totality of American life. What it has
brought, however, is none the less clear: "religious group-
ings throughout [American] society [have been] stamped
with recognizably 'American' qualities,"[31] to an extent indeed where foreign observers sometimes find the various
American religions more like each other than they are like
their European counterparts.[32]

Under the influence of the American environment the historic Jewish and Christian faiths have tended to become
secularized in the sense of becoming integrated as parts
within a larger whole defined by the American Way of
Life. "There is a marked tendency," Williams writes in his
discussion of the relations of religion to other institutions in
the United States, "to regard religion as a good because it
is useful in furthering other major values—in other words,
to reverse the ends-means relation implied in the conception
of religion as an ultimate value."[33] In this reversal the
Christian and Jewish faiths tend to be prized because they
help promote ideals and standards that all Americans are
expected to share on a deeper level than merely "official"
religion. Insofar as any reference is made to the God in
whom all Americans "believe" and of whom the "official"
religions speak, it is primarily as sanction and underpinning
for the supreme values of the faith embodied in the Ameri-

can Way of Life. Secularization of religion could hardly go further.

As a consequence, in some cases of its own origins, but primarily of the widespread influence of the American environment, religion in America has tended toward a marked disparagement of "forms," whether theological or liturgical. Even the highly liturgical and theological churches have felt the effects of this spirit to the degree that they have become thoroughly acculturated. Indeed, the anti-theological, anti-liturgical bias is still pervasive despite the recent upsurge of theological concern and despite the greater interest being shown in liturgy because of its psychological power and "emotional richness."

American religion is (within the limits set by the particular traditions of the churches) non-theological and non-liturgical; it is activistic and occupied with the things of the world to a degree that has become a byword among European churchmen. With this activism has gone a certain "latitudinarianism," associated with the de-emphasis of theology and doctrine: Americans tend to believe that "ethical behavior and a good life, rather than adherence to a specific creed, [will] earn a share in the heavenly kingdom."[34] The activism of American religion has manifested itself in many forms throughout our history: in the Puritan concern for the total life of the community; in the passionate championing of all sorts of reform causes by the evangelical movements of the first half of the nineteenth century; in the "social gospel" of more recent times; in the ill-starred Prohibition "crusade"; in the advanced "progressive" attitudes on social questions taken by the National Council of Churches, the National Catholic Welfare Conference, and the various rabbinical associations; in the strong social emphasis of American Protestant "neo-orthodoxy." This activism, which many Europeans seem to regard as the distinguishing feature of American religion, both reflects the dynamic temper of the American Way of Life and has been a principal factor in its development.

It is hardly necessary to continue this analysis much farther along these general lines. The optimism, moralism, and idealism of Jewish and Christian faith in America are

plain evidence of the profound effect of the American outlook on American religion. Indeed, such evidence is amply
provided by any tabulation of the distinctive features of religion in America,[35] and needs no special emphasis at this
point.

What is perhaps of crucial importance, and requires a
more detailed examination, is the new attitude toward religion and the new conception of the church that have
emerged in America.[36]

Americans believe in religion in a way that perhaps no
other people do. It may indeed be said that the primary
religious affirmation of the American people, in harmony
with the American Way of Life, is that religion is a "good
thing," a supremely "good thing," for the individual and
the community. And "religion" here means not so much any
particular religion, but religion as such, religion-in-general.
"Our government makes no sense," President Eisenhower
recently declared, "unless it is founded in a deeply felt religious faith—*and I don't care what it is*" (emphasis
added).[37] In saying this, the President was saying something that almost any American could understand and ap-
prove, but which must seem like a deplorable heresy to the
European churchman. Every American could understand,
first, that Mr. Eisenhower's apparent indifferentism ("and
I don't care what it is") was not indifferentism at all, but
the expression of the conviction that at bottom the "three
great faiths" were really "saying the same thing" in affirming the "spiritual ideals" and "moral values" of the American Way of Life. Every American, moreover, could understand that what Mr. Eisenhower was emphasizing so
vehemently was the indispensability of religion as the foundation of society. This is one aspect of what Americans
mean when they say that they "believe in religion." The
object of devotion of this kind of religion, however, is "not
God but 'religion.' . . . The faith is not in God but in faith;
we worship not God but our own worshiping."[38] When
Americans think of themselves as a profoundly religious
people, whose "first allegiance" is "reserved . . . to the
kingdom of the spirit,"[39] this is, by and large, what they

mean, and not any commitment to the doctrines or traditions of the historic faiths.

With this view of religion is associated a closely analo-
gous view of the church. For America, the celebrated
dichotomy of "church" and "sect,"[40] however pertinent it
may be to European conditions, has only a secondary significance. The concept of the church as the nation religiously organized, established socially, if not always legally,
has only an oblique relevance to American reality; and
though America does know sects in the sense of "fringe"
groups of the "disinherited," it does not understand these
groups and their relation to the more conventional churches
the way Europe does. An entirely new conception of church
and church institutions has emerged in America.

It must be remembered that in America the variety and
multiplicity of churches did not, as in Europe, come with
the breakdown of a single established national church; in
America, taking the nation as a whole, the variety and
multiplicity of churches was almost the original condition
and coeval with the emergence of the new society. In America religious pluralism is thus not merely a historical and
political fact; it is, in the mind of the American, the pri-
mordial condition of things, an essential aspect of the American Way of Life, and therefore in itself an aspect of religious belief.[41] Americans, in other words, believe that the
plurality of religious groups is a proper and legitimate condition. However much he may be attached to his own
church, however dimly he may regard the beliefs and
practices of other churches, the American tends to feel
rather strongly that total religious uniformity, even with his
own church benefiting thereby, would be something undesirable and wrong, indeed scarcely conceivable. Pluralism
of religions and churches is something quite axiomatic to
the American. This feeling, more than anything else, is the
foundation of the American doctrine of the "separation of
church and state," for it is the heart of this doctrine that
the government may not do anything that implies the pre-
eminence or superior legitimacy of one church over another.

This means that outside the Old World distinction of
church and sect America has given birth to a new type of

religious structure—the denomination.[42] The denomination
as we know it is a stable, settled church, enjoying a
legitimate and recognized place in a larger aggregate
of churches, each recognizing the proper status of the
others.[43] The denomination is the "non-conformist sect" become central and normative. It differs from the church in
the European understanding of the term in that it would
never dream of claiming to be *the* national ecclesiastical institution; it differs from the sect in that it is socially established, thoroughly institutionalized, and nuclear to the
society in which it is found. The European dichotomy becomes meaningless, and instead we have the nuclear denomination on the one side, and the peripheral sect on the
way to becoming a denomination on the other. So firmly
entrenched is this denominational idea in the mind of the
American that even American Catholics have come to think
in such terms; theologically the Catholic Church of course
continues to regard itself as the one true church, but in their
actual social attitudes American Catholics, hardly less than
American Protestants or Jews, tend to think of their church
as a denomination existing side by side with other denominations in a pluralistic harmony that is felt to be somehow
of the texture of American life.[44]

Denominational pluralism, as the American idea of the
church may be called, obviously implies that no church can
look to the state for its members or support. Voluntarism
and evangelism are thus the immediate consequences of the
American idea: for their maintenance, for their very existence, churches must depend on the voluntary adherence of
their members, and they are therefore moved to pursue a
vigorous evangelistic work to win people to their ranks. The
accommodation of the church to American reality extends
even to its inner polity. "As the polity of the Roman church
followed the pattern of the Roman empire," H. Richard
Niebuhr points out, "so the American churches incline to
organize themselves [along representative lines] in conformity with the system of state and national legislatures
and executives."[45] Even the Roman Catholic Church, with
its fixed hierarchical structure, has not been totally immune
to American influence of this kind.[46]

The denominational idea is fundamental to American thinking about religion, but it is not the last word. Americans think of their various churches as denominations, but they also feel that somehow the denominations fall into larger wholes which we have called religious communities. This kind of denominational aggregation is, of course, something that pertains primarily to Protestantism and to a lesser degree to Judaism; both have more or less organized denominations which, taken together, form the religious communities. Catholicism, on the other hand, has no such overt inner divisions, but American Catholics readily understand the phenomenon when they see it among Protestants and Jews. Denominations are felt to be somehow a matter of individual preference, and movement between denominations is not uncommon; the religious community, on the other hand, is taken as something more objective and given, something in which, by and large, one is born, lives, and dies, something that (to recall our earlier analysis) identifies and defines one's position in American society.[47] Since the religious community in its present form is a recent social emergent, its relations to the denominations properly so-called are still relatively fluid and undefined but the main lines of development would seem to be fairly clear.

When the plurality of denominations comprehended in religious communities is seen from the standpoint of the "common faith" of American society, what emerges is the conception of the three "communions"—Protestantism, Catholicism, Judaism—as three diverse, but equally legitimate, equally American, expressions of an over-all American religion, standing for essentially the same "moral ideals" and "spiritual values." This conception, whatever may be thought of it theologically, is in fact held, though hardly in explicit form, by many devout and religiously sophisticated Americans. It would seem to be the obvious meaning of the title, *The Religions of Democracy*, given to a recent authoritative statement of the Protestant, Catholic, and Jewish positions.[48] "Democracy" apparently has its religions which fall under it as species fall under the genus of which they are part. And in this usage "democracy" is obviously a synonym for the American Way of Life.

It is but one more step, though a most fateful one, to proceed from "the religions of democracy" to "democracy as religion" and consciously to erect "democracy" into a super-faith above and embracing the three recognized religions. This step has been taken by a number of thinkers in recent years. Thus, Professor J. Paul Williams has been urging a program of religious reconstruction in which he insists that: "Americans must come to look on the democratic ideal (not necessarily the American practice of it) as the Will of God, or if they please, of Nature. . . . Americans must be brought to the conviction that democracy is the very Law of Life. . . . The state must be brought into the picture; governmental agencies must teach the democratic ideal *as religion* . . . primary responsibility for teaching democracy as religion must be given to the public school, for instance . . ."[49]

Professor Horace M. Kallen reaches very much the same conclusion from another direction. "For the communicants of the democratic faith," he writes, "it is the religion *of* and *for* religions. . . . [It is] the religion of religions, all may freely come together in it."[50]

It is not our purpose, at this point, to draw the theological implications of this super-religion of "democracy" as the "religion of religions"; it is only necessary to point out that it marks a radical break with the fundamental presuppositions of both Judaism and Christianity, to which it must appear as a particularly insidious kind of idolatry. What is merely implicit and perhaps never intended in the acceptance of the American Way of Life as the "common religion" of American society is here brought to its logical conclusion and made to reveal its true inner meaning.

By and large, the "common faith" of American society remains implicit and is never carried to the logical conclusion to which a few ideologists have pushed it. By the great mass of the American people the American Way of Life is not avowed as a super-faith above and embracing the historic religions. It operates as a "common faith" at deeper levels, through its pervasive influence on the patterns of American thought and feeling. It makes no pretensions to override or supplant the recognized religions, to which it assigns a place of great eminence and honor in the American scheme of things. But all the implications are there . . .

IV

The "common faith" of American society is not merely a civic religion to celebrate the values and convictions of the American people as a corporate entity. It has its inner, personal aspects as well; or rather, side by side and in intimate relation with the civic religion of the American Way of Life, there has developed, primarily through a devitalization of the historic faiths, an inner, personal religion that promises salvation to the disoriented, tormented souls of a society in crisis.

This inner, personal religion is based on the American's *faith in faith*. We have seen that a primary religious affirmation of the American is his belief in religion. The American believes that religion is something very important for the community; he also believes that "faith," or what we may call religiosity, is a kind of "miracle drug" that can cure all the ailments of the spirit. It is not faith in *anything* that is so powerful, just faith, the "magic of believing." "It was back in those days," a prominent American churchman writes, recalling his early years, "that I formed a habit that I have never broken. I began saying in the morning two words, 'I believe.' Those two words *with nothing added* . . . give me a running start for my day, and for every day" (emphasis not in original).[51]

The cult of faith takes two forms, which we might designate as introvert and extrovert. In its introvert form faith is trusted to bring mental health and "peace of mind," to dissipate anxiety and guilt, and to translate the soul to the blessed land of "normality" and "self-acceptance." In earlier times this cult of faith was quite literally a cult of "faith healing," best expressed in what H. Richard Niebuhr has described as the "man-centered, this-worldly, lift-your-selves-by-your-own-bootstraps doctrine of New Thought and Christian Science."[52] Latterly it has come to vest itself in the fashionable vocabulary of psychoanalysis and is offering a synthesis of religion and psychiatry.[53] But at bottom it is the same cult of faith in faith, the same promise that through "those two words, 'I believe,' with nothing added," all our troubles will be dissipated and inner peace and harmony restored.

The cult of faith has also its extrovert form, and that is known as "positive thinking." "Positive thinking," thinking that is "affirmative" and avoids the corrosions of "negativity" and "skepticism," thinking that "has faith," is recommended as a powerful force in the world of struggle and achievement.[54] Here again it is not so much faith in anything, certainly not the theocentric faith of the historic religions, that is supposed to confer this power—but just faith, the psychological attitude of having faith, so to speak. And here too the cult is largely the product of the inner disintegration and enfeeblement of the historic religions; the familiar words are retained, but the old meaning is voided. "Have faith," "don't lose faith," and the like, were once injunctions to preserve one's unwavering trust in the God from Whom comes both the power to live and the "peace that passeth understanding." Gradually these phrases have come to be an appeal to maintain a "positive" attitude to life and not to lose confidence in oneself and one's activities. "To believe in yourself and in everything you do": such, at bottom, is the meaning of the contemporary cult of faith, whether it is proclaimed by devout men from distinguished pulpits or offered as the "secret of success" by self-styled psychologists who claim to have discovered the "hidden powers" of man.[55] What is important is faith, faith in faith. Even where the classical symbols and formulas are still retained, that is very often what is meant and what is understood.

Such are some major aspects of the social, cultural, and spiritual environment in which religion in America moves and has its being. And religion in America means the three great religious communities, the Protestant, the Catholic, and the Jewish. These three religious communities must now be examined and the main features characterizing each of them in turn described.

FOOTNOTES

1. *Belief in God:* 97 per cent—"Do Americans Believe in God?", *The Catholic Digest*, November 1952; 96 per cent—Gallup poll, *Public Opinion News Service*, December 18, 1954; 95 per cent—Lincoln Barnett, "God and the American People," *Ladies' Home Journal*, November 1948, p. 37. According to the *Catholic Digest* poll 89 per cent of Americans believe in the Trinity ("How Many in the U. S. Believe in the Trinity?", *The Catholic Digest*, July 1953) and 80 per cent think of Christ as divine ("What We Americans Think of Our Lord," *The Catholic Digest*, August 1953).

2. *Church membership and attendance:* see above, chap. iv, pp. 47–50.

3. *Prayer:* 92 per cent answer yes to the question, "Do you ever pray to God?" ("Americans and Prayer," *The Catholic Digest*, November 1953); 90 per cent say they pray, 56 per cent "frequently"—Barnett, "God and the American People," *Ladies' Home Journal*, November 1948, p. 37.

4. *Life after death:* 77 per cent believe in afterlife, 7 per cent don't, 16 per cent don't know—"What Do Americans Think of Heaven and Hell?", *The Catholic Digest*, March 1953; 76 per cent say yes, 13 per cent no, 11 per cent don't know—Gallup poll, *Public Opinion News Service*, December 11, 1944; 73 per cent say yes, 15 per cent no, 12 per cent no opinion—Barnett, "God and the American People," *Ladies' Home Journal*, November 1948, pp. 230–31; 74 per cent believe in life after death—Gallup poll, *Public Opinion News Service*, April 19, 1957.

Heaven and Hell: 72 per cent believe in heaven, 58 per cent in hell—*The Catholic Digest*, as above; 52 per cent think that "life after death is divided into heaven and hell," though heaven looms larger in their minds than hell—Barnett, "God and the American People," *Ladies' Home Journal*, November 1948, p. 231; 61 per cent believe there is a devil—Gallup poll, *Public Opinion News Service*, April 19, 1957.

5. *Opinion about church and clergymen:* 75 per cent deny the allegation that the church is too much concerned about money—"Is the Church Too Much Concerned About Money?", *The Catholic Digest*, March 1954; 68 per cent regard clergymen as "very understanding," 21 per cent as "fairly understanding"—"How Understanding Are Clergymen?", *The Catholic Digest*, December 1953; clergymen rank at the top in the scale of those who "do most good"—see above, chap. iv, p. 51.

6. *Bible:* 86 per cent regard it as divinely inspired, the "word of God"—"What Do Americans Think of the Bible?", *The Catholic Digest*, May 1954; a survey conducted by the *British Weekly*

gives the figure for Americans who regard the Bible as divinely inspired as 86.5 per cent (see *Information Service* [National Council of Churches of Christ], December 27, 1952).

7. *Religious instruction:* 98 per cent say yes—"Do Americans Want Their Children to Receive Religious Instruction?", *The Catholic Digest*, September 1953. *Children raised as church members:* 72 per cent say yes—"How Important Is Religion to Americans?", *The Catholic Digest*, February 1953.

8. *Importance of religion:* 75 per cent regard it as "very important," 20 per cent as "fairly important"—"How Important Is Religion to Americans?", *The Catholic Digest*, February 1953; 69 per cent think that the influence of religion is increasing and 81 per cent believe that religion can answer "most of today's problems"—Gallup poll, *Public Opinion News Service*, April 21, 1957. The religiosity of the American people appears even more striking when it is contrasted with the much more "skeptical" views held by the British; see the series of comparative surveys conducted by the Gallup organization, *Public Opinion News Service*, April 16, 17, 18, 19, 21, 1957.

9. Barnett, "God and the American People," *Ladies' Home Journal*, November 1948, p. 234.

10. "What the U. S. Thinks of Life Here and Hereafter," *The Catholic Digest*, May 1953.

11. Barnett, "God and the American People," *Ladies' Home Journal*, November 1948, pp. 233, 234, 235.

12. Barnett, "God and the American People," *Ladies' Home Journal*, November 1948, p. 234.

13. See particularly the statement of Father George B. Ford, in Barnett, "God and the American People," *Ladies' Home Journal*, November 1948, p. 237.

14. Robin M. Williams, Jr., *American Society: A Sociological Interpretation* (Knopf, 1951), p. 312.

15. Williams, *American Society*, p. 320 n.

16. Williams, *American Society*, p. 344.

17. When an American tourist comes upon the inadequate sanitary arrangements in certain parts of Europe and discovers what seems to him the careless attitude of the inhabitants in matters of personal hygiene, he is inclined to feel what he experiences not simply as a shortcoming in modern living conveniences but as a *moral defect*, on a par with irreligion, caste rigidity, and the absence of American representative democracy. Cp. the following placard displayed by many restaurants in the midwest: "Sanitation is a way of life. As a way of life, it must be nourished from within and grow as an ideal in human relations."

18. Barnett, "God and the American People," *Ladies' Home Journal*, November 1948, pp. 235–36.

19. Where this "principle" of the American Way of Life is flagrantly violated by local prescription, as in the case of racial attitudes in the south and elsewhere, festering "bad conscience" and a destructive defensive aggressiveness are the result.

20. "Differences in religion make a difference in social conduct" (Williams, *American Society*, p. 311). Investigating belief-systems from this angle would seem to be a good way of discovering what the "religion" of an individual or a group really is.

21. Discussing the European background of such churches, H. Richard Niebuhr writes: "These churches are doctrinal and liturgical in character, regarding conformity to creed and ritual as the essential requirements of Christianity" (*The Social Sources of Denominationalism* [Holt, 1929], p. 126).

22. For a discussion of the "religions of the disinherited," see below, chap. vi, pp. 122–23, chap. ix, pp. 216–19.

23. See the illuminating account of Memorial Day as an "American sacred ceremony" in W. Lloyd Warner, *Structure of American Life* (Edinburgh, 1952), chap. x. Warner writes: "The Memorial Day ceremonies and subsidiary rites, such as those of Armistice Day, of today, yesterday, and tomorrow, are rituals which are a sacred symbol system which functions periodically to integrate the whole community, with its conflicting symbols and its opposing autonomous churches and associations. . . . Memorial Day is a cult of the dead which organizes and integrates the various faiths, ethnic and class groups, into a sacred unity" (p. 214). As to the "saints" of the American Way of Life, Warner quotes a Memorial Day orator: "No character except the Carpenter of Nazareth has ever been honored the way Washington and Lincoln have been in New England. Virtue, freedom from sin, and righteousness were qualities possessed by Washington and Lincoln, and in possessing these qualities both were true Americans, and we would do well to emulate them. Let us first be true Americans" (p. 220). The theological implications of this statement are sensational: Washington and Lincoln, as "true Americans," are credited with the moral and spiritual qualities ("virtue, freedom from sin, and righteousness") traditionally associated with Christ, and we are all urged to "emulate" them!

24. For the quotations, as well as a general account of Mr. Eisenhower's religion, see Paul Hutchinson, "The President's Religious Faith," *The Christian Century*, March 24, 1954. For a sharp critique, see William Lee Miller, "Piety Along the Potomac," *The Reporter*, August 17, 1954.

25. For a penetrating examination of the sources and expressions of the American conviction of a "new order of things" in the New World, see Reinhold Niebuhr, *The Irony of American History* (Scribner's, 1952).

26. Dorothy Canfield Fisher, *Vermont Tradition* (Little, Brown, 1953). For a comprehensive survey of American life, see Max Lerner, *America as a Civilization: Life and Thought in the United States Today* (Simon and Schuster, 1957); see also Elting E. Morison, ed., *The American Style: Essays in Value and Performance* (Harper, 1958).

27. "America is a middle-class country, and the middle-class values and styles of perception reach into all levels except perhaps the fringes at the very top and the very bottom" (David Riesman, *Individualism Reconsidered* [Free Press, 1954], p. 499).

28. Riesman sees the immigrant generations as an important source of replenishment of old-line middle-class inner-directedness in American society (*Individualism Reconsidered*, pp. 289, 290).

29. See H. Richard Niebuhr, *The Kingdom of God in America* (Willett, Clark, 1937), pp. 76–83.

30. See F. E. Mayer, *The Religious Bodies of America* (Concordia, 1954), pp. 352–53, 354, 378 n.

31. Williams, *American Society*, p. 319. See also Roy F. Nichols, *Religion and American Democracy* (Louisiana State University Press, 1959) and William Lee Miller, "Religion and the American Way of Life," in *Religion and the Free Society* (Fund for the Republic, 1958).

32. "European visitors are able to detect better than we ourselves the emergence of a 'typically American' form of Christian worship" (Herbert Wallace Schneider, *Religion in 20th Century America* [Harvard, 1952], p. 170). "As many have noticed, the Protestant churches in America, even though brought from Europe, show more qualities in common than any one retains with its European stem. And they feel that in America, the synagogue is no longer an alien. Even the Catholic Church in America acquires a tone unlike Catholicism in Europe" (Perry Miller, "The Location of American Religious Freedom," in *Religion and Freedom of Thought* [Doubleday, 1954], p. 21).

33. Williams, *American Society*, p. 337. Something of the shift involved in this secularization of Jewish-Christian faith is suggested by Ralph Barton Perry in his apologia for Protestant "liberalism": "If it does not stress the love of God, it does at least embrace the love of neighbor. If it neglects the fatherhood of God, it at any rate proclaims the fraternity of men. If it disparages the church along with other corporate entities, it is because it is so insistent on the finality of the human person. The independence of this moral ideal in no way argues *against* theism . . ." (Ralph Barton Perry, *Characteristically American* [Knopf, 1949], p. 117).

34. Oscar Handlin, *The Uprooted* (Little, Brown, 1951), p. 128.

35. See, e.g., the section, "Relatively Distinctive Features of American Religious Institutions," in Williams, *American Society*, pp. 315–51.

36. Two recent studies of contemporary American religion are of major importance: A. Roy Eckardt, *The Surge of American Piety* (Association Press, 1958) and Martin E. Marty, *The New Shape of American Religion* (Harper, 1959). See also Lerner, *America as a Civilization*, chap. x, sec. 1, "God and the Churches" (pp. 703–17) and William H. Whyte, Jr., *The Organization Man* (Simon and Schuster, 1956), Part VII, chap. 26, "The Church of Suburbia" (pp. 365–81).

37. *The New York Times*, December 23, 1952; see also G. Elson Ruff, *The Dilemma of Church and State* (Muhlenberg, 1954), p. 85. Cp. the very similar sentiment expressed by Robert C. Ruark: "Although I am not a practicing religionist, I have a great respect for organized religion, no matter what shape it takes" ("Scoff-religious," *New York World Telegram*, October 10, 1955).

38. Miller, "Piety Along the Potomac," *The Reporter*, August 17, 1954. Mr. Miller continues: "If the object of devotion is not God but 'religion' . . . then the resulting religiosity may become simply the instrument of more substantial commitments." The most "substantial" commitment of the American people, to which their "religiosity" is instrumental, is the American Way of Life. Once more to quote Mr. Eisenhower: "I am the most intensely religious man I know. Nobody goes through six years of war without faith. A democracy cannot exist without a religious base. I believe in democracy" (*New York Times*, May 4, 1948).

39. Dwight D. Eisenhower, quoted in Paul Hutchinson, "The President's Religious Faith," *The Christian Century*, March 24, 1954.

40. See Ernst Troeltsch, *The Social Teaching of the Christian Churches* (1911; tr. by Olive Wyon, Macmillan, 1931), Vol. I, pp. 331–49, Vol. II, pp. 691–728; also J. Milton Yinger, *Religion in the Struggle for Power* (Duke, 1946), pp. 16–50.

41. Williams speaks of a "value-consensus in which religious differences are subsidiary to the values of religious liberty" (*American Society*, p. 345).

42. "The Mormons, the Orthodox Jews, and a few small religious communities are religiously organized peoples, but almost all other religious bodies in the United States, including the Roman Catholic Church, are neither national churches nor sects; they are commonly known as denominations or 'communions'" (Schneider, *Religion in 20th Century America*, p. 22). Even the groups Schneider mentions as exceptions, insofar as

they have become acculturated to American life, would seem to fall into the same pattern.

43. Since most American denominations emerged from earlier sects, denominations have sometimes been defined as "simply sects in an advanced stage of development and adjustment to each other and the secular world" (Leopold von Wiese, *Systematic Sociology*, adapted and amplified by Howard Becker [Wiley, 1932], p. 626). There is, of course, a good deal of truth in this definition; its defect, however, is that it regards the denomination as essentially transitional between sect and church, which is emphatically not the case with denominations in the American sense. American denominations have indeed, by and large, developed out of sects, but they represent the final stage of development, rather than a transitional stage to something else ("church" in the European sense). For a more general discussion, see Joachim Wach, *Types of Religious Experience* (Routledge and Kegan Paul, 1951), chap. ix, "Church, Denomination, and Sect."

44. In a number of European countries (Germany, Holland, Switzerland), Protestant and Catholic churches have reached a kind of balance in which neither can pretend to be "the" national church. But where this is the case, it is simply a social and historical fact, not the proper and normative condition. In America, on the other hand, the plurality of churches is held to be proper and normative; in this the American situation differs fundamentally from the European, even where the latter seems to resemble it most.

45. H. Richard Niebuhr, *The Social Sources of Denominationalism*, p. 207. "The Church in our time, like the Church in any place at any time, is deeply influenced in its institutional forms by the political and economic society with which it lives in conjunction. As the polity of all the churches, whether they are episcopal, presbyterian, or congregational by tradition, has been modified in the direction of the political structure of Canada and the United States, so the institutional status and authority of the ministry are being modified in the direction of the democratic type of political, educational, and economic executive or managerial authority" (H. Richard Niebuhr, *The Purpose of the Church and Its Ministry* [Harper, 1956], p. 90). Cf. the statement of Franklin Clark Fry, president of the United Lutheran Church of America: "The polity of our church as a whole is frankly constructed on a secular model. Its prototype is the government of the United States" (quoted in H.E.F., "Lutherans Centralize," *The Christian Century*, October 27, 1954).

46. Thus McAvoy speaks of the "practical and parochial character of American Catholicism"; the "parochial" character

he relates to the "American tradition of disestablishment," while for the "practical" aspect of American Catholicism, he notes that "some observers have claimed that [it] is the product of the puritanism dominant in American Protestantism" (Thomas T. McAvoy, "The Catholic Church in the United States," in Waldemar Gurian and M. A. Fitzsimons, *The Catholic Church in World Affairs* [Notre Dame, 1954], pp. 361, 364).

47. Despite all the instability of American life, fully 96 per cent of Americans were found in 1955 still belonging to the religious community of their birth (see *Public Opinion News Service*, March 20, 1955).

48. Louis Finkelstein, J. Elliot Ross, and William Adams Brown, *The Religions of Democracy: Judaism, Catholicism, and Protestantism in Creed and Life* (Devin-Adair, 1946). One of the clearest expressions of this conception by a layman was voiced by Admiral William F. Halsey, principal speaker at the fifth annual "four chaplains award dinner." "This picture," Admiral Halsey declared, "is symbolic of our national life. Protestant, Catholic, and Jew, each group has given, when called upon, the full measure of devotion in defense of our [American democratic] way of life" (*The New York Times*, February 6, 1955).

49. J. Paul Williams, *What Americans Believe and How They Worship* (Harper, 1952), pp. 71, 78, 368, 374; see the critical review of this book by J. H. Nichols, *The Christian Century*, September 3, 1952. (A strong tendency toward this kind of "religion of democracy" is to be found in Jewish Reconstructionism; see Ira Eisenstein and Eugene Kohn, *Mordecai M. Kaplan: An Evaluation* [Jewish Reconstructionist Foundation, 1952], p. 259). "The religion of the American majority is democracy. . . . In fact, the religion of public education is a more powerful factor in American life today than that of the churches. The only religion with which the great majority of American youth have ever come in contact is the religion of public education" (Conrad Moehlman, *School and Church: The American Way* [Harper, 1944], pp. ix, x). David Riesman speaks of "new ways of using the school as a kind of community center, as the chapel of a secular religion perhaps" (*Individualism Reconsidered*, p. 211).

50. H. M. Kallen, "Democracy's True Religion," *Saturday Review of Literature*, July 28, 1951.

51. Daniel A. Poling, "A Running Start for Every Day," *Parade: The Sunday Picture Magazine*, September 19, 1954.

52. H. Richard Niebuhr, *The Social Sources of Denominationalism*, p. 104. Niebuhr thus describes this type of religiosity in which the old Puritan spirituality has terminated: "In its final phase, the development of this religious movement exhibits the complete enervation of the once virile force . . . the problem

of evil [has been] simplified out of existence, and for the mysterious will of the Sovereign of life and death and sin and salvation [has been substituted] the sweet benevolence of a Father-Mother God or the vague goodness of the All. Here the concern for self has been secularized to its last degree; the conflicts of sick souls have been replaced by the struggles of sick minds and bodies; the Puritan passion for perfection has become a seeking after the kingdom of health and mental peace and its comforts" (p. 105).

53. The most celebrated effort along these lines is undoubtedly Joshua Loth Liebman, *Peace of Mind* (Simon and Schuster, 1946).

54. Norman Vincent Peale, *The Power of Positive Thinking* (Prentice-Hall, 1952). For a careful study of American religious literature reflecting both the "peace of mind" and the "positive thinking" gospels, see Louis Schneider and Sanford M. Dornbusch, *Popular Religion: Inspirational Books in America* (University of Chicago Press, 1958).

55. A salesman writes to Norman Vincent Peale in the latter's regular question page in *Look:* "I have lost my faith and enthusiasm. How can I get them back?" To which Dr. Peale replies: "Every morning, give thanks for the new day and its opportunities. Think outgoingly of every prospect you will call on. . . . Affirm aloud that you are going to have a great day. Flush out all depressing, negative, and tired thoughts. Start thinking faith, enthusiasm and joy . . ." ("Norman Vincent Peale Answers Your Questions," *Look*, August 10, 1954). This may be compared with an advertisement for a quite "secular" self-help book in *The New York Times Magazine* for May 8, 1949:

DON'T WORRY
If you don't acknowledge it,
it isn't so!
Develop the Art of Adaptability

VI. *Protestantism in America*

The story of American Protestantism[1] is the story of a religious movement following the advancing frontier and subduing it, periodically crystallizing into established denominations, yet always in some way breaking through them again, until it comes face to face with what has so far proved an insurmountable challenge, the urbanized, industrialized America of today. In fact, the story may profitably be interpreted in terms of challenge and response, expanding America providing the challenge, Protestantism meeting the challenge in creative response as long as that challenge bore the familiar features of the frontier. The end of the frontier and the emergence of an urbanized culture brought Protestantism up against a new America in which it has made a place for itself very different from the position it occupied in the two centuries when it was religious America on the march.

I

Most of the better known Protestant groups in this country began as transplantations from Europe, but in the New World they had to operate in a social, cultural, and religious environment radically different, which very soon transformed them in structure and spirit. Aside from Anglicanism, which for a time established itself in Virginia and other southern colonies, virtually all of the churches that made their way to these shores in the seventeenth and early eighteenth centuries were dissenting churches, more or less in opposition to the established institutions in the old country. Pilgrims and Puritans, Baptists and Quakers, Presbyterians and Catholics (from England and Ireland), Mennonites, Moravians, and the other Continental sects, even many of the early Lutherans, came here as non-conformist groups, excluded if not actually persecuted in their homeland. Here most of them expected to establish their freedom as a church and develop their own religious and ecclesiastical life as they had not been permitted to do in the lands of their birth. But their expectations, and their best efforts to realize these expectations, were set at naught by the pressures and demands of the new environment. In New England the Puritans sought to plant a "new Israel" in the wilderness, a "holy community" bound together by common faith and covenant; in effect, what they were doing was attempting to establish as a national church the "gathered" church in which membership was limited to the converted who could give satisfactory evidence of their conversion in terms of "experimental religion." This led in the beginning to the persecution and exile of dissidents in an effort to maintain the "gathered" character of the church and yet keep it identical with the community; but before very long the compulsions of the secular order made themselves felt, the church lost its rigorously "gathered" character, admitting those who though professed Christians could not give "experimental" evidence of their "new birth," and finally settled down to the status of a kind of established denomination, tolerating other religious groups within the Protestant fold. In the middle colonies the diversity was greater from the very beginning, leading to a kind of denominational "coexistence" if not always full freedom. The South was in many ways nearer to the English pattern, especially where the Anglican Church was legally established; but here too the dissenting groups were numerous and influential, and by the middle of the eighteenth century the situation was not altogether different from that which prevailed in the other colonies on the Atlantic seaboard.

In one respect all the colonies, whatever churches and establishments they possessed, found themselves in a situation utterly different from what they had been familiar with in the old country: they were face to face with the open frontier. At first the frontier simply meant the wilderness and the Indians. In striking contrast to the Catholics elsewhere on the continent, the Puritans showed little active interest in evangelizing the aborigines, and many of the other religious groups displayed even less. They were mostly concerned with planting and consolidating their own religious institutions along lines dictated by their traditions and convictions. Some missionary activity was carried on but it never loomed large in the total scheme of the early settlers.

But very soon the frontier began to assume another meaning. It came to signify the advancing front of the European settlers penetrating into the wilderness and bringing it into subjection to the white man. It was this new frontier that played havoc with the expectations of the colonists to transplant the settled life of the Old World to the New, for this frontier meant a radical restructuring of the ways of life and thought of the Europeans who pushed it ever further into the wilderness across the continent.

By the beginning of the eighteenth century the original Puritan fervor in New England had declined. Men had become totally absorbed in their worldly enterprises; conversions were fewer, the churches were full of those who had never "experienced" God, and the number of the unchurched was very great.[2] To judge by contemporary denunciations, morality too was at a low ebb. Yet there was restlessness and longing in the air. It was in this atmosphere that the Great Awakening, the first of the momentous revival movements in American Protestant history, got under way. It was initiated by a series of sermons which Jonathan Edwards, a profound scholar and theologian, preached at Northampton, Massachusetts, in December 1734. It is still difficult to understand the shattering effect of these sermons, so learned, so carefully prepared, so closely reasoned, so utterly theological. But as the sermons progressed the effects were sensational. Men and women were stirred into violent manifestations of repentance; hundreds were converted and gave fervent testimony of their conversion. The movement spread from New England and New Jersey, where sporadic revivals had already broken out, to New York and Pennsylvania and the other colonies. The separate revival movements were, so to speak, bound together by George Whitefield, the great Methodist preacher, who arrived in 1739 and toured the colonies till his departure for England the following year. Denominational lines were overpassed; all were caught up in the movement. A great "ingathering of souls" resulted: it has been estimated that nearly 50,000 people joined the church in New England alone, and the effect was very much the same elsewhere. Colleges and Indian missions were established; the public conscience was quickened, and the real beginnings of the anti-slavery agitation are to be traced to the Great Awakening.

But the Great Awakening, which so unexpectedly overflowed the established denominational landmarks and gave rise to so much that was new and unfamiliar, also brought dissension and schism in its wake. The very notion of revivalism, alien to the settled traditions of the churches, roused vehement opposition, which was fed by the emotional extravagances of some of the revivalists and their audiences. A furious polemic broke out, in which Jonathan Edwards defended revivalism as in effect (to use modern language) an appeal to the whole man for an existential decision. Charles Chauncy, on the other hand, championed respectability, sobriety, and reason in the Christian life. The dispute was not resolved by these learned polemics; it was to go on for another two centuries, to our own day. But of decisive importance was the fact that in the course of the Great Awakening a widening gulf became visible between the established religion of the respectable folk in the settled communities and the "religion of the proletariat," the religion of the frontier and the submerged poor. "The heir of the movement," H. Richard Niebuhr has pointed out, "was the Baptist church."[3] The older Rhode Island Baptists had themselves been suspicious of the revival movement but they could not hold their churches in leash. Large numbers of religious groups came into being during the Great Awakening outside the bounds of the official Congregational churches, and many of the older congregations broke away. The freedom and fluidity characteristic of the Baptists just suited their purpose, and "henceforth the Baptists became the exponents of the religion of the frontier in New England. . . . As the settlements pushed ever further westward, the Baptist church seemed to become the frontier branch of Congregationalism."[4] In other parts of colonial

America it was the Presbyterians and the newly emerging Methodists who profited by the revival.

The Great Awakening, despite the fact that it began in settled communities, was essentially a frontier phenomenon and in a general sort of way fixed the pattern of revivalism and frontier religion. It was but the opening of a wave of revival movements that was to go on for another century and change the face of the land.

The next great outburst of revivalism came shortly after the establishment of independence. It was a movement that brought religion to and beyond the Appalachian frontier. Religious and moral conditions of frontier life were everywhere described as deplorable. The great mass of the people were unchurched and indifferent; among the educated classes, in the older East as well as the frontier West, deism and unbelief were prevalent.[5] In 1793, indeed, the Kentucky Legislature felt that it no longer needed a chaplain.[6] It was in Kentucky that the Great Revival, the second powerful revival movement, came into being, although it had its counterpart in the eastern centers as well. In the East, particularly in New England, it scored its best successes in the colleges and universities; deism was stopped and numerous conversions took place. But the movement really showed its power on the frontier. Organized religion, which "previous to the revivals . . . had been largely an upper-class affair . . . now became increasingly a concern of the common man."[7] Some of the older churches were involved, notably the Presbyterian, but, by and large, the revival movement was the work of groups that were peculiarly suited to the task and that grew into vast bodies as a result of the evangelization of frontier America.

The Baptists and the Methodists both represented "religions of the disinherited" and so were the better able to understand and meet the challenge that the frontier offered to Protestantism.[8] The religion they brought was fervent, emotional, and personal; their institutional forms were fluid and they were ready to modify them freely at need. Their clergy and active workers were usually from the same social and cultural classes as the people they evangelized; and in the Baptist preacher and Methodist circuit rider they possessed indefatigable workers whose energy and devotion overcame all obstacles.[9] "The Methodist preacher crossed the mountains into Kentucky only ten years after Daniel Boone, and he gained on Boone's successors. He reached Oregon and California ahead of the first division of the oncoming migration."[10] The camp meeting, which the Presbyterians had devised but had abandoned when its excesses caused alarm, was taken up by the Methodists and Baptists, who found it particularly suited to the conditions of the frontier.[11] Methodism and Baptism were "in tune with the spirit of the frontier to begin with" and so they were able to "cultivate that spirit wholeheartedly."[12]

Yet Methodists and Baptists had both to make certain adjustments and accommodations before they could meet and overcome the frontier. Baptism had to abandon its extreme sectarianism and allow for some stability and cooperation in the work of evangelizing, while Methodism had to "relinquish part of its inheritance as the child of Anglicanism and the autocratic Wesley."[13] The adaptation was successful and both groups grew tremendously. They not only brought in scores of thousands of the unchurched, but they also absorbed large numbers who, for social, cultural, or religious reasons, found the older denominations increasingly uncongenial. The Great Revival, initiated in 1795 and continuing for some fifteen or twenty years, devastated the Presbyterian churches in Kentucky, parts of Tennessee, and elsewhere on the southwestern frontier, just as the Great Awakening sixty years before had made serious inroads into Congregationalism.[14]

The revival movement, in irregular rhythm, went on almost continuously with the advancing frontier. In 1830 the third of the great evangelical denominations appeared, the Disciples of Christ. This group was entirely American, emerging in response to American conditions. It arose as a secession from the Presbyterians, one of several of the time, in protest against those features of established Presbyterianism which, in the opinion of Alexander Campbell and others, prevented the Presbyterian churches from bringing the faith to the people. There was no intention of founding another denomination, any more than there had been in the original impulse that gave rise to Methodism. But another denomination, and a significant one, it soon became.

The Great Revival and subsequent movements transformed the face of American Protestantism. "At the end of the colonial period, the Congregationalists and the Presbyterians ranked, respectively, first and second in numbers and influence; the Baptists and the Episcopalians were third and fourth, while the Lutherans and Reformed (Dutch and German), the Quakers, the German sectaries, and the Methodists followed in about that order. By 1850 the last had become first, at least in numbers, for the Methodists in that year had a membership of 1,324,000. The Baptists came next with 815,000 members; the Presbyterians ranked third with 487,000; the Congregationalists, fourth with 197,000; the Lutherans, fifth with 163,000; the Disciples of Christ, after only twenty years as a separate body, had a membership of 118,000; and the Episcopalians came last with 90,000."[15]

Baptists and Methodists, and later Disciples, frequently found themselves on the same frontier, in rivalry yet often co-operating in revival enterprises. But before long a kind of geographical division of labor came to be roughly defined. The Baptist missionary carried the evangelical message vigorously to the South and Southwest, but somehow he did not move so freely beyond the Missouri. The Methodist circuit rider followed, on the whole, a somewhat different course; he took over the Midwest and went on to the Northwest. The Disciples, emerging on the frontier, established themselves in the West and Midwest. The Disciples remained localized as one of the smaller churches, but the Baptists and Methodists soon became the largest and most characteristic bodies in American Protestantism.[16]

It was not only in numbers and organization that the revival movement changed the aspect of American Protestantism. It radically modified its outlook, its theology, its worship, and its spirit. "The frontier," H. Richard Niebuhr indicates, "not only divided its pioneers from the established churches of the East, but also impressed upon them a common pattern of religious life and a common religious symbolism."[17] The old Puritan insistence on religion as a corporate activity in which all human enterprises, personal and social, were to be brought under the sovereignty of God gave way to a profound theological individualism, in which the individual was held to be sovereign and the deep stirring of his religious emotions was understood to be the most authentic working of faith. Impatience with institutional forms, creeds, theologies, and liturgies constituted another aspect of this attitude, for these were all held to invade the rights of the sovereign individual and to inhibit the free flow of spirit. "Deeds, not creeds" was the cry, where "deeds" covered pious exertions, "right living," strenuous moral crusades, and (later) social action alike. Even more repugnant than theology, liturgy, and institutional order was any separation between clergy and laity, particularly such as is involved in an educated and specially placed ministry. In all these respects and others that might be mentioned, frontier religion, the religion manifesting itself in the great evangelical denominations, was a true reflection of the frontier spirit with its individualism, emotionalism, pragmatism, and impatience of forms and restraints.[18] But it was not merely frontier religion in the stricter sense that was thus fashioned in the image of the frontier. Since all vital American Protestantism began as frontier religion or very soon became involved in the revivalist movement, all American Protestantism has retained the marks of the frontier, however overlaid and modified by subsequent changes in American life.

One of the most significant features of the revivalist movement was the way it overran denominational lines and led to supra-denominational efforts and enterprises. It was in the wake of the Great Revival that the first mission societies, transcending denominational rivalries, were formed, along with home mission movements. The Great Revival stimulated education, both public and religious. Above all, it gave a tremendous impetus to the social causes and reform movements that multiplied in the second quarter of the nineteenth century, and left its impress on all later history. In this period, at least, revivalism really represented a religious *movement* overflowing into many other areas of national life.

"The distinction between religious 'bodies,' or denominations, and religious 'movements,'" Herbert W. Schneider points out, "is more important for American culture [than the European distinction between church and sect]. A religious body is a stable institution with a heritage which it cherishes, a government which gives organized expression to its faith, and a body of members whose duties and values are generally recognized. Most movements culminate in bodies, as most faiths become creeds. A movement is endangered when it does not create a body, and a body is endangered when it ceases to move."[19] Most of the colonial churches were transplanted and began their career in the new world as religious bodies, but under conditions of the open frontier they either underwent transformation into movements or else gave way before movements that arose to meet the challenge of the new environment. The succession of revivals, beginning with the Great Awakening in the 1730s and continuing for perhaps a century and a half, kept Protestantism in America in a state of permanent revolution, fluid, dynamic, creative. Frontier religion provided a striking confirmation of Ernst Troeltsch's insight that "the really creative, church-forming religious movements are the work of the lower strata."[20] Frontier religion was eminently the work of the "lower strata," although the "lower strata" on the American frontier were rather different from the disinherited proletariat and peasantry of Europe whom Troeltsch had in mind. These "lower strata" of the frontier were the bearers of an outgoing movement, a movement which, impatient of forms and traditions, appealed to immediacy against hierarchies and sacraments, took its stand on the Bible against man-made creeds and theologies, insisted on the efficacy of religion in radically transforming lives, broke through or overpassed established denominational boundaries, and gave rise to many new forms, agencies, and activities of evangelical work. It even succeeded in stirring into motion some of the older religious bodies, which, because of their reluctance or inability to

adapt themselves to the conditions of the frontier, were falling behind in the evangelization of America.

But every religious movement carries within itself its own
inner contradiction. Its very success tends to rob it of its
dynamic and to harden into set forms what was once fluid
and open. Religious revivals, of their very nature, are passionate stirrings of the spirit, brief and tempestuous. When
the passion is spent, reaction sets in; after the revivalists
come the organizers and institutionalizers, who understand
their responsibility as that of conserving the gains of the
movement. Denominational lines are consolidated and become all-important again. The immediacy of spirit becomes an institutionalized form; indeed, a kind of institutionalized revival is itself incorporated into the system.[21] The
liberating appeal to the Bible becomes a routinized bibli-
cism; the radical transformation of life is reduced to an
often graceless legalism and moralism: "a loveless legalism
is always the mark of a dying evangelicalism."[22] In part,
this process is the inevitable congealing of the religious
movement into religious institutions, without which no kind
of social survival or continuity would be possible. But in
part too it reflects the pattern of social and economic transformation which the frontier underwent as it advanced
across the continent. In good measure through the disci-
plining effects of religion,[23] the foot-loose, propertyless
frontiersmen became respectable farmers and small merchants and the next generation moved even higher up the
social scale. Frontier religion, essentially the religion of the
"religious proletariat," imperceptibly became transformed
into more or less conventional denominationalism, still bear-
ing the old names but harboring a very different social and
spiritual content. "Protestantism was the religion of the
common man in the days of the American frontier. But as
frontiersmen graduated into the middle class, the Protestant
Church tended to move up one rung in the social ladder.
. . . As the frontier grew in stability and prosperity, and as
the frontiersmen became the solid middle class of the
American commonwealth, the 'first fine careless rapture' of
Evangelical Christianity was lost . . ."[24] The sense of common venture in conquering the land for Christ gave way to

a circumspect concern for denominational standing, prestige, and power. "With the loss of the sense of the common task in proclaiming the kingdom of Christ, sectional, racial, and cultural differences assumed increasing importance. The more attention was concentrated upon the church, the greater became the tendency toward schism."[25] As the force of the great revivals spent itself, splits took place in virtually every American Protestant body, largely reflecting the sectional, cultural, and ethnic interests that now loomed so large. The most fateful source of division was the conflict over slavery. The schisms this conflict produced resulted in the sundering of the Baptists, Methodists, Presbyterians, and other Protestant bodies into Northern and Southern divisions; only in recent years has this breach begun to be healed.

The conversion of the frontier religious movement into an established rural church did not, of course, take place all at once. As the frontier advanced, it left behind it thriving churches and denominations reducing to order the ground that had been gained. Meanwhile, the movement went forward with the frontier, and as long as the movement continued even the settled churches of the hinterland were filled with the revivalistic spirit. Reinhold Niebuhr believes that "the greatest religious vitality in America developed in the first half of the nineteenth century" and that after 1850 it "began to wane."[26] Perhaps the terminal date might be set rather later. At any rate, the frontier movement continued for some decades at least after the Civil War. A significant development was the Mormon settlement in Utah and nearby regions. Mormonism ran directly counter to the basic pattern of frontier religion: it was hierarchical, collectivistic, in its own way highly theological; yet in its earlier days it was genuinely a movement and shared some of the dynamic features of Protestant revivalism. It too, after a time, began to settle down, first into a closed religious community, and then in the twentieth century into a denomination along more or less typical American lines.

By the last third of the nineteenth century the drive and dynamic of frontier religion was very largely gone. By this

time, too, the fusion of Protestantism with the American
Way of Life had been pretty well completed.[27] Protestantism now came up against a new kind of frontier, very different indeed from the expanding geographical frontier it
had met so effectively. This new frontier was the frontier of
the urbanized, industrialized society into which the older
America was being rapidly transformed. Here American
Protestantism was confronted with a challenge for which it
was not prepared and which has so far proved very nearly
beyond its capacity to meet.

II

The religious movement represented by American Protestantism encountered two problems of a very different order, each in its way reflecting the uniquely diverse ethnic
character of the American people. The churches of the immigrants and of the Negroes made a significant contribution
to the emerging pattern of American denominationalism.

The immigrant churches, the churches of the non-
English-speaking immigrants in particular, represented a
fusion of religion and culture that was of the very texture
of immigrant life. These churches, especially the Lutheran
and Reformed, often had strong doctrinal positions and
allegiances; creeds and confessions and theological statements generally played a big part in their religious life.
Yet national-cultural bonds, defined in terms of language,
were potent. "Many an immigrant church became more a
racial and cultural than a religious institution in the new
world. Its parochial schools were fostered not only that the
children might receive instruction in religion, but also that
they might learn the mother-tongue, and with it the attitudes and social ideals of the old homeland."[28] Indeed, language and cultural influences often proved predominant.
Churches with substantially the same creed and confession,
such as German and Dutch Reformed or German and
Scandinavian Lutheran, could not unite; while schemes
of union of German-language Lutheran and Reformed
churches were broached, and it was even proposed that a
German-language college be set up in Pennsylvania un-

der joint Lutheran-Reformed auspices.[29] Even among the English-speaking Presbyterians the forces of ethnic origin and culture were not without effect, making for approaches and divisions cutting across confessional lines.

Yet the forces of acculturation were relentlessly at work. The American environment demanded accommodation at the pain of extinction, and "the choice between accommodation and extinction finally [became] a forced choice. Though churches [might] delay the moment of their surrender, few [elected] to perish with their mother tongue."[30] The adoption of English as church language was bitterly resisted, but with the rise of the second and third generations it could not be withstood. With the introduction of English as church language other changes inevitably set in. The old religion and the foreign culture in which it was embedded became increasingly distinct as the latter grew increasingly obsolescent. The process of accommodation was, of course, not without its cost. It was often frantically resisted by those who dreamed of perpetuating the foreign culture on American soil, and it led to widespread division and conflict. Succeeding waves of immigration renewed and multiplied these conflicts, setting later immigrants against earlier, and dividing still further churches already divided.[31] In the end, the forces of Americanization won out almost everywhere, under the impact not only of the American cultural environment but also of the revival movement, which broke through ethnic as it did denominational lines and united Christians of all origins and cultures in the same cause. Accommodation to American life was inevitable and necessary, yet for many it meant a tragic loss in the religious "substance" of their faith, so thoroughly had religion and culture been fused in their experience and tradition.[32]

Advancing Americanization overcame certain barriers, but it did not completely eliminate dissension and schism among the rival churches. On the contrary, it sometimes added new sources of conflict. As language and cultural distinctions declined, doctrinal and liturgical distinctions were often accentuated as defensive and competitive devices.[33] In any case, a residual ethnic impress remained. Lutheran churches are still divided according to whether they are "German" or "Scandinavian" or made up largely of the descendants of colonial Lutheranism,[34] and most of the German sectarian groups, such as Mennonites, Brethren, Moravians, and the like, are essentially "family" societies, belonging to which is a matter of ethnic background and family tradition. There is even a lingering Scotch and Scotch-Irish aura about Presbyterianism; nor has the "English" background of the Episcopalian and Congregational churches entirely disappeared.

Yet, by and large, Protestantism in America has become thoroughly and characteristically American. The process of cultural accommodation has resulted in a kind of religious Americanization. "So the Americanization of the immigrant churches has gone on. Adapting themselves to a common mold, they have grown very much like each other, and have made notable progress toward the foundation of that American Christianity which will inevitably appear when the melting pot has completed its synthetic work."[35] In terms of our own conception, what has emerged is an American Protestantism that serves as one of America's three great "population pools" in the land of the "triple melting pot."

The segmentation that has resulted in the establishment of the powerful Negro churches that form a significant part of American Protestantism has operated not along language or cultural lines but along lines of race and color. Before the Civil War, Negro slaves, as they became Christians, found themselves in the same churches as the whites, though of course segregated from them. Such was the case, too, with most of the free Negroes in the North. Considerations of Christian unity in Christ and the patriarchal responsibility of master for slave, combined with a natural reluctance to allow Negro slaves to develop independent institutions, helped bring about a very limited kind of fellowship in worship. The revival movement reached the Negroes in large numbers and swept them into the Methodist and Baptist churches as these spread in the South and Southwest.

Even before the Civil War, however, there were here and there beginnings of separate Negro churches, usually the result of resentment of free Negroes in the North at segregation and other discriminatory practices.[36] But it was not until after the war that independent Negro churches emerged on a large scale. The Civil War and emancipation removed the restrictions which had fettered independent Negro organization and released the energies of the former slaves. At the same time, the war and postwar conflicts exacerbated the bitterness between the races and intensified the "color" consciousness of the whites. The newly emancipated Negroes carried out the work of separation and independent organization with astounding energy and success. The colored members of the Methodist Episcopal Church, South, left in vast numbers to join the African M.E. and African M.E. Zion churches, which had been formed as small groups in the North in 1816 and 1821 respectively. Of the 208,000 Negro members of the Southern Methodist Church in 1860, only 49,000 remained in 1866, and these soon departed to form the Colored Methodist Episcopal Church. Another Negro church came into being with the division of the Presbyterians, and still another with the separation of the Baptists, both in the decade and a half after the Civil War. The Northern Methodist Church and the Episcopal Church resisted division but could not avoid a great measure of inner segregation.[37]

The Negro churches have grown perhaps faster than Protestant churches in general. About 1953, reports indicate, there were 7,600,000 members in nine all-Negro Baptist denominations, 2,500,000 in six all-Negro Methodist denominations, 90,000 in three all-Negro Presbyterian denominations, and about 12,000 in the Negro Lutheran missions.[38] This would make something over 10,000,000 Negroes in well-established Negro churches. In addition, there were about 900,000 in more or less mixed churches (including about 350,000 Roman Catholics), and an uncertain though not inconsiderable number in small, unaffiliated churches of the "fringe" type. All in all, available figures suggest a total of over 11,500,000 Negro church members in the United States, apparently around 75 per cent of the 15,500,000 Negroes in this country reported in the 1950 census.

"The church," as Sweet points out, "has meant more to

the Negro than any other institution, since only in his
church has he had an opportunity for self-expression."[39]
The Negro church, though it has followed the general institutional lines of its parent white churches, has developed
significant distinctive features of its own, retaining in many
cases residual elements of the revivalism of an earlier day.[40]

The churches of the immigrants ultimately became
American churches and an integral, often indistinguishable,
part of the American denominational scheme. The Negro
churches, entirely American to start with, still stand outside the general system, just as the Negro still stands largely
outside the general pattern of American life. According to
studies mentioned by Liston Pope, "less than one per cent
of the white congregations had any Negro members . . .
and less than one-half of one per cent of the Negro Protestants who belonged to 'white denominations' worshiped
regularly with white persons."[41] The racial segregation of
white and colored Protestants, within the same church as
well as between churches, denounced by Protestant spokesmen with growing frequency as a "sin" and a "scandal,"
shows some signs of abating. Religious desegregation, however, will probably lag considerably behind the desegregation of other aspects of American life, since influential
groups of Negroes have themselves developed a strong interest, emotional and social, in the maintenance of separate
Negro churches, and these churches play a more creative
role in the lives of the masses of Negro Americans than
does any other segregated institution. In any case, the
existence of the Negro church as a segregated division of
American Protestantism constitutes an anomaly of considerable importance in the general sociological scheme of the
"triple melting pot" along lines of religious community
presented in earlier chapters.

III

Until the latter part of the nineteenth century the United
States remained predominantly rural. Cities and towns
were important but were not really America. Until the
Moody-Sankey revival got under way in Brooklyn in 1874,

the revival movement had been largely rural, with the cities barely on the fringe. But by 1900 nearly half of the nation was urban, and by mid-century, 57 per cent of the American people were living in the urban-suburban complexes of the metropolitan centers of the country.

The urbanization of America was an aspect of the far-reaching economic changes that took place in the decades after the Civil War. Modern industry seized possession of the country, and by the twentieth century it became increasingly mass-production industry. The metropolitan centers grew; industrial towns multiplied; large concentrations of industrial wage workers, fed by successive waves of immigration, emerged on the eastern seaboard, in the Midwest, and later in the Far West as well. Under the impact of the urban-industrial revolution rural life was transformed. The automobile immensely accelerated geographical mobility, broke down the isolation of country life, and gave rise to a growing number of rootless, homeless people always on the move. Some time in the new century a reverse movement from the cities to the suburbs set in, creating the urban-suburban combination, frequently with its rural fringe, so characteristic of American life today. The America of 1950 seemed centuries away from the America of a hundred years before.[42]

It was this emerging America, with its industry and industrial workers, its big cities and concentrated immigrant masses, that Protestantism faced after the Civil War. And in this new America it faced a challenge that required a response it was somehow not capable of giving.[43] Its very success in winning the frontier and spreading over the face of the country in the century and a half after the Great Awakening seemed to incapacitate it for meeting the challenge that now confronted it.[44]

The revival movement had made the Protestant church, outside the older centers, largely a church of the lower classes. The economic development of the country and the social mobility characteristic of American life transformed it into a middle-class church, established, respectable, self-satisfied, preoccupied with itself as an institution of standing in middle-class America. It grew increasingly remote from the outlook and hopes of the urban industrial masses, and it cultivated its own self-sufficiency. It was no longer open, as the Protestant movement had been open in the days of its great advance.

In evangelizing the country in the wake of the advancing frontier Protestantism had become a church of the older immigration—English, Scotch and Scotch-Irish, German, Dutch, Scandinavian. To its social and cultural remoteness from the urban and industrial masses was thus added a kind of ethnic exclusiveness, with its sense of racial superiority over against the "alien stocks" of the new immigration. The two kinds of exclusiveness sustained and confirmed each other, for as the lower classes of the older America moved upward in the social scale their place at the bottom was taken by the newer immigrants, reflecting "the remarkable fluidity of [the American] social system, in which each new group pushed upward the level of its predecessors."[45] In the great coal and iron fields of Pennsylvania, for example, the earlier Welshmen and Cornishmen, moving up to supervisory positions or leaving for other, better regarded occupations, were replaced successively by Irish and Germans, Slavs and Italians. Between the Protestant church as it came to be constituted toward the end of the century and the urban, industrial masses, a gulf had arisen which was to grow wider with time. For one thing, the new immigration was largely non-Protestant in origin; for another, it came directly to an industrial America, without passing through the frontier.

Because of its origins in frontier religion American Protestantism was almost from the beginning geared to an individualistic piety, in which right living by the individual was stressed, with the expectation that social justice would naturally follow. As long as Protestantism remained a movement of the masses in the earlier America "right living" was interpreted in sufficiently profound terms to produce an overflow of evangelical piety into the larger areas of social life, thus stimulating the many reform movements of the earlier nineteenth century. But as American social life became more complex, and as Protestantism itself became more and more an institutional reflection of certain strata of middle-class America, the religious individualism remaining from frontier religion began to serve as a means of ignoring and evading the social problems that were arising in the New America of big cities and modern industry. The shibboleths appropriate to the rural life of the first half of the century were repeated in a new situation, where they acquired a very different significance. Protestantism exhausted its crusading spirit in campaigns to improve individual morality, refusing to see that the genuinely moral problems of the time were social problems that could not be adequately dealt with merely from the standpoint of personal betterment. There were other voices in American Protestantism, as we shall see, but they were neither very numerous nor very effective.

By and large, then, it may be said that the very success of American Protestantism in evangelizing the earlier America hampered its effectiveness in meeting the challenge of the new time.[46] Its success had removed it from the newer currents of American life and had engendered certain attitudes of social and ethnic exclusiveness which made difficult indeed any genuinely outgoing movement of evangelization under the new conditions. Thus did American Protestantism, as it approached the new century, offer another confirmation of the Toynbeean law of the "idolization of the ephemeral."[47]

There were many in Protestant ranks, however, particularly among theologians and church leaders, who were deeply uncomfortable about this situation. Their Christian conscience was troubled, and their concern was aroused by the fact that the spokesmen of the urban, industrial masses, insofar as spokesmen there were, bitterly protested against the callousness of representative Protestants to the suffering of the masses and their hostility to the rising labor movement.[48] City missions had already been initiated in the decade following the Civil War, but these were felt to be utterly insufficient. The YMCA and YWCA, which began to flourish about the same time, had been established in part at least for the evangelization and religious education of the young people in the cities. In the 1880s the "institutional church" emerged, fostered particularly by Episcopalians and Congregationalists, with the purpose of providing centers of culture, recreation, and religious education for the urban poor who were now inhabiting the sections of the city in which these churches were located. Settlement houses were part of the same program, though increasingly they came to be operated under secular auspices. But the most significant effort of American Protestantism to meet the challenge of the new America was the "social gospel" and the social action agencies that went along with it.

The Christian Socialist movement, originating in England, had begun to make some impression on certain sections of American Protestantism. Washington Gladden, a distinguished Congregational minister, was already in the early 1870s preaching against the inequities of an uncontrolled capitalism and urging a more understanding attitude toward the labor movement. He never ceased emphasizing that economic questions were really at bottom moral questions and confronted the church with a serious responsibility. George D. Herron preached the "reconstruction of society on the basis of New Testament teaching." During the last years of the nineteenth century a concerted effort got under way to provide a theological basis for this new sense of social criticism and social responsibility in modern industrial society.[49] Shailer Mathews, F. G. Peabody, and others wrote studies and treatises; Charles M. Sheldon, a minister, fictionalized the new concern in his best-selling novel, *In His Steps*. But in many ways the most impressive and influential exponent of the "social gospel" was Walter Rauschenbusch.

In his pioneer work, *Christianity and the Social Crisis* (1907), and in his more systematic treatise, *A Theology for the Social Gospel* (1917), as well as in many other writings and addresses, Rauschenbusch made a serious attempt to adapt the evangelical Protestant message to urban, industrial America. He preached a gospel of redeeming not only individuals but also institutions and social systems. Increasingly, Rauschenbusch, and especially his followers, were led to identify co-operative and collectivist economics uniquely with the social demand of the Christian faith; the Christian gospel soon became indistinguishable from a gospel of social reform.[50] Rauschenbusch's teaching had a powerful effect on large sections of the younger generation of Protestant leaders.

The institutional side of the "social gospel" was the social action agency. As far back as 1887 the Episcopal Church had set up the Church Association for the Advancement of the Interests of Labor. The first Protestant church to appoint a full-time secretary concerned with social problems was the Presbyterian Church, which in 1904 set up its Department of Church and Labor under the direction of the redoubtable Charles Stelzle. The Episcopal and the Congregational churches followed soon after, and then the Northern Methodist, the Unitarian, and the Northern Baptist. (In some cases the agencies could not be fully official because of the decentralized character of the churches.) By 1912 eleven other denominations had taken similar steps. When in 1908 the Federal Council of Churches was established, representing twenty-five Protestant denominations with about two thirds of the Protestants in this country, it began to function as a social action agency almost immediately. The interest in social action has remained an abiding one, though with time the older "liberal" theology has become more or less discredited and been replaced by a more sophisticated attitude which spurs social concern, yet forbids a simple identification of Christian faith with any social or economic order.[51]

In recent years these various approaches have been supplemented by experiments in industrial chaplaincy and by church-labor associations and conferences in which Protestant leaders are able to establish close relations with influential spokesmen of the trade union movement.[52] No one today can say that the Protestant church, at least at its upper levels, is unconcerned with the "social problem" of modern industrial society.

And yet, all this concern, all this thought and action, has had very little effect. Nothing like the earlier movement to evangelize America has appeared. The revivalists, such as Billy Graham and Charles Templeton, for all the power and fervor of their crusades, still speak the language of individualistic piety, which in lesser men frequently degenerates into a smug and nagging moralism.[53] On the other hand, the social action movements possess no evangelizing drive and are concerned mostly with the analysis of social problems and the formulation of social policy. The two have hitherto made almost no contact whatever. Protestantism has definitely not succeeded in regaining its dynamic so as to meet the challenge of the urban-industrial frontier.

A clue to this failure may perhaps be found by looking back at the evangelization of the old frontier. Who evangelized the continent, who made Protestantism, for the time, the church of the "common man"? The lay preacher, the circuit rider, the evangelist who was himself a "common man." "It was not the least of Methodism's advantages," H. Richard Niebuhr has pointed out, "that its missionaries were distinguished in no way from the people with whom they dealt, save in the fervor of their piety and the purity of their lives."[54] The poor were evangelized by the poor, by people of their own kind who lived and suffered with them. When Protestantism came face to face with the city poor and the industrial wage worker, however, this could no longer be said. It is not without significance that the first churches to be troubled about the city poor and the industrial workers were the Congregational and Episcopalian churches, which had mighty few poor or workers in their ranks. The Protestant approach to the urban-industrial frontier has been, and very largely remains, the approach of morally sensitive middle-class people striving to do something for the "underprivileged." The spirit of *noblesse oblige* and Christian charity are curiously compounded in this concern, but there is little trace either of the evangelical fervor or of the movement from within the people themselves that won the continent for Christianity. Experiments like the East Harlem Protestant Parish, the Oak Street Christian Parish of New Haven, the West Side Christian Parish in Chicago, and the Inner-City Protestant Parish in

Cleveland reveal a different spirit, more akin to the earlier evangelism, but they are few and have so far had little effect on Protestantism as a whole.[55]

So the Protestant movement has not been resumed. But it should not be concluded that Protestantism is not making headway among the urban population. Recent migrations of southern Negroes and whites to industrial centers have considerably augmented the sections of the working class that have a Protestant background, and have given the Protestant churches access to workers in basic mass-production industries, whereas formerly workers in their ranks were largely mechanics and skilled artisans. But most effective of all has been the operation of the social forces described in earlier chapters. Wherever the industrial workers have become sufficiently American to be caught up in the common pattern of American life, wherever, in other words, religious identification has become a primary necessity of social location, large numbers are joining the churches. This tendency is, of course, even more marked among the white-collar and professional groups and the new middle-class society of the suburbs.[56] Church membership, as we have seen, is growing, but it is an institutional growth, part of the contemporary sociological picture, not a resumption of the great movement that evangelized the continent.

Nor has the cessation of the Protestant movement led to intellectual stagnation. On the contrary, the past quarter of a century has witnessed what is probably the most impressive renewal of Protestant religious thinking since the days of Jonathan Edwards. Reinhold Niebuhr and Paul Tillich are the outstanding representatives of this trend, but they are by no means alone; an increasing company of men, mostly of the younger generation, are contributing to the contemporary theological renaissance in American Protestantism and bringing it into line with the best of Continental and English theology. Yet this theological revival has hitherto affected but a small segment of American Protestants; it has not, or not yet, had much effect in restoring an inner dynamic to American Protestantism.

Religious movements that dimly recall the old evangelical crusade are to be found among some of the "fringe"
sects. As Protestantism began to settle down to a stable,
respectable, "domesticated" existence and to lose its appeal
to the poor, sectarian groups began to make their appearance at the periphery, expressing in somewhat deterio-
rated form the "religion of the disinherited." These sects,
springing up outside the bounds of official Protestantism,
have generally been the products of "eras of economic and
social pressures, moral decline, wars, and . . . distressing
conditions";[57] the great depression of the early thirties and
the convulsions of war stimulated their growth very considerably. Their appeal is largely to those sections of the
urban and rural poor who feel themselves rejected in contemporary society, deprived of status and prestige, de-
valuated, "proletarianized" in Toynbee's sense. The sects
come to these people with very much the same message
that the earlier Methodists and Baptists brought to the
frontier—direct "spiritual" religion, sanctification, and mil-
lennial expectations[58]—and these words still stir a profound
evangelical fervor. Pentecostal, "holiness," and millenial
groups[59] are numerous throughout the country, though how
large they are is hard to estimate.[60]

It requires an effort to recall that today's great Methodist, Baptist, and Disciples churches were once sects of this
kind, teaching very much the same doctrine and making
very much the same appeal. But the times are different.
Whereas the Methodists and Baptists and Disciples have
become great churches, indeed among the pillars of Protestantism, the peripheral sects of today seem to be denied
such possibilities. They emerge on the fringe of Protestantism but never appear able to get much closer to the center.
As, in response to what may be called "Wesley's Law,"[61]
accentuated by the extraordinary mobility of American life,
the members of these sects become more prosperous and
socially accepted and move up in the social scale, many
leave the sects and join denominations more congenial to
their new status; but sometimes what happens is that the
lower-class sect itself becomes a respectable middle-class
church, with appropriate changes of outlook, beliefs, pro-

cedures, and organization. Such was the case in earlier times with the Baptists and Methodists and Disciples, and very much the same is taking place today with the Nazarenes, the Assemblies of God, and other "fringe" groups of yesterday. But even though they become denominations, they become very minor denominations, hardly affecting the total picture. Protestantism no longer has the openness and fluidity it once possessed; there is no longer any possibility, or at least so it seems, for a radical breakthrough by any new "church of the poor."

Between the big established churches on the one side and the peripheral sects on the other, there are the Protestant unchurched. These people are not anti-church; on the contrary, they identify themselves religiously and often think of themselves as church members. Indeed, as several observers have had occasion to point out, "these unchurched Protestants are, as a whole, conservative, have more sympathy for fundamentalism than for modernism, and are not slow to express their disapproval of what they call 'newfangled ideas' . . ."[62] Under pressure of social and cultural forces they are increasingly joining the churches, but in effect there is not much difference between the "churched" and the "unchurched." Whether they actually belong to a church or do not belong, they associate themselves with Protestantism as a matter of self-identification and social location. It was very different when Protestantism meant "the sovereignty of God, the kingship of Christ, and the coming kingdom,"[63] the transformation of life and the promise of salvation.

IV

Protestantism in 1958 counted 61,505,000 members in the ranks of the churches—about 56 per cent of the 109,557,000 Americans religiously affiliated. Although more than 200 bodies were listed, the great bulk of the Protestants were to be found in the seven top denominational families (Baptist, Methodist, Lutheran, Presbyterian, Episcopalian, Disciples, Congregational).[64] The denominational divisions constitute a perplexing problem for contemporary Protestantism. In most cases the old sense of exclusive loyalty is gone; American Protestants experience no difficulty in passing from one denomination to another when social or personal convenience requires, nor are there ever any real difficulties in intermarriage. Yet the denominations, or at least the denominational families, do represent differing historical traditions, often reveal diverse social and cultural structures, and frequently represent distinct and important institutional interests. The "fragmentation" of Protestantism has aroused the concern of many who are deeply disturbed at what they believe to be the effect of this fragmentation in depriving it of evangelical power and in weakening it in the face of a united Roman Catholic Church. Federative and unionist movements at various levels of Protestant organization are multiplying;[65] at the very highest level, thirty bodies, with a membership of 35,542,000, are joined in the National Council of the Churches of Christ in the United States of America, formed in 1950.[66]

About thirty years ago, in 1927, André Siegfried described Protestantism as America's "only national religion" and warned that "to ignore that fact is to view the country from a false angle."[67] In a certain sense this is still true today. Protestantism remains the most numerous and the most widespread of the three religious communities; there is no part of the country in which it is not to be found, and there are many parts of the nation in which it is virtually identical with the American people.[68] Yet, by the same token, nowhere in the United States are Protestants unaware that they are not the whole of America. They are particularly conscious, perhaps, of their coexistence with the Roman Catholics, but they are also generally ready to acknowledge the legitimacy of the Jewish community as a thoroughly American institution. In net effect, Protestantism today no longer regards itself either as a religious movement sweeping the continent or as a national church representing the religious life of the people; Protestantism understands itself today primarily as one of the three religious communities in which twentieth-century America has come to be divided. The "denominational" system—the word "denomination" here referring both to the religious community and to the denomination in its more restricted sense —has become part of the basic assumptions of Protestants about America, as it has become part of the basic assumptions of all Americans.

"In a very general sense," wrote H. Richard Niebuhr in his classic study of American denominationalism, "it is true that under the influence of frontier conditions, the churches of Europe, after migrating to America, have tended to become sects, and that with the passage of the frontier and the establishment of ordered society, the sects of Europe and America have tended to become churches."[69] Altering the last word of this passage to "denominations," and remembering that all Protestant denominations are now seen as part of a larger Protestant community, Professor Niebuhr's formula may be taken as a profound description of the dialectic of American Protestantism.

FOOTNOTES

1. For this chapter detailed documentation is neither necessary nor possible. Attention may be called, however, to the following works to which this account is particularly indebted: the authoritative histories by William W. Sweet, *Religion on the American Frontier*, 4 vols. (University of Chicago, 1931, 1936, 1939, 1946), *The Story of Religion in America*, rev. ed. (Harper, 1939), *American Churches: An Interpretation* (Abingdon-Cokesbury, 1948); Kenneth Scott Latourette, *A History of the Expansion of Christianity* (Harper, 1937–45), Vol. IV, chaps. vi–xii; Jerald C. Brauer, *Protestantism in America* (Westminster, 1953); F. E. Mayer, *The Religious Bodies of America* (Concordia, 1954), a comprehensive presentation of the credal and theological positions of American religious groups; Ray H. Abrams, ed., "Organized Religion in the United States," *The Annals of the American Academy of Political and Social Science*, Vol. 256, March 1948; Willard L. Sperry, *Religion in America* (Macmillan, 1946); and the classic studies by H. Richard Niebuhr, *The Social Sources of Denominationalism* (Holt, 1929) and *The Kingdom of God in America* (Willett, Clark, 1937). Three articles by Sidney E. Mead are particularly noteworthy: "From Coercion to Persuasion: Another Look at the Rise of Religious Liberty and the Emergence of Denominationalism," *Church History*, Vol. XXV, No. 2, December 1956; "Denomina-

tionalism: The Shape of Protestantism in America," *Church History*, Vol. XXIII, No. 4, December 1954; and "American Protestantism Since the Civil War: From Denominationalism to Americanism," *The Journal of Religion*, Vol. XXXVI, No. 1, January 1956. A volume on American Protestantism in the Chicago History of American Civilization (edited by Daniel J. Boorstin) is promised for the near future.

2. Sweet says that until the third decade of the eighteenth century the lower classes in the American colonies "were little influenced by religion . . . there came to be more unchurched people in America, in proportion to the population, than was to be found in any country in Christendom" (Sweet, *The Story of Religion in America*, pp. 7–8). For a perceptive account of the Great Awakening, see Edwin Scott Gaustad, *The Great Awakening in New England* (Harper, 1957). Perry Miller's brilliant work, *Errand into the Wilderness* (Harvard, 1956) also deals with this period.

3. H. Richard Niebuhr, *The Social Sources of Denominationalism*, pp. 151–52.

4. H. Richard Niebuhr, *The Social Sources of Denominationalism*, p. 168.

5. Crèvecoeur speaks bitingly of the "selfishness . . . religious indifference" of the farmer in the "middle settlements" (J. Hector de Crèvecoeur, *Letters From An American Farmer* [1782; 1904 ed. Fox Duffield], pp. 57–58).

6. Brauer, *Protestantism in America*, p. 92.

7. Sweet, "The Protestant Churches," in "Religion in the United States," *Annals*, p. 44. For an authoritative account of Protestant revivalism in America, see W. W. Sweet, *Revivalism in America: Its Origin, Growth, and Decline* (Harper, 1944); also Bernard A. Weisberger, *They Gathered at the River: The Story of the Great Revivalists and Their Impact upon Religion in America* (Little, Brown, 1958).

8. "By virtue of the affinity between the religious movements of the poor and those of the frontier, Methodists and Baptists found the advancing Western settlements of America congenial soil for their methods of cultivation" (H. Richard Niebuhr, *The Social Sources of Denominationalism*, pp. 165–66; see also pp. 141 ff.). "The Baptist emphasis on the sovereignty of the individual made a strong appeal to the 'common man,' to the socially and economically 'disinherited,' and has been an important factor in making the Baptists, originally a despised sect, one of the largest bodies in America" (Mayer, *The Religious Bodies of America*, p. 258).

9. "With its fervent piety, its lay preaching, its early sectarian polity, it [Methodism] accorded well with the spirit of the West, while the itinerary and the circuit system were admirable

devices for the evangelization of the frontier" (H. Richard Niebuhr, *The Social Sources of Denominationalism*, p. 171). See also Winfred E. Garrison, "Characteristics of American Organized Religion," *Annals*, p. 19; Sweet, *Religion on the American Frontier*, Vol. IV, pp. 41 ff.

10. H. Richard Niebuhr, *The Social Sources of Denominationalism*, p. 176.

11. So well suited, indeed, was the camp meeting to the frontier, that it was soon turned to political purposes. The political camp meeting became a widespread feature of the election campaigns on the frontier in the decades before the Civil War. See Chas. A. Johnson, *The Frontier Camp Meeting: Religion's Harvest Time* (S.M.U. Press, 1955).

12. H. Richard Niebuhr, *The Social Sources of Denominationalism*, p. 176.

13. H. Richard Niebuhr, *The Social Sources of Denominationalism*, pp. 171–72.

14. "Between 1790 and 1830, substantially every older denomination had experienced a schism due to the fact that the main body could not keep up with the more radical spirit of the frontier" (H. Paul Douglass, *Church Unity Movements in the United States* [Institute of Social and Religious Research, New York, 1934], p. 33).

15. Sweet, "The Protestant Churches," *Annals*, p. 45.

16. H. Richard Niebuhr speaks of "these three denominations —the churches of the Methodists, and Baptists, and Disciples of Christ" as the "outstanding examples of frontier religion. . . . With the Baptists and the Methodists, the Disciples used the methods of revival, fostered immediacy in religious experience through appeal to the emotions, adopted lay preaching, ordained their clergymen without requiring theological education, and organized their churches on the sectarian principle" (*The Social Sources of Denominationalism*, pp. 165, 178–79).

17. H. Richard Niebuhr, *The Social Sources of Denominationalism*, p. 179.

18. "The religion of the frontier was the same as the rest of frontier life. It was uninhibited, emotional, extremely personal, lacking in all formality" (Brauer, *Protestantism in America*, p. 111). For an account of frontier religion against its social background, see H. Richard Niebuhr, *The Social Sources of Denominationalism*, chaps. vi and vii, pp. 135–99. Mayer finds a certain "rationalistic" element in frontier religion along with the "subjective, revivalistic elements so congenial to the American frontiersman of the early decades of the nineteenth century" (*The Religious Bodies of America*, p. 358). Among the Disciples, this becomes explicit in their view that "faith is an intellectual ac-

ceptance of the Scriptural evidence of Christ" (Mayer, *The Religious Bodies of America*, p. 370, note 3). It is a curious fact that, as Brauer points out, "the mild deists, such as Franklin and Jefferson, were in agreement with the Christian revivalists on many things. Both wanted to destroy state-established church relations as contrary to true religion. Both were suspicious of clergymen who controlled politics. Both emphasized that religion was not concerned with doctrine but with right living as outlined in Jesus' teachings" (*Protestantism in America*, p. 84).

19. Herbert W. Schneider, *Religion in 20th Century America* (Harvard, 1952), p. 22.

20. Ernst Troeltsch, *The Social Teachings of the Christian Churches* (1911; translated by Olive Wyon, Macmillan, 1931), Vol. I.

21. "For two hundred years, a conventional type of revivalism was the chief external feature of American Protestantism" (Douglass, *Church Unity Movements in the United States*, p. 34). A critical account of the later revivalism may be found in William G. McLoughlin, *Modern Revivalism: Charles Grandison Finney to Billy Graham* (Ronald, 1959).

22. Reinhold Niebuhr, "The Impact of Protestantism Today," *The Atlantic Monthly*, February 1948. The process of the "institutionalization and secularization" of the religious movement of American Protestantism is brilliantly described in H. Richard Niebuhr, *The Kingdom of God in America*, chap. v.

23. John Wesley, with keen insight, saw the inner contradiction in every revival of religion. "Wherever riches have increased," he pointed out, "the essence of religion has decreased in the same proportion. Therefore I do not see how it is possible in the nature of things for any revival of religion to continue long. For religion must necessarily produce both industry and frugality, and these cannot but produce riches. But as riches increase, so will pride, anger, and love of the world in all its branches. How then is it possible that Methodism, that is a religion of the heart, though it flourishes now as the green bay tree, should continue in this state? For the Methodists in every place grow diligent and frugal; consequently they increase in goods. Hence, they proportionately increase in pride, in anger, in the desire of the flesh, the desire of the eyes, and the pride of life. So, although the form of religion remains, the spirit is swiftly vanishing away. Is there no way to prevent this—this continual decay of pure religion?" (quoted in Robert Southey, *Life of Wesley and the Rise and Progress of Methodism* [1820; 2nd Amer. edition, Harper, 1847], Vol. II, p. 308). Wesley thought he saw a solution of the dilemma in the formula: "Gain all you can, save all you can, give all you can." That this formula is

hardly adequate, and that it has difficulties of its own, need no more than be mentioned.

24. Reinhold Niebuhr, "The Impact of Protestantism Today," *The Atlantic Monthly*, February 1948. See also H. Richard Niebuhr, *The Social Sources of Denominationalism*, pp. 170, 181–87.

25. H. Richard Niebuhr, *The Kingdom of God in America*, p. 178.

26. Reinhold Niebuhr, "The Impact of Protestantism Today," *The Atlantic Monthly*, February 1948.

27. "What was not so obvious at the time [the latter part of the nineteenth century] was that the United States, in effect, had two religions, or at least two different forms of the same religion, and that the prevailing Protestant ideology represented a syncretistic mingling of the two. The first was the religion of the denominations, which was commonly articulated in the terms of scholastic Protestant orthodoxy and almost universally practiced in terms of the experimental religion of pietistic revivalism . . . The second was the religion of the democratic society and nation. This . . . was articulated in terms of the destiny of America, under God, to be fulfilled by perfecting the democratic way of life for the example and betterment of all mankind" (Sidney E. Mead, "American Protestantism Since the Civil War: From Denominationalism to Americanism," *Journal of Religion*, Vol. XXXVI, No. 1, January 1956). Catholics and Jews, still very much foreigners in those days, were not swept up by this syncretistic movement. In the succeeding decades, however, these two communities became rapidly Americanized, and as they became Americanized they took over the Protestant pattern Mead describes, thus helping bring about the religio-cultural structure discussed in the previous chapter. For a suggestive view of the Protestant "movement" which carries it into the twentieth century, see Robert T. Handy, "The Protestant Quest for a Christian America," *Church History*, Vol. XXII, No. 1, March 1953.

28. H. Richard Niebuhr, *The Social Sources of Denominationalism*, pp. 223–24.

29. See H. Richard Niebuhr, *The Social Sources of Denominationalism*, pp. 217, 233.

30. H. Richard Niebuhr, *The Social Sources of Denominationalism*, p. 212. What frequently happened was that the American, or at least Americanized, elements went off to form their own "English" church (often so designated by name) side by side with the foreign-language churches in the denomination; as time went on these "English" churches grew in number and membership at the expense of the others. Thus, in 1825, the "First English Evangelical Lutheran Church" was formed in

Baltimore "to meet the need for ministering in the English language to Lutheran Christians in this important city of a young nation. Within twenty years, it had established two additional English-speaking congregations" (statement in the order of service of the First English Evangelical Lutheran Church, Baltimore, Maryland).

31. See H. Richard Niebuhr, *The Social Sources of Denominationalism*, pp. 214–17, 224–29.

32. See Mayer, *The Religious Bodies of America*, p. 179.

33. See H. Richard Niebuhr, *The Social Sources of Denominationalism*, pp. 229–30.

34. See Sweet, "The Protestant Churches," *Annals*, pp. 47–48; Mayer, *The Religious Bodies of America*, pp. 180–87.

35. H. Richard Niebuhr, *The Social Sources of Denominationalism*, p. 220.

36. See H. Richard Niebuhr, *The Social Sources of Denominationalism*, pp. 255–57.

37. See H. Richard Niebuhr, *The Social Sources of Denominationalism*, pp. 257–59; Brauer, *Protestantism in America*, p. 49.

38. See *Yearbook of American Churches*, edition for 1955, ed. by Benson Y. Landis (National Council of Churches of Christ, 1954), pp. 255–60; also *The Negro Handbook*, ed. by Florence Murray (Macmillan, 1949), pp. 288–89. For the period 1916–52 "the membership of 126 Protestant bodies in Continental U.S. [showed] a gain of 94.2 per cent. Four of [the] denominations with predominantly Negro membership reported gains of 129 per cent in this period" ("Trends in Church Membership, 1916–1952," *Information Service* [National Council of Churches of Christ], April 9, 1955). In 1957, there were reported about 575,000 Negro Catholics in the United States (*The 1959 National Catholic Almanac* [Paterson, N.J.: St. Anthony's Guild, 1959], p. 455).

39. Sweet, "The Protestant Churches," *Annals*, p. 49.

40. For recent studies of the Negro church, see Benj. E. Mays and J. W. Nicholson, *The Negro's Church* (Institute of Social and Religious Research, New York, 1933); A. H. Fauset, *Black Gods of the Metropolis* (University of Pennsylvania, 1944); Frank Loescher, *The Protestant Church and the Negro* (Association Press, 1948); Leonard L. Haynes, *The Negro Community Within American Protestantism* (Boston: Christopher Publishing House, 1953); Ruby Funchess Johnston, *The Religion of Negro Protestants* (Philosophical Library, 1956).

41. Liston Pope, "Religion and the Class Structure," *Annals*, pp. 90–91. There has been significant but not decisive increase since.

42. See Glen W. Trimble, "Two Worlds of Church Life in the United States," *Information Service*, March 28, 1959. Two recent books on the suburban development are: William A. Dobriner, ed., *The Suburban Community*. (Putnam, 1958) and Robert C. Wood, *Suburbia: Its People and Their Politics* (Houghton Mifflin, 1959). A considerable literature has arisen on Suburbia and its religion, of which the following are outstanding: Gibson Winter, "The Church in Suburban Captivity," *Christian Century*, September 28, 1955 (Protestant); and Neil P. Hurley, S.J., "The Church in Suburbia," *America*, November 16, 1957, "Suburbanism and the Church," *Worship*, January 1959 (Catholic).

43. See Sweet, "The Protestant Churches," *Annals*, p. 47.

44. Both "challenge" and "response" are discussed in Aaron Ignatius Abell, *The Urban Impact on American Protestantism, 1865–1900* (Harvard, 1943).

45. Oscar Handlin, *The Uprooted* (Little, Brown, 1951), p. 4, also pp. 68, 72.

46. Daniel Jenkins is of the opinion that the "sectarian" (in Troeltsch's sense) form of organization of American Protestantism has hampered its adaptation to the new situation. "Sectarian Christianity," he writes, "has many virtues, virtues of enthusiasm and fellowship and of emphasis on individual responsibility. . . . But among its many limitations is the very relevant one that it has not shown itself capable of adapting itself for effective working in large-scale modern society, where political and economic organization becomes increasingly centralized. It flourishes best in a small community with a simple organization . . ." (*Europe and America: Their Contributions to the World Church* [Westminster, 1951], p. 23).

47. Arnold J. Toynbee, *A Study of History*, abridgment of Volumes I–VI by D. C. Somervell (Oxford, 1947), pp. 307–26.

48. See Charles H. Hopkins, *The Rise of the Social Gospel in American Protestantism, 1865–1915* (Yale, 1940), pp. 85–86. Hopkins quotes the reply given by Samuel Gompers in 1898 to a query by the Rev. H. Francis Perry as to why workingmen were being alienated from the church: "My associates have come to look upon the church and the ministry as the apologists and defenders of the wrong committed against the interest of the people, simply because the perpetrators are possessors of wealth . . . whose real god is the almighty dollar, and who contribute a few of their idols to suborn the intellect and eloquence of the divines, and make even their otherwise generous hearts callous to the suffering of the poor and struggling workers, so that they may use their exalted positions to discourage and discountenance all practical efforts of the toilers to lift themselves out of the slough of despondency and despair."

49. For a survey of the "social gospel" and its influence upon American Protestantism, see Hopkins, *The Rise of the Social Gospel in American Protestantism, 1865–1915;* Henry F. May, *Protestant Churches and Industrial America* (Harper, 1949); Neal Hughley, *Trends in Protestant Social Idealism* (King's Crown, 1948); Paul A. Carter, *The Decline and Revival of the Social Gospel* (Cornell, 1954); J. Milton Yinger, *Religion in the Struggle for Power* (Duke, 1946), pp. 130–42; James Hastings Nichols, *Democracy and the Churches* (Westminster, 1951), pp. 212–44.

50. Rauschenbusch went so far as to identify the "communistic" (i.e., socialistic) principle as "essentially Christian." "The Church," he wrote, "should help public opinion understand clearly the difference between the moral qualities of the competitive and the communistic principle, and enlist religious enthusiasm on behalf of that which is essentially Christian" (*Christianity and the Social Crisis* [Macmillan, 1907], p. 398).

51. This change, which reflects the reorientation of Protestant theology in recent years, is largely the work of such men as Reinhold Niebuhr, John C. Bennett, Liston Pope, and others at Union Theological Seminary and Yale Divinity School; see Nichols, *Democracy and the Churches,* pp. 231–44. The recent statement of the National Council of Churches, "Christian Principles and Assumptions for Economic Life" (including thirteen "norms for guidance") is a good example of the newer and more sophisticated approach (see *The Christian Century,* October 13, 1954; *The New York Times,* September 16, 1954). An instructive comparison of this document with the 1932 statement of the Federal Council of Churches on "Social Ideals of the Churches" may be found in Robert T. Handy, "From 'Social Ideals' to 'Norms for Guidance,'" *Christianity and Crisis,* Vol. XIV, No. 24, January 24, 1955. See also Paul Ramsey, "A Theology of Social Action," *Social Action,* Vol. XII, No. 8, October 15, 1948.

52. For recent experiments in the industrial chaplaincy, see *Information Service* (National Council of Churches of Christ), October 24, 1953 and September 4, 1954; Clair M. Cook, "A New Industrial Chaplaincy," *The Christian Century,* September 1, 1954; Marshal Scott, "The Industrial Chaplain," *The City Church,* Vol. 5, No. 2, March–April 1954. For the new type of church-labor relations, see: *Report of the National Study Conference on the Church and Economic Life,* Pittsburgh, February 18–20, 1947 (Federal Council of Churches, 1947); *National Study Conference on the Church and Economic Life,* Detroit, February 16–19, 1950 (Federal Council, 1950); *Report of the North American Lay Conference on the Christian and His Daily Work,* Buffalo, February 21–24, 1952 (National Council of Churches, 1952); see also "In the Kingdom of God All Men Are

Brothers: A Report on the Second Conference on Church and Economic Life," *Ammunition* (published by the United Automobile Workers—CIO), March 1950.

53. A curious upper-bracket revivalistic movement is to be found in Moral Re-Armament (MRA). Initiated in the early 1920s by Frank N. Buchman, a former Lutheran minister, it cultivates a kind of sophisticated pietism in a house-party atmosphere and stresses direct divine guidance as a resource in the affairs of everyday life. MRA possesses two large establishments, one at Caux, near Geneva, and the other, Island Home, on Mackinac Island, Michigan; at both, house parties and conferences, attended by diplomats, politicians, financiers, industrialists, labor leaders, even theologians, are frequently held. Many, if not most, of the supporters of MRA belong to the regular churches. See Mayer, *The Religious Bodies of America*, pp. 490–92; Walter H. Clark, *The Oxford Group: Its History and Significance* (Bookman Associates, 1951).

54. H. Richard Niebuhr, *The Social Sources of Denominationalism*, p. 172.

55. For these ventures, see Brauer, *Protestantism in America*, pp. 284–85; also William Harlan Yale, "Going Down This Street, Lord . . ." *The Reporter*, January 13, 1955. Two noteworthy studies of Protestantism in the city are: Frederick A. Shippey, *Church Work in the City* (Abingdon, 1952) and Ross W. Sanderson, *The Church Serves the Changing City* (Harper, 1955).

56. "Strange as it may sound, numbers are also a problem in this [suburban] milieu. Families are joining 'active' churches faster than any staff of clergy or nucleus lay fellowship can train and assimilate them" (Gibson Winter, "The Church in Suburban Captivity," *Christian Century*, September 28, 1955). On the other hand: "Rural Areas, Cities Lose Membership" (*New York World Telegram*, January 26, 1957; headline of an article by Louis Cassels about the "uneven impact of the back-to-church movement" in American Protestantism).

57. Mayer, *The Religious Bodies of America*, pp. 419–20. See also Brauer, *Protestantism in America*, p. 266.

58. "Premillennialism and the doctrines, formerly emphasized especially among the Methodists, of holiness and the 'second blessing,' and the necessity of conversion, are the doctrines stressed by these 'churches of the disinherited,' and these are now often characterized as the poor man's doctrines" (Sweet, "The Protestant Churches," *Annals*, p. 47).

59. For these groups, see Mayer, *The Religious Bodies of America*, pp. 319–39, 419–70; Charles S. Braden, "The Sects," *Annals*, pp. 53–62; Elmer T. Clark, *Small Sects in America*

(Abingdon-Cokesbury, 1949); Charles S. Braden, *They Also Believe* (Macmillan, 1949); Marcus Bach, *They Have Found a Faith* (Bobbs-Merrill, 1946). For an appreciative estimate of the "fringe" groups as Christendom's "third force," see Henry P. Van Dusen, "[The Third] Force's Lessons for Others," *Life*, June 9, 1958; "Caribbean Holiday," *Christian Century*, August 17, 1955.

60. A survey of the churches of twenty-three metropolitan districts, conducted by the Committee for Cooperative Field Research, indicates that the "exceptional" Protestant churches constituted 24.6 per cent of the total number of churches (31.3 per cent in the Far West), but had only about 7 per cent of the membership (*Information Service*, January 21, 1950). A similar survey, conducted by the same agency, of rural churches "shows a preponderant rural strength of the nationally major denominations, the slender contribution of the minor ones, and the insignificance of the irregular types, measured by membership" (*Information Service*, February 4, 1950).

61. See above, note 23.

62. Sweet, "The Protestant Churches," *Annals*, p. 50; Sweet adds: "Often, too, anti-Catholic feeling is strong among them." Not a few of the unchurched find solace in such "peace of mind" cults as Unity, Psychiana, etc., which, however, probably count as many devotees inside the churches as outside (see Mayer, *The Religious Bodies of America*, pp. 537–45, 547–59).

63. These are the three themes in terms of which H. Richard Niebuhr presents the Protestant movement (*The Kingdom of God in America*).

64. See *Yearbook of American Churches*, edition for 1960, pp. 253–58, 281; Mayer, *The Religious Bodies of America*, p. 568.

65. Detailed information as to moves for denominational union are to be found in the news columns of *The Christian Century*. See also Brauer, *Protestantism in America*, pp. 249–52, 259, 276–78.

66. See *Yearbook of American Churches*, edition for 1955, p. 273. The membership had increased to 39,256,000 by 1958 (*Yearbook of American Churches*, edition for 1960, p. 275). A report, "Notes on the State of the Churches," submitted by Roy G. Ross, general secretary, and Roswell P. Barnes, associate general secretary, to the third Assembly of the National Council of Churches, will be found in *Information Service*, December 25, 1954.

67. André Siegfried, *America Comes of Age* (Harcourt, Brace, 1927), p. 33.

68. Thus in North Carolina there are said to be fewer Catho-

lics proportionately than anywhere else in the world, including Africa and the Far East; Jews are to be found only in some of the larger cities.

69. H. Richard Niebuhr, *The Social Sources of Denominationalism*, p. 145.

VII. *Catholicism in America*

Unlike American Protestantism, Catholicism in America[1] never was a religious movement. Its story is that of a foreign church, or rather a conglomerate of foreign churches, recruited from the successive waves of overseas immigration, finally emerging into one of the three great "American religions." This remarkable transformation of a group socially and culturally alien into a thoroughly American religious community provides a significant clue to the inner history of Catholicism in the United States.

I

Strictly speaking, of course, Catholicism was no more foreign to the American colonies than any of the Protestant denominations. True, the United States was never a Catholic country, as were all the nations of western Europe at some point of their history, but a permanent and successful Catholic settlement was established in Maryland in the second quarter of the seventeenth century, very early in our colonial history. With the acquisition of the trans-Mississippi territories under the Louisiana Purchase of 1803, the United States acquired another center of native Catholicism in New Orleans; later acquisitions from Mexico in the Southwest in 1848 added still a third. Maryland, New Orleans, and New Mexico—English, French, and Spanish respectively—provided the nearest thing the United States has had to an old-established native Catholicism, with its "old families" enjoying wealth, respectability, and assured social position. But these early centers, while they have played their part, did not themselves become the substance of American Catholicism; that was supplied by the great immigration of the nineteenth century. Catholicism in America is essentially the product of this immigration.

Catholics had by no means an easy time of it in colonial America. Their church was proscribed in most of the colonies and actively persecuted in some. Only in Pennsylvania, New York, and Rhode Island were they tolerated, and in Maryland for a brief period; some relaxation set in during the latter part of the eighteenth century; but there was no real relief till the Revolution and the Constitution assured them a secure and equal status under the federal government. (Some states continued discriminatory laws and practices until well into the nineteenth century.) At the time of the Revolution there were perhaps 25,000 Catholics in the colonies—16,000 in Maryland, about 6,000 in Pennsylvania, and the rest scattered. In 1789, when, after some hesitation, the Holy See established the first diocese in the United States with John Carroll as Bishop of Baltimore, his jurisdiction extended over all the states and territories, with a Catholic population of perhaps 40,000 in a total of some 4,000,000.

The outlook was not very promising. Through the seventeenth and eighteenth centuries there had been heavy defections on the part of Catholic immigrants. "A good many Irish had come out during the Cromwellian period, but they had to go untended by clergy, particularly in New England. Two hundred and fifty thousand Catholic immigrants are reported to have been lost to the church during the eighteenth century . . ."[2] These huge losses are generally attributed to the lack of clergy and the absence of anything but the most rudimentary church organization. Even more basic perhaps was the fact that these Catholic immigrants came to a country almost entirely Protestant, where Protestantism was generally identified with the new American character. Acculturation, becoming an American, meant getting rid of one's foreignness, and of this Catholicism was felt to be a part. Some Catholic immigrants actually became Protestants; many more simply lapsed and remained unchurched. This was a problem that was to prove perennial. In 1836 Bishop England calculated that "had the church been able to hold her own people up to that time, the Catholic population would have been, even then, 4,000,000," instead of hardly more than 650,000.[3] As late

as the 1850s and 1860s the same laments at mass defections
were to be heard.[4] In the early decades of the nineteenth
century the Catholic Church appeared to have no future
in the United States; it seemed doomed to stagnate in its
three or four older centers, leaving America to the Protestant movement that was sweeping the country. That this
did not take place was thanks largely to the vast influx of
Catholic immigrants in the course of the century, above all,
to the role the Irish came to play in the life of America
and American Catholicism. The Irish Americanized and
"plebeianized" the Catholic Church in America, and so set
it on the path it was to follow thereafter.

I I

The hegemony of the Irish in American Catholicism was
established not without a protracted struggle. Colonial
Catholicism was English and to some extent German; the
Irish at first played little significant part in the life of the
church. The huge Irish immigration of the nineteenth century shifted the balance of forces, and the conflict over
"Trusteeism" that racked the church for some forty years
after Bishop Carroll's death in 1815 provided the circumstances under which the Irish predominance became in-
stitutionally established.

Without much clerical supervision, the early Catholics
in America had established a pattern of church government considerably influenced by the ubiquitous Protestant
model. Parochial affairs were largely in the hands of the
laity. Parish trustees, laymen, held title to church buildings
and other church property and consequently managed the
secular affairs of the church. Nor did they always restrict
themselves to the merely secular affairs; it was only natural
that with the church property under their control they
should, like their Protestant neighbors, feel that they had
the right to intervene in the selection of their spiritual
leaders and the direction of the general activities of the
church. These pretensions ran directly counter to the
established system of Roman Catholicism, and conflict was
inevitable. It began when Bishop Carroll tried to bring

some order into his diocese; but the violent phase of the
struggle developed in the decades following his death.[5]

The conflict over church government was characteristically intertwined with a complex of other factors rooted
in ethnic and cultural antagonisms. The earliest clergy had
been English; German clergy there were, but they tended
to their own people who were settled in Pennsylvania and
one or two other colonies. After the French Revolution
there was a considerable influx of priests from France, who
soon rose to positions of influence. Carroll's successor in
Baltimore (following Leonard Neale, who occupied the see
from 1815 to 1817) was a Frenchman, Archbishop Am-
brose Maréchal; indeed, in 1817 all the bishops in the
United States save one were French. The French bishops
and priests did not get along any too well with the "old
Catholics" of colonial stock; but they were in perpetual
warfare with the Irish immigrants, who were beginning
to form a preponderant part of their flocks. No greater
incompatibility could be imagined than that between the
cultured, aristocratic Catholicism of the French hierarchy
and the kind of Catholicism that the Irish immigrants
brought with them and transplanted to this country. Archbishop Maréchal spoke contemptuously of *"la canaille
irlandaise"* and protested because Rome gave him "Irish
priests" as missionaries. The Irish lay people, on their side,
with the few priests they had of their own, were restive and
rebellious. In the first phase of the struggle over "Trusteeism" it was the Irish who took up the cause of lay
autonomy; indeed, belligerent Irishmen in Norfolk, Virginia, did not hesitate to send a declaration to Rome an-
nouncing that "in consequence of our inalienable right of
patronage, our first bishop will be elected by us." The
movement spread to Charleston, South Carolina, and for
a time there was talk of setting up a church "independent
of Maréchal." The firmness and diplomacy of Bishop John
England of Charleston averted the crisis, though not without minor schisms.

The final victory of the hierarchy over the movement to
force a radical change in the structure and government of
the church along American Protestant models came only

when the Irish began to lose their disaffection as a result of the rapid replacement of the French clergy by priests of their own at the various levels of the clergy. With the loyalty of the Irish restored, the victory of the church was assured. In 1829 the First Provincial Council of Baltimore issued decrees calculated to establish the authority of the hierarchy; these decrees were reaffirmed by subsequent councils and were extended by the First Plenary Council in Baltimore in 1852. By this time the battle was virtually over, although the Third Plenary Council in 1884 still found it necessary to make a pronouncement on the question. Since then the issue has arisen sporadically, generally as the expression of resentments on quite other grounds arraying the laity against clergy and hierarchy.[6]

The conflict over "Trusteeism," which for some decades tore apart the Catholic Church in this country, probably constituted "the most serious crisis in the whole history of American Catholicism," for it was in effect "an attempt to set up an Independent Catholic Church in America, free of all reference to Rome,"[7] along the lines of the nationally autonomous Protestant churches. The long struggle that led to the defeat of this attempt had diverse and unforeseen consequences: it clearly established the lines which Catholic development would take in America; it brought the Irish into the strategic leadership of the church and helped give American Catholicism its Irish character; it also "meant the damaging of the original American Catholic spirit [of clerical-lay co-operation],"[8] which some see as still a problem for the church in this country. It was an episode thoroughly revealing of the conditions under which Catholicism had to operate in the United States.

One of the factors that helped the hierarchy allay the dissension over "Trusteeism" was the repeated outbursts of anti-Catholic rancor that punctuated the three decades before the Civil War, culminating in the Know-Nothing movement. In the period immediately following the Revolution, American Catholics enjoyed friendly relations with their Protestant neighbors. The Catholic Church was small, apparently limited to a few respectable old families and some thousands of European immigrants, primarily Germans, whose way of life did not bring them into too much contact with the general population. Non-Catholic citizens contributed to Catholic funds and on certain public occasions even attended Catholic services. But when the heavy deluge of Irish immigration began to inundate the country, the entire picture underwent a rapid change. Between 1820 and 1865 something like 1,900,000 Irish came to the United States, almost all Catholics. In the decade 1840 to 1850 the church grew from 650,000 to 1,600,000 members; the accessions were predominantly Irish, although Germans made a considerable contribution. The Irish, precisely because in language, manners, and culture, they were so like and yet so different from the native Americans, seemed to the latter a far greater peril than the more obvious foreigners from the Continent; moreover, they settled in great urban centers, such as New York, Boston, and Philadelphia, concentrating in ghetto-like quarters, and so were particularly "visible" to the unsympathetic eyes of the natives. Feeling grew tense; friction developed in many areas, and anti-Catholic passion was fed by rabble-rousers and agitators, who were responsible for a flood of incendiary books, pamphlets, and newspapers. Catholics were embittered by the fact that the schools and public institutions to which they were compelled to resort were avowedly Protestant and were often employed to break down the Catholic faith they cherished for themselves and their children. In the 1830s violence began. In 1831 St. Mary's Catholic Church in New York was burned down, and three years later a crowd attacked, pillaged, and destroyed a convent in Charlestown, near Boston. Sporadic rioting continued through the decade and came to a climax in Philadelphia in 1844, where for three days the city was in chaos. Thirteen persons were killed, scores injured; the Catholic seminary, two churches, and whole blocks of Catholic dwellings went up in flames. Anti-Catholic agitation was renewed in the early 1850s, particularly in connection with the arrival of Archbishop Bedini as Apostolic Visitor in 1853. In 1854 rioters in St. Louis killed ten men; a year later, on "Bloody Monday" at Louisville, Kentucky, nearly a hundred Catholics were slain and scores of houses burned to the ground. By this time anti-Catholicism had become a leading principle of the so-called Know-Nothing Party. The Civil War crisis suddenly threw everything else into the background, and when the anti-Catholic movement was resumed in the latter part of the century it bore a very different character.[9]

The anti-Catholic movement before the Civil War was essentially nativist; it was an uprising of "native" Americans (many themselves of recent immigrant stock) against "foreigners," who, they felt, were imperiling their livelihood, their culture, their religion, their American way of life. And by "foreigners" they meant the Irish. It was the Irish who were confronted with such notices as "Men Wanted—No Irish Need Apply." It was the Irish whom the nativist bigots so particularly resented. "At the height of the Philadelphia riots," it has been pointed out, "when Irish Catholic churches were burned to the ground, even though guarded by militia, a German Catholic church remained unguarded and unattacked, though it stood within a few blocks of the actual rioting."[10] Apparently, in the American mind, Irish and Catholic had already become synonymous, and this identification has continued well into our own day. The three decades of nativist crusading against the Irish as foreigners and Catholics completed the process which the struggle against "Trusteeism" had initiated. The Irish began self-consciously to organize as a religio-ethnic group (in 1860 the Irish Catholic Benevolent Union was formed on a national basis); their loyalty to their church was cemented by persecution; and the Irish character of American Catholicism was strongly reinforced.

III

"Already in the 1830s, Irish names were prominent in the priesthood, although not yet among the bishops. Soon thereafter, the full impact of the great migration transformed American Catholicism. Church membership became overwhelmingly Irish in composition, and Irish-Americans assumed some of the most distinguished places in the hierarchy in the United States. . . . By the 1890s, the hierarchy was almost entirely of Irish descent."[11] The Catholic Church in the United States as we know it today is largely the achievement of the Irish Catholic immigrant, and it bears his mark.[12]

It is indeed doubtful if the church could have reached its present position in the United States had it not been for the Irish and the part they played. It is certain that this role was most strategic. For the Irish in effect performed an indispensable task in mediating between the Catholic Church as a strange and alien body and the emerging American culture. The Irish were peculiarly equipped for this task. They were foreigners themselves, yet they spoke English and came from an English-speaking land. They became citizens, it was facetiously remarked, just as soon as they got off the boat. Though largely peasants at home, they quickly adapted themselves to American urban life. They became active in local politics and soon acquired considerable influence in public affairs. As they Americanized themselves—and they did so with amazing facility— they carried the whole church along with them and made it an American church. "Not the least of the contributions of the Irish," a Catholic historian suggests, "was their work of Americanizing Catholics of other nationalities."[13] The Irish set the pattern; increasing numbers of the other immigrant groups followed. It is hard to see how, in the absence of the Irish, the work could have been done so expeditiously and so completely.[14]

Nevertheless, the Americanization of the Catholic Church did not proceed smoothly; it was achieved through another great crisis, rivaling the struggle over "Trusteeism" in depth and intensity. Before the Catholic Church in this country, composed as it was of immigrants from every part of Europe and from many parts of the other continents, could become American, it had to frustrate the attempts to convert it into a loose federation of semi-autonomous immigrant national churches. Such attempts in one form or another were repeatedly made, since to the immigrant, as we have seen, his church was inescapably part of the "old home" transplanted to the New World, where he could hear the mother tongue spoken, meet fellow countrymen, and find security in the old familiar ways and practices. The earliest German Catholics had little difficulty in establishing their own parishes, but those who came later, settling in localities where the Irish were already dominant, found themselves in churches they could not regard as their own. The plight of the Italians and Slavs, who began to arrive toward the end of the century, was even more painful, since the Irish church they found in America appeared to them even more remote from what they had been accustomed to at home and what they so longed to re-establish in the New World. "The result was a struggle, parish by parish, between the old Catholics and the new, a struggle that involved the nationality of the priest, the language to be used, the saints' days to be observed, and even the name of the church."[15]

But of course the struggle was not confined to the parish. German priests in America addressed appeals to the Pope complaining against the unsympathetic, even hostile, attitude of the episcopal authorities. Lay leaders of the newer ethnic groups joined in the movement, which came to a head in 1890 in a petition addressed to the Holy See by Peter Paul Cahensly, a German concerned with the difficulties of German Catholic immigrants in America. Cahensly, who was secretary of the Archangel Raphael Society in Germany, warned that the church in America was suffering from enormous leakages because it failed to provide the immigrant with a church he could recognize as his own. (There was a distinct suggestion that the Catholic culture of the German immigrant was much superior to the American, and especially to what the immigrant encountered in the Irish-American church.) Cahensly therefore urged the establishment of dioceses in the United States not along geographical lines but along lines of nationality and culture: a German diocese with German parishes for German immigrants, an Italian diocese with Italian parishes for Italian immigrants, and so on. In effect, this was a proposal to establish in America a system of quasi-independent national Catholic churches with only a federative bond at the top. It was obviously predicated on the mistaken assumption that the immigrant groups in America were destined to perpetuate their particular ethnic-cultural character from generation to generation. Against this scheme both the Irish and the American bishops united, and it was rejected by the Holy See.[16] This did not end the movement, which appeared again and again among immigrant Catholic groups and led to minor schisms and defections. But, by and large, the unity of the church was preserved as well as its capacity to adapt itself to the developing pattern of American life.[17] Having routed Cahenslyism, the American hierarchy attempted in a number of ways to provide the immigrant with a church he could feel at home in; "national" parishes with priests from the same ethnic group were permitted, sometimes even encouraged; lay societies of all sorts were established along ethnic lines; the church availed itself of the immigrant's language in its religious and educational work. Little by little, as the second and third generations emerged and the old-line ethnic groups began to dissolve, the old discontent disappeared and the American church prevailed as an American institution, increasingly free from the taint of foreignness. The defeat of Cahenslyism saved the Catholic Church in this country from the kind of fragmentation along ethnic-cultural lines that American Protestantism has had to undergo.[18] And it left the Irish, or rather the Irish-Americans, in an even stronger position and the Irish influence upon American Catholicism even more deeply marked.

Due to this predominant Irish influence, Catholicism in America soon acquired a special character which, however equivocal it may have seemed from the European standpoint, indubitably helped it survive and adapt itself to American reality. In the first place, the Catholicism the Irish brought with them seemed less foreign to American eyes than any other type except the old Maryland variety. It was English-speaking, "puritanical," democratic, popular, and activistic, with little of the traditional Catholic inwardness, but also with little of the aristocratic conservatism or the baroque excesses that characterized so much of nineteenth-century Continental Catholicism;[19] Americans could "understand" it better, and it proved more viable as Ameri-

can generations followed immigrant forebears.[20] Coming
from a country where the aristocracy was largely alien in
religion and allegiance, and where the priest was virtually
the only man of education and standing in a peasant
community, the Irish immigrants brought to this country
an attitude of intense reverence for the clergy very different
indeed from the more "relaxed" attitude prevalent in England and on the Continent. The undisputed leadership the
priests enjoyed in the Irish immigrant communities enabled
them to hold these communities together in the face of
Americanization. It enabled the Irish to form a strong
religio-ethnic group without the aid of a distinct and sepa-
rating language, and it gave the Irish clergy a preponderant
position in the Catholic community as a whole. American
Catholicism has had this Irish trait deeply imprinted upon
its character, as most European observers have been quick
to note.[21] It has proved a significant factor in survival.

But perhaps the most distinctive feature of Irish Catholicism, and a feature that has proved most influential in the
development of Catholicism in America, was the fusion of
religion and nationalism in the Irish mind. In the centuries
of struggle against an alien and Protestant master, national
loyalty came to take on an intense religious coloring, even
a kind of "mystical" quality, utterly unintelligible to the
Continental mind. To be a Catholic was to be a true Irishman; to be an Irishman was to be a true Catholic. This
equation helped the Irish Catholic to survive and prevail
in the New World, but what was perhaps even more important, it enabled the Irish Catholic to become a passionately patriotic American while retaining much of his age-
old hostility to Protestantism. Despite the hatred and
persecution he encountered, or perhaps for that very reason, the Irish Catholic newcomer—after some hesitation—
adopted this country as his own and transferred his deeply
emotional nationalism to his adopted land. His Americanism
took on the same religious fervor and soon came to be
identified with his Catholicism. It was almost as though to
be a Catholic meant somehow to be an American, even
though it was obvious that the converse was not as true as
it had been in Ireland. The alienation the Irish Catholic had

suffered in the "old country" and in the early days of immigrant life was thus overcome with a vengeance: Irish, Catholic, and American became almost identical in the Irish-American mind, and the Americanism of the Irish Catholic developed into something much more than merely the sense of national "belonging." To a greater or lesser degree all American Catholicism has tended to take on this peculiar nationalistic coloration. It unquestionably has its dubious side, which critics have been ready to point out,[22] but it has obviously facilitated the rapid Americanization of the church and its transformation into a genuinely American institution.

In any case, it was under Irish hegemony, and largely through the advantages which their distinctive background gave to the Irish clergy, that the Catholic Church in America was consolidated into an American religious community. "Out of the bewildering diversity and the sharply conflicting traditions brought by an immigration from every Roman Catholic group in Europe and from several of those of Asia and Africa," Latourette notes, "a unified church was progressively developed, and when the obstacles are considered, with amazing rapidity."[23] The large-scale defections that had so troubled Catholic leaders in the early nineteenth century were stopped; in spite of the sweep of the Protestant movement and "the expenditure by Protestant churches of millions of dollars in religious and social efforts for the immigrants, largely of the Roman Catholic form of the faith, no large movements of Roman Catholics to Protestantism occurred. . . . In the main, the Catholic Church, while winning comparatively few who were not traditionally of the faith, retained the allegiance of the large majority of immigrants who in Europe had been in its fold."[24] By the opening of the twentieth century, certainly by the time of World War I, the Catholic Church in this country had achieved a secure status and a dynamic adaptation to American society. In this process the "Irish tradition" played the part of "catalyst," if not actually of "determinant."[25]

The Americanization of the church, and its secure establishment in American society, was considerably accelerated by the fairly rapid advancement in social and cultural status of the Irish, German, and other Catholic ethnic groups. The transformation of the original "shanty" Irish into the "lace-curtain" Irish of the second and third generations is a familiar American story,[26] and very much the same change took place, though somewhat more slowly and not so spectacularly, among the Germans, and rather later among the Italian and Slavic groups as well. In this process, which is of course characteristic of the American pattern of life, the church played a crucial role. Not only was the church "used as vehicle for the social, economic, and political ambitions of . . . immigrant groups . . . bent on building themselves from identification as poor foreigners to recognition as middle-class Americans";[27] through its widespread network of institutions and activities the church actually provided the ambitious immigrant with effective means and instruments for his advancement. The Catholic school has been singularly effective in this respect. The Catholic school, particularly the Catholic college, though established to help preserve and perpetuate the faith, has, as Evelyn Waugh notes, served "to transform the proletariat into a bourgeoisie"[28] culturally and thereby also economically and socially. This effort has been manifestly successful. Aside from some "old families" in the earliest centers, American Catholicism originally possessed no middle or upper class; the clergy, and even the hierarchy, came from the lower classes who made up almost the entirety of Catholic lay-folk. It was only within this century that a substantial middle class began to emerge. With the emergence of a middle class, the entire body of Catholics became more American—America is pre-eminently a middle-class country; and with the advancement of large segments of the Catholic community, the church too advanced, becoming on its part more middle-class and more American[29]—without, however, losing its contact with the lower classes or the ethnically unassimilated. It thus became possible to be an American not only without falling away from the church but (if one may so put it) precisely through and by way of being a Catholic.[30] In this momentous development the long-range policy of the Irish-dominated church fell in with the underlying trends of contemporary American society, each reinforcing the other.

IV

The Americanization of the church under Irish influence meant a substantial reshaping of its outlook and activities in a way that reflected the influence of certain salient features of the American environment. The American church has tended to be activist in a way that almost borders on what Pius XII in 1950 described as the "heresy of action": the notion that "the world can be saved by . . . external activity."[31] Archbishop John Ireland of St. Paul, one of American Catholicism's great churchmen, had not hesitated to declare: "An honest ballot and social decorum will do more for God's glory and the salvation of souls than midnight flagellations or Compostellian pilgrimages."[32] Somewhat later, in the controversy over "Americanism," the same issue emerged. In an apostolic letter, *Testem benevolentiae,* which Leo XIII directed to Cardinal Gibbons in 1899, the Pope warned against certain tendencies which a number of European theologians claimed to discover in the American church. Among these were overemphasis on the active virtues at the expense of humility, charity, and obedience; putting natural virtues above the supernatural; and employing untried methods of attracting non-Catholics to the faith. Although Cardinal Gibbons immediately replied that no one in America—prelates, priests, or laity—held these views, and a few years later the Pope told Archbishop Ireland to forget the whole matter,[33] there can be little doubt that what Leo XIII was warning against was not altogether unrelated, if not to the explicit beliefs, then to the implicit patterns of behavior, of the American church half a century ago as well as today. It is part of the Americanness of American Catholicism, something which it shares with American Protestantism and American Judaism, as one of the three "religions of [American] democracy." No institution can remain part of American life without being extrovert and activistic, and the Catholic Church, which so aspires to be

American, cannot help but take on the color of the American environment.

Another aspect of the Americanization of American Catholicism was the radical revision of Catholic thinking on the problem of church and state so as to bring such thinking in line with American experience and tradition. The conventional position, affirming the union of church and state on the model of the Catholic monarchies of the seventeenth and eighteenth centuries, still remained normative in the manuals,[34] but the pronouncements of prelates, and more recently the writings of theologians, began to take a new line, obviously reflecting American conditions. Cardinal Gibbons could declare without hesitation: "Sixteen millions of Catholics . . . prefer [the American] form of government before any other. They admire its institutions and its laws. They accept the Constitution without reserve, with no desire as Catholics to see it changed in any feature. The separation of church and state in this country seems to them the natural, inevitable, and best conceivable plan, the one that would work best among us, both for the good of religion and of the state. Any change in their relations they would contemplate with dread. They are well aware, indeed, that the church here enjoys a larger liberty, and a more secure position, than in any country today where church and state are united. No establishment of religion is being dreamed of here, of course, by anyone; but were it to be attempted, it would meet with united opposition from the Catholic people, priests, and prelates."[35] Some decades later Archbishop John T. McNicholas, speaking for the entire American hierarchy, declared: "We deny absolutely and without qualification that the Catholic Bishops of the United States are seeking a union of church and state by any endeavors whatsoever, either proximate or remote. If tomorrow Catholics constituted a majority in our country, they would not seek a union of church and state . . ."[36] As far as official pronouncements and general lay attitudes are concerned, Catholic opinion was by the second quarter of the present century substantially in line with the American tradition embodied in the First Amendment. The many disputes as to the meaning and extent of "separation" that have embittered relations between Catholics and non-Catholics in recent years must not be permitted to obscure this fact.

Perhaps even more important has been the reorientation of Catholic thinking on this matter on the theological level. John Courtney Murray, S.J., one of American Catholicism's outstanding theologians, undertook a systematic re-examination of Catholic teaching on church and state, and soon developed a viewpoint and approach capable of relating basic Catholic doctrine to American democracy in a way that would do violence to neither. The brilliance and cogency of his achievement made a deep impression beyond the limits of the church. Murray's thinking, it is true, met with sharp opposition from more conventional-minded European theologians, and some American as well, but there was evidence that in the Vatican, too, new currents of thought were beginning to make themselves felt.[37]

The most striking evidence of the Americanization of the Catholic Church in this country probably came when American Catholics began to regard their church as one of the three great American religious communities and themselves as devotees of religion in one of its three American forms. This did not at any point involve an explicit rejection of the church's claim to be the one true and universal church; rejection, or even questioning, of this claim would obviously be impossible for a Catholic. What it did involve was a deep-lying, though often unarticulated, conception of American social reality. Though the theologians might protest, the average American Catholic—to the degree that he became American—could not help but regard American society as intrinsically pluralistic, and his own church as one among several. At first this emphasis on pluralism was a kind of spontaneous strategy of survival, a protection against Protestant engulfment. As time went on it became identified with the emerging conception of American society as an over-all community of religious communities, the conception we have called the "triple melting pot." By the second quarter of the present century the American Catholic, like every other American, was thinking of his church as one of the three "religions of de-

mocracy," side by side with the other two; he could hardly
imagine an America without Protestants and Jews—even
though he might be deeply suspicious of Protestants and
not altogether free of anti-Semitism. With his customary
insight, Evelyn Waugh noted this significant difference between Europe and America on his recent visit to this country. "I saw both in London and Chicago," he reported in
his article in *Life*, "the Italian film *Paisan*, one incident of
which portrays, with fewer anomalies than usual, the life of
a small Franciscan community in a remote mountain dis-
trict. Three American chaplains arrive there and are
warmly welcomed. It transpires that only one is Catholic,
the other two being respectively a Protestant and a Jew.
The friars are disconcerted and impose a fast on themselves for the conversion of their non-Catholic guests. In
London, the audience was mainly non-Catholic, but its
sympathy was plainly with the friars. In Chicago, the
audience was composed mainly of Italian speakers, presumably Catholics of a sort, and to them the friars seemed
purely comic."[38] There is no reason to sneer at the Catholicism of these "Italian speakers," presumably first- and
second-generation Italian immigrants; most other American Catholics would have responded the same way, for to
them, like to all Americans, it would have seemed right
and proper that there should be *three* chaplains—one Catholic, the other Protestant, and the third Jewish—and to them
too the conversion of the non-Catholic clergymen to Catholicism, while no doubt eminently desirable religiously,
would have appeared slightly absurd in terms of American
reality.

Thus, under pressure of the American environment to
which they so successfully adapted themselves, American
Catholics—like American Jews and in part even American
Protestants—learned to operate with a double vision: in
terms of a self-enclosed microcosmic community within
their own church and its complex of Catholic institutions;
and in terms of a tripartite macrocosm in which Catholics,
Protestants, and Jews were conceived as living in harmoni-
ous coexistence, if not co-operation, under the benevolent
aegis of American democracy.[39] The earlier separatism,

that had arisen out of the deep necessities of a persecuted and submerged minority trying to preserve itself and its faith in a hostile environment, passed over almost imperceptibly into the very different kind of community separatism that the emerging structure of American society seemed to demand. It was the Irish Catholic, situated so strategically at the boundary between Europe and America, between the foreign and the native, between the new and the old, who led the church in achieving this difficult transition.

V

In 1957 the Catholic Church in America[40] counted about 36,023,000 members in 111 dioceses and 27 archdioceses. They constituted about 21 per cent of the American people and just over 34 per cent of the country's church-affiliated population. The hierarchy consisted of four cardinals (after the elevations at the consistory held in December 1958), 34 archbishops, and 183 bishops; some 17,000 parishes were cared for by a priesthood that numbered more than 50,000. Over 190,000 were in religious orders (164,000 sisters), most of them engaged in teaching and other activities in the world.[41] American Catholics had always tended to be urban and had become more so in the course of the past century, reflecting the increasing urbanization of the nation. The great centers of Catholic strength were the cities, some of which (Buffalo, Boston, Newark, Chicago) showed an actual majority, or very nearly a majority, of Catholics, and others very strong minorities. It was weak on the countryside, particularly in the South (except for Maryland and Louisiana), but taking the country as a whole, it was far and away America's largest single denomination. As late as 1908 the church in the United States was still part of the missionary field, under the jurisdiction of the Roman Congregation of the Propagation of the Faith; today it is the richest, most powerful, and one of the most numerous divisions of the world-wide Roman Catholic communion.

The Catholic Church in America operates a vast network of institutions of almost every type and variety. The

social and recreational activities in the Catholic parish—
from baseball teams to sewing circles, from bowling leagues
to religious study groups—are only a beginning. Every interest, activity, and function of the Catholic faithful is
provided with some Catholic institution and furnished with
Catholic direction. There are Catholic hospitals, homes,
and orphanages; Catholic schools and colleges; Catholic
charities and welfare agencies; Catholic Boy Scouts and
War Veterans; Catholic associations of doctors, lawyers,
teachers, students, and philosophers; Catholic leagues of
policemen, firemen, and sanitary workers; Catholic lunch-
eon clubs and recreation fellowships; there is the Catholic
Youth Organization, with some six million members; there
is even a Catholic Audio-Visual Educators Association.
This immense system constitutes at one and the same time
a self-contained Catholic world with its own complex in-
terior economy and American Catholicism's resources of
participation in the larger American community.

Perhaps the most impressive aspect of this vast institutional structure is the system of Catholic education that
the church has developed in the past century. Walter J.
Ong is not far from right when he says that "never in the
history of Christianity, including the height of the Middle
Ages, has the church as such been charged with an
organized educational program which even remotely compares with that in the present United States."[42] There are
today in this country nearly four million pupils in the
church's elementary schools—about half of the Catholic
children of elementary school age—over 780,000 in secondary schools, and about 271,000 in Catholic universities
and other institutions at the collegiate level.[43] In many
communities the church's educational system constitutes a
substantial, if not predominant, part of available educational facilities.

The National Catholic Welfare Conference, established
in 1919 as an outgrowth of the wartime National Catholic
War Council, has come to serve as an over-all agency guiding the church's temporal activities.[44] At the top essentially an official annual gathering of the hierarchy, the
NCWC serves as the voice of the American church on all

social and cultural matters. Its various departments, staffed by specialists in direct contact with the ongoing life of the country, provide a clearing house and co-ordinating center for the church's far-flung work in the world. Over against the nation as a whole, it interprets the church's purposes and conducts the church's public relations. In its entire set-up it reflects the double orientation of the Catholic Church in America.

The remarkable combination of discipline and diversity with which the Catholic Church conducts its work has always been a source of bafflement to the outsider. "Rome remains an enigma in theology and in politics," confesses the Protestant church historian, F. E. Mayer. "The Roman Church is the most dogmatic and at the same time the least doctrinal church. There is a fixed dogmatic limit, but within this limit there is room for divergent and often contradictory opinions. . . . There is probably no church which has the capacity for harboring so many widely divergent points of view as the Roman Church."[45] American Catholicism finds room for the most diverse social, political, and cultural outlooks, provided they remain measurably within the dogmatic framework of the faith. Catholics in politics have been the mainstay of corrupt political machines in many cities; on the other hand, they have supplied leadership and strength to American liberalism in recent years.[46] The Catholic press varies all the way from super-nationalistic publications with strong isolationist leanings to such a paper as *The Catholic Worker,* the exponent of semi-anarchistic Christian pacifism. The Catholic laity is largely conventional-minded in social and cultural matters, yet some of the most vigorous new thinking in these fields is being done by Catholic clerics and laymen in this country today.[47] This diversity cannot be denied and should not be underestimated; at the same time, one must not overlook the fact that in certain areas the Catholic Church has had a line which has been more or less consistently followed through many decades.

This has been particularly the case in the field of labor and social policy. The Catholic Church in America has, at least until recently, been overwhelmingly lower-class in composition, predominantly working-class, with emphasis on the basic industries of the country. In the years after the turn of the century, it has been estimated, about two thirds of the membership, and a substantial part of the leadership, of organized labor was Catholic. The decisive point in fixing the church's policy toward labor came in the late 1880s. The Canadian hierarchy had obtained a Papal condemnation of the Knights of Labor on the ground that it was a secret society, infected with "socialism," and given to violence. A similar condemnation for the United States was being contemplated. Gibbons, however, had already established friendly relations with Terence V. Powderly, the Catholic head of the Knights, and when he went to Rome in 1887 to receive his cardinal's hat, he was able to convince Leo XIII that such a condemnation would be both unjust and disastrous.[48] The path which Gibbons thus blazed was followed by the church, despite many hesitations and uncertainties. The Catholic Church has remained, by and large, pro-labor and has shown a deep concern for retaining the allegiance of its working people. It very early adopted the approach later formulated by Pius XI in *Quadragesimo anno* (1931)—"The first and immediate apostles to the working man must themselves be working men"—and it could follow this injunction, where American Protestantism could not, because so many of its clergy and lay leaders were themselves of working-class origin and background. As a result, the church has managed to develop, especially in recent decades, extensive activities in connection with the labor movement, implemented by a considerable number of "labor priests" and such agencies as the Association of Catholic Trade Unionists, the Young Christian Workers, and the Jesuit labor schools.[49]

The church's social policy, too, has served it well. The influence of John A. Ryan, who, as professor at Catholic University and first director of the social action department of the NCWC, pioneered in developing a progressive social program for the church, is still felt. American Jesuits in particular have made Catholic social policy their concern, and they have won wide recognition for their consistent championship of a constructive social outlook, at once liberal and realistic. It should not be assumed, however, that in its social and labor programs the church has had the support of its entire membership. Opposition, resistance, particularly indifference, have always been rife, and practice has not invariably followed in the line of policy. But, by and large, the church has managed to establish itself as a significant and progressive force in the fields of labor and social welfare.

The Catholic community today is one of the three great "melting pots," or population "pools," into which America is divided. Within the Catholic community the innumerable ethnic elements that made up the immigrant church during the nineteenth and early twentieth century are being gradually amalgamated, and a new type of American Catholic, rather along the Irish-American model, is emerging. Thomas Sugrue recalls that in his youth, "an attempt at marriage between an Irish boy and an Italian girl [both Catholics, of course] so shocked the Irish of the parish that the affair was broken up."[50] Today, with the social and cultural advancement of the Italian Catholics, and the Americanization of both Irish and Italians, such obstacles are rapidly disappearing, and so too are the old ethnic groups into which American Catholics were once so obviously divided. It is still possible to find in an American town a whole array of "ethnic" Catholic churches—an Irish church (St. Patrick's), a French-Canadian (Sacré Coeur), an Italian (Our Lady of Carmel), a Hungarian (St. Stephen's), a Croatian (Sts. Cyril and Methodius), a German (St. Boniface's)—but these churches are now usually English-speaking and quite mixed in their membership. It is still possible to find survivals of the many diverse patterns of Catholic life and worship that more than a century of immigration brought to these shores, but merely as survivals; here, too, there has emerged an American pattern along Irish-American lines into which what remains of the onetime diversity is being absorbed. There are those who see in this continuing dissolution of the "national" groups a serious weakening of the church,[51] but there are others who point out that this process is not only inevitable but is precisely the way in which the Catholic Church in America has ceased to be foreign and has become an American institution. It is, in effect, the logical end of the road which American Catholicism took up when it so decisively rejected the program of Cahenslyism.

The advancing Americanization of the later immigrant groups and the increasing ethnic amalgamation within the Catholic community are naturally not without their effect in producing a change in the composition of the hierarchy and priesthood. All four American cardinals are of Irish extraction. A great majority of the 217 bishops and archbishops are still of Irish background. No figures about the priesthood are available, but there seems to be general agreement that the proportion of Irish is declining, both in the hierarchy and the clergy.[52] Yet the "Irish problem"— the problem, as Evelyn Waugh puts it, of "guarding them [the Irish] from the huge presumption of treating the Universal Church as a friendly association of their own"[53]—has not been solved by any means. The Catholic Church in America continues Irish in temper, tradition, and leadership.

Two groups still remain almost entirely unassimilated in the Catholic community—the small group (575,000) of Negro Catholics and the much larger group of Latin Americans, whether Mexicans in the Southwest or Puerto Ricans in New York. These groups present the church with a problem in many ways different from that which it dealt with so effectively in the past: America is no longer a land of immigrants, and both the Negro and the Spanish-speaking groups are by no means so directly assimilable as were the Irish, or the Germans, or even the Italians in the past century. Often in the face of strong lay opposition the church has fought segregation of the Negroes, especially in religion and education, and is vigorously supporting the present desegregation movement. It is yet too soon to judge how successful it will be in keeping the Latin Americans, particularly the Puerto Ricans, in the church and assimilating them into the general Catholic community.

Along with ethnic amalgamation, certain social and cultural trends must be noted insofar as they have significantly affected the structure of American Catholicism. The Catholic community in this country, it should be remembered, is today no longer overwhelmingly lower-class in composition; it has developed an important middle class, which is well represented in business, management, public service, and the professions (pre-eminently in law and teaching). The old Catholic boast that its hierarchy and priesthood come very largely from poor working-class families is no longer as true as it once was. The emergence of a middle class with substantial standing in the general community has, of course, enhanced the position and influence of the church in the nation, but it has precipitated certain vexing problems. Americanization, ethnic amalgamation, and "bourgeoisification" have opened the Catholic community to the outside world in a way that was manifestly impossible when American Catholicism was made up almost entirely of lower-class immigrant groups at the periphery of American society, forced to huddle together for mere survival.[54] Intermarriage has become a serious problem, though how far it leads to defections from the church is not altogether clear.[55] So also, to some extent, has the so-called "suburban trend," for it seems that middle-class Catholics at the professional or junior executive level, as they move out to the suburbs, show some tendency to drop out of the church and adopt an affiliation which they feel to be more in consonance with their new status and the community of which they are a part, especially if the only available Catholic church is such that membership in it would imply a downgrading in status. By and large, however, American Catholicism seems to be successfully coping with the difficulties and perils that its changed position in American society has brought.

Paradoxical evidence of the enhanced cultural status of American Catholics may be found in the rising tide of complaint on the part of eminent Catholic thinkers about the low intellectual level of the American Catholic community and its insufficient concern for learning and scholarship, especially in secular fields.[56] This preoccupation with the intellectual life, however justified the complaints, is one of the best indications of the cultural progress achieved by what was once overwhelmingly an uneducated lower-class community.

That American Catholicism is indeed weathering the crisis of Americanization and "bourgeoisification" is evidenced by the fact that neither Protestantism nor Catholicism has been gaining very markedly at the expense of the other in the past three decades. Both have been growing, because of the general growth of church membership in this period, but not in such a way as to indicate serious inroads on either side.

	Percentage of total population[57]	
	Protestants	Catholics
1926	27.0	16.0
1940	28.7	16.1
1950	33.8	18.9
1955	35.5	20.3
1958	35.5	22.8

Protestant increase has been about 32 per cent, Catholic increase approximately 42 per cent, but in relation to these figures the difference is not decisive. Conversions from one community to the other take place, but they seem to be very small and do not appreciably affect the over-all picture.[58] In general, it would seem to be the case that the growth of both Protestantism and Catholicism is the result of the natural increase of each community and the churching of those hitherto identified but not affiliated with them. In other words, Protestantism and Catholicism seem to have struck pretty much of a balance as things stand. If Catholicism is not carrying everything before it, as some enthusiastic Catholics predicted it would in the days of the great immigration, neither is it disintegrating with the dissolution of its ethnic solidarities. As we have stressed more than once, American Catholicism has successfully negotiated the transition from a foreign church to an American religious community. It is now part of the American Way of Life.

The new status of the Catholic Church, and its openness to the outside world, is reflected in the fact that today it speaks to, and is heard by, the entire nation, and not merely its own community, as was so frequently the case in the past. When the American hierarchy declares itself against "secularism" and "atheistic materialism,"[59] it is received and discussed by Americans as a general "religious" pronouncement rather than as a sectarian address. Fulton Sheen, though appareled in his bishop's cassock, is followed by a vast radio audience consisting of many non-Catholics as well as Catholics. The Christopher movement makes the same general appeal.[60] This new kind of attention that the American people give to the Catholic Church does not mean either a lessening of the tensions between Catholics and non-Catholics (such tensions seem to have mounted in recent years) or any particular readiness of the American people to come over to Catholicism. It merely means that the Catholic Church is recognized as a genuinely American religious community, speaking to the American people not in terms of a unique treasure of revelation entrusted to it alone but in terms of those "ideals and values" which the American feels is at the bottom of all religion. It is because it has become one of the three great "religions of democracy," and not because of its claim to speak as the Universal Church, that American Catholicism is today listened to with such respect and attention by the American people.

FOOTNOTES

1. There is, unfortunately, no adequate history of American Catholicism reaching to our own day, although John Tracy Ellis' perceptive essay, *American Catholicism* (Chicago, 1956), may be regarded as an outline and program for such a work. The history of the church through the nineteenth century may be found in: John Gilmary Shea, *History of the Catholic Church in the United States,* 4 vols. (privately printed, New York, 1886–92); Donald Shearer, *Pontificia Americana: A Documentary History of the Catholic Church in the United States, 1784–1884* (Catholic University, 1933); Martin I. J. Griffin, *Documents Relating to the History of the Catholic Church in the United States* (United States Catholic Historical Society, n.d.). Standard biographies of church leaders are most useful: Peter Guilday, *The Life and Times of John Carroll,* 2 vols.

162   *Protestant – Catholic – Jew*

(Encyclopedia Press, 1922); Peter Guilday, *The Life and Times of John England,* 2 vols. (America Press, 1927); John T. Ellis, *The Life of James Cardinal Gibbons,* 2 vols. (Bruce, 1952); James H. Moynihan, *The Life of Archbishop John Ireland* (Harper, 1953); Fred J. Zwerlein, *The Life and Letters of Bishop McQuaid,* 3 vols. (Art Print Shop, Rochester, N.Y., 1925–27). Two short histories may be mentioned: Theodore Roemer, *The Catholic Church in the United States* (Herder, 1950); and Theodore Maynard, *The Story of American Catholicism* (Macmillan, 1941). Three chapters (Chaps. 12, 13, and 14) of E. E. Y. Hales, *The Catholic Church in the Modern World* (Hanover House, 1958) will be found relevant. An informed and critical survey of contemporary Catholicism is provided by *Catholicism in America: A Series of Articles from the Commonweal* (Harcourt, Brace, 1953); see also Louis J. Putz, ed., *The Catholic Church U.S.A.* (Fides, 1956) and W. J. Ong, *Frontiers in American Catholicism* (Macmillan, 1957). Ludwig Hertling, *Geschichte der katholischen Kirche in den Vereinigten Staaten* (Morus, Berlin, 1953) is a valuable study. Three important sociological studies are Joseph H. Fichter, *Southern Parish: The Dynamics of a City Church* (Chicago, 1951), *Social Relations in the Urban Parish* (Chicago, 1954), and *Parochial School: A Sociological Study* (Notre Dame, 1959); see also C. J. Nuesse and T. S. Harte, eds., *Sociology of the Parish* (Bruce, 1951). Thomas F. O'Dea, "The Catholic Immigrant and the American Scene," *Thought,* Vol. XXXI, No. 121, Summer 1956, well focuses this crucial aspect of American Catholic history. Valuable material will be found in the *American Catholic Sociological Review,* issued quarterly by the American Catholic Sociological Society.

2. "Consequently, the Church had suffered here a loss of 240,-000 members or possible members by 1790" (Gerald Shaughnessy, *Has the Immigrant Kept the Faith* [Macmillan, 1925], p. 52).

3. Sperry, *Religion in America,* p. 215, also p. 204.

4. Sperry, *Religion in America,* p. 215.

5. For the story of "Trusteeism," see Peter K. Guilday, *Trusteeism* (American Catholic Historical Society, New York, 1928); Guilday, *Life and Times of John England;* Patrick J. Dignan, *History of the Legal Incorporation of Catholic Church Property in the United States* (Catholic University, 1933). See also Roemer, *The Catholic Church in the United States,* pp. 140–60, 163, 220; Maynard, *The Story of American Catholicism,* pp. 187–96, 236–37.

6. Thus *The Christian Century,* in its June 23, 1954 issue, reported: "The old question of the right of Roman Catholic laymen to control church property has cropped up again in a law-

suit in La Union, New Mexico. It seems that a new priest there, a refugee from Lithuania, applied canon law to excommunicate forty residents who protested against having title to the church taken away from a local association."

7. Sperry, *Religion in America*, p. 207.

8. Bishop Robert J. Dwyer, "The American Laity," *The Commonweal*, August 27, 1954.

9. For the story of the anti-Catholic movement before the Civil War, see Ray Allen Billington, *The Protestant Crusade, 1800-1860* (Macmillan, 1938). See also Roemer, *The Catholic Church in the United States*, pp. 194, 217–19, 239–44; Maynard, *The Story of American Catholicism*, pp. 276–306.

10. John J. Kane, "Catholic Separatism," *Catholicism in America*, p. 50.

11. Oscar Handlin, *The Uprooted* (Little, Brown, 1951), pp. 131–32, 135. "Thus, when the first Plenary Council of Baltimore was convened in 1852, the American hierarchy consisted of six foreign-born archbishops and seventeen foreign-born bishops. . . . The chief archiepiscopal sees—New York, Baltimore, Cincinnati, and St. Louis—were occupied by prelates of Irish birth. In point of fact, this Irish domination represented the numerical composition of the Catholic body at this time" (Thomas T. McAvoy, "The Formation of the Catholic Minority in the United States, 1820–1860," *The Review of Politics*, Vol. X, No. 1, January 1948).

12. Maynard thus describes the rise of the Irish to leadership in the church: "Over a hundred native Irishmen have been made bishops, and those who were Irish in blood, though not by birth, at least double this number. It is unquestionable not only that they have supplied the majority of the members of the American hierarchy, but that they have occupied the most important sees. New York has always been held by an Irishman (except for Dubois); Boston (except for Cheverus and the Marylander Fenwick) has always been so held; Baltimore (except for the Frenchman Maréchal and the Englishman Whitfield) has been an Irish preserve. The same thing is true of the other great dioceses. . . . Upon the whole, it is incontestable that the guiding hands of the church in the United States have been Irish" (*The Story of American Catholicism*, pp. 506–07). (For Baltimore, Maynard should have added the old Marylanders Carroll, Neale, and Spalding to his list of non-Irish.)

13. Maynard, *The Story of American Catholicism*, p. 285.

14. "In America too, the Irish supplied the numbers that made Catholicism for the first time a major factor in American life. But they did something much more important. They established the precedents for all future Catholic immigrants. They gave the Church in America a great deal of its mentality and

atmosphere. From among them came the first great numbers of clergy and a major part of the hierarchy up to this day. Above all, both priests and people accepted without inhibitions the great American adventure with all its implications. They were democrats. . . . They spoke English as their mother tongue. . . . When the other waves of Catholic immigrants arrived, the die had been cast and all the important decisions made. . . ." (Desmond Fennell, "Continental and Oceanic Catholicism," *America*, March 26, 1955.) For the view that English and American Catholics, who preceded the Irish, had worked out a culturally superior type of accommodation, see McAvoy, "Formation of the Catholic Minority in the United States," *The Review of Politics*, Vol. X, No. 1, January 1948. But McAvoy adds: "Even though the more dominant immigrant groups were of lower strain culturally, their staunch defense of their religion created in this country the most militant Catholic organization in the English-speaking world. Before the change, the Anglo-American Catholics, like their English brethren, did not show themselves active apologists of the Catholic position, and in striving to advance the faith by Catholic pre-eminence in cultural matters, they had continued the defeatist attitude of the English minority group of colonial days."

15. Handlin, *The Uprooted*, p. 135.

16. For a story of Cahenslyism which is really a defense of Cahensly, see Coleman J. Barry, *The Catholic Church and German Americans* (Bruce, 1953); see also Hertling, *Geschichte der katholischen Kirche in den Vereinigten Staaten*, pp. 162, 175–79, 216–21.

17. Resistance to Americanization, in varying degrees, though by no means as extreme as Cahenslyism, came from certain sections of the Irish clergy as well, such as Archbishops Hughes and Corrigan of New York and Bishop McQuaid of Rochester, but the influence of such men as Archbishops Ireland of St. Paul and Gibbons of Baltimore and Bishop Spalding of Peoria prevailed. It was Archbishop Ireland who formulated the position of the dominant group in these terms: "It will not do to understand the thirteenth century better than the nineteenth. . . . We should speak to our age; we should be in it and of it, if we would have its ear. For the same reason, there is needed a thorough sympathy with the country. The church of America must be, of course, as Catholic as even in Jerusalem or Rome; but as far as her garments assume color from the local landscape, she must be American" (quoted by Sperry, *Religion in America*, p. 219). Native-born Catholics, and of course the few "Yankee" converts, were eager to speed the Americanization of Catholicism, but in the beginning they met with considerable resistance. "Perhaps none of these [converts] outshone in their zeal Isaac Thomas Hecker and Orestes A. Brownson, both of whom be-

came notable for their efforts to show that Catholicism and Americanism were not only compatible but complementary. . . . The native-born Catholics, including the older Irish, looked forward to the day when the immigrant would cease to be looked upon as a foreigner. Brownson, a militant Yankee, wanted to eliminate this distinction at once. Archbishop Hughes objected to Brownson's reasonings because he feared that the loss in faith in a hasty adoption of American ways would outweigh any social gain. Later on, the Americanized Irish would use Brownson's argument against the Germans, Poles, and French Canadians . . ." (McAvoy, "The Formation of the Catholic Minority in the United States, 1820–1860," *The Review of Politics,* Vol. X, No. 1, January 1948).

18. For the effect of ethnic-cultural loyalties in fragmenting American Protestantism, see H. Richard Niebuhr, *The Social Sources of Denominationalism* (Holt, 1929), esp. chap. viii, pp. 200–35.

19. For a penetrating comparison between "Continental" and "Oceanic" (English-speaking, predominantly Irish) Catholicism, see Fennell, "Continental and Oceanic Catholicism," *America,* March 26, 1955.

20. Walter J. Ong even finds an affinity in temperament: "There is a curious affinity, which I do not pretend to explain, between the hail-fellow-well-met Irish friendliness and the cordiality of the larger American tradition . . ." ("American Catholicism and America," *Thought,* Vol. XXVII, No. 107, Winter 1952–53).

21. Thus Evelyn Waugh, in his acute comments on Catholicism in America, notes the extreme "deference with which they [the clergy] are treated on purely social occasions" and accounts for it along the lines I have suggested ("The American Epoch in the Catholic Church," *Life,* September 19, 1949).

22. In his rather unbalanced criticism of the Catholic Church in America, for example, Thomas Sugrue rebukes the "Irish clergy" for setting the "pattern which oriented newcomers first to Americanism, then to American Catholicism" (*A Catholic Speaks His Mind on America's Religious Conflict* [Harper, 1951], p. 45). This is the line generally taken in many European Catholic criticisms of the American Catholic Church.

23. Kenneth Scott Latourette, *A History of the Expansion of Christianity* (Harper, 1937–45), Vol. IV, p. 253.

24. Latourette, *A History of the Expansion of Christianity,* Vol. IV, pp. 255, 283. Theodore Abel, writing in 1933, estimated that: "If we take the available figures at their face value, the most that can be claimed by American churches engaged in mission work among Catholic immigrants is a total membership of between 50,000 and 60,000. This estimated total includes,

besides converts from Catholicism, the children and grandchildren of converts who have not themselves been brought up in Catholicism, and also persons of Protestant stock" (*Protestant Home Missions to Catholic Immigrants* [Institute of Social and Religious Research, New York, 1933], p. 33). The leakage due to unchurching has been considerably greater, but nowhere as great as in the eighteenth and early nineteenth centuries.

25. "The Irish tradition does not so much directly determine the character of American Catholicism as afford a meeting point for the general American tradition and the Church in America. . . . The Irish tradition is less a determinant than a catalyst" (Ong, "American Catholicism and America," *Thought*, Vol. XXVII, No. 107, Winter 1952–53).

26. The classic comic strip, "Bringing Up Father," by George McManus, memorializes this transformation. Jiggs and Maggie began as "shanty Irish," but then Jiggs made his fortune (as a building contractor) and they moved up in the social scale, Jiggs somewhat ruefully, Maggie with an almost neurotic anxiety. Their daughter, however, shows none of these traits: she is American, sophisticated, and bourgeois, as to the manner born. The process has here been somewhat speeded up for effect, but the pattern is substantially true to life.

27. Sugrue, *A Catholic Speaks His Mind*, p. 7.

28. Waugh, "The American Epoch in the Catholic Church," *Life*, September 19, 1949. A careful sociological study of the parochial school is to be found in Joseph H. Fichter, *Parochial School* (Notre Dame, 1959).

29. Indeed, in certain European eyes, altogether too much so. Thus, a report on American Catholicism presented in the January 1951 issue of *Au Service de Tout*, a French Catholic Action magazine, declared: "It [the American church] is at present very wealthy and its faithful are citizens esteemed by their compatriots. Catholicism has become the religion of a large portion of the middle class." See also the series of articles on American Catholicism by Georges Escoulin in *Le Monde* (Paris) for January 10, 11, and 12, 1950; and Erik von Kuehnelt-Leddihn, "American Catholics Revisited," *The Tablet* (London), April 22, 1950. Thomas Sugrue and other American critics of the church make the same point (*A Catholic Speaks His Mind*, pp. 53–56, and *passim*).

30. David Riesman notes "the rise in the social position of American Catholics in the last several decades," and goes on: "Everett C. Hughes . . . has pointed out that one of the greatest sources of anxieties among middle-class Catholics is the problem of the relation between their church affiliation and their social mobility. Because they are mobile, these Catholics have looked for the definition of 'good American' in the past largely to non-

Catholics. . . . But as Catholics have increasingly moved into the managerial and professional classes, they have been able greatly to influence the definition of 'good American,' and have taken the lead, since they were among the 'earliest arrivals,' in the crusade against Communism, in defining the 'bad un-American' as well. At the same time, non-Catholic opinion-leaders . . . do not define the middle- and upper-class style of life in such a way as to exclude good Catholics—save, perhaps, for the still differentiating and hence exceedingly anxiety-provoking issue of birth control" (*Individualism Reconsidered* [Free Press, 1954], p. 391).

31. Apostolic Adhortation, "Menti Nostrae," September 23, 1950 (*The Catholic Mind*, Vol. XLIX, No. 1057, January 1951).

32. Quoted in Sperry, *Religion in America*, p. 218.

33. For the much misunderstood story of the Papal condemnation of "Americanism," see: Raymond Corrigan, *The Church and the Nineteenth Century* (Bruce, 1938), pp. 276 ff.; Thomas T. McAvoy, *The Great Crisis in American Catholic History, 1895–1900* (Regnery, 1957); E. E. Y. Hales, *The Catholic Church in the Modern World* (Hanover House, 1958), pp. 166–75; John J. Wynne, *The Great Encyclical Letters of Pope Leo XIII* (Benziger, 1903), pp. 441–53; Roemer, *The Catholic Church in the United States*, pp. 309–11; Maynard, *The Story of American Catholicism*, pp. 498–511; James M. O'Neill, *Catholicism and American Freedom* (Harper, 1952), pp. 70–73. It is necessary to point out two things: (1) the "heresy" seems to have been held explicitly more by certain French "liberals," including "liberal" Catholics, than by any American churchmen; and (2) the Pope specifically excluded from his condemnation "the characteristic qualities . . . special [to America] and the condition of your [the American] commonwealths, or the laws and customs that prevail in them" (Wynne, *The Great Encyclical Letters*, p. 452).

34. E.g., John A. Ryan and Moorhouse F. X. Millar, *The State and the Church* (Macmillan, 1922), esp. p. 35; John A. Ryan and Francis J. Boland, *Catholic Principles of Politics: The State and the Church* (Macmillan, 1948), pp. 311–12, 315–21.

35. James Cardinal Gibbons, "The Church and the Republic," *Retrospect of Fifty Years* (John Murphy, Baltimore, 1916), Vol. I, pp. 210–11. Catholic approval of American constitutional arrangements with respect to religion go back to the early days of the Republic, as can be seen from the pronouncements of Bishop Carroll and Bishop England.

36. "The Catholic Church in American Democracy," press release of the National Catholic Welfare Conference, January 26, 1948; see also O'Neill, *Catholicism and American Freedom*, pp. 34–36.

37. John Courtney Murray's writings will be found in the columns of *Theological Studies,* the journal he edits; also, "On the Structure of the Church-State Problem," *The Catholic Church in World Affairs,* ed. by Waldemar Gurian and M. A. Fitzsimons (Notre Dame, 1954), pp. 11–32; "The Problem of Pluralism in America," *Thought,* Vol. XXIX, No. 113, Summer 1954; "A Church-State Anthology: The Work of Father Murray," ed. by Victor R. Yanitelli, *Thought,* Vol. XXVII, No. 104, Spring 1952; "Reflections on the Religiously Pluralist Society: Selected Articles and Addresses," *Catholic Mind,* Vol. LVII, No. 1143, May–June 1959; also Gustave Weigel, "The Church and the Democratic State," *Thought,* Vol. XXVII, No. 105, Summer 1952. The various viewpoints on the question are extracted and presented in Mario Delmirani, "Church and State: Positions in the Controversy," *The Theologian,* Vol. VIII, No. 2, Spring 1953. For recent Papal pronouncements, see *Pope Pius XII on the World Community,* with commentaries by Edward A. Conway and Gustave Weigel, edited by Charles Keenan (America Press, 1954).

38. Waugh, "The American Epoch in the Catholic Church," *Life,* September 19, 1949.

39. "This accounts in great part for the indistinguishability of the [American] Catholic in the ordinary activities of life. In the office, in the factory, in the professions, and in social intercourse, the Catholic is rarely distinguished from his non-Catholic fellows. The behavior of both is the same. The Catholic has striven so hard and so long to be accepted by the American community that he has taken on the color and habits of the general environment . . . Now that he is accepted, he is very loath to do anything which would isolate him . . . The American Catholic's attempt at adaptation to his milieu has been successful, perhaps too successful" (Gustave Weigel, "An Introduction to American Catholicism," in Louis J. Putz, ed., *The Catholic Church U.S.A.*).

40. For a valuable survey of "The Catholic Church in the United States," see Thomas T. McAvoy, in Waldemar Gurian and M. A. Fitzsimons, eds., *The Catholic Church in World Affairs,* chap. xiv, pp. 358–76, and Louis J. Putz, ed., *The Catholic Church U.S.A.* A map showing the location of Catholic dioceses and archdioceses in the United States is to be found in Roemer, *The Catholic Church in the United States,* facing p. 384; see also Appendices II and III, pp. 401–12, 413–14, for lists of the hierarchy and ecclesiastical provinces. See also *Official Catholic Directory, 1958* (Kenedy, 1958).

41. See *The 1959 National Catholic Almanac* (Paterson, N.J.: St. Anthony's Guild, 1959), pp. 407–11; *Yearbook of American Churches,* edition for 1959, pp. 296–97. A useful compilation of facts and figures, based on the *Official Catholic Directory* for

1955, will be found in "The Roman Catholic Church in the U.S.," *Information Service*, January 7, 1956. The *Yearbook of American Churches*, edition for 1960, gives the number of Catholics in 1958 as 39,509,508 (p. 282).

42. Ong, "American Catholicism and America," *Thought*, Vol. XXVII, No. 107, Winter 1952–53.

43. See *The 1959 National Catholic Almanac*, pp. 470–72.

44. See *Official Catholic Directory*, 1954, pp. 723–24.

45. F. E. Mayer, *The Religious Bodies of America* (Concordia, 1954), pp. 30, 36, 107. And a Catholic historian pretty much agrees: "No minority group in the United States is probably so formless, and yet at the same time so rigid, as the American membership of the Roman Catholic Church. The rigidity of the Catholic organization arises from the fact that there has never been a real heresy during the three centuries and more of Catholic life within the boundaries of the United States. . . . In startling contrast to this unity in dogma and morals has been the extreme divergence among American Catholics in political beliefs and in economic and social status" (McAvoy, "The Formation of the Catholic Minority in the United States, 1820–1860," *The Review of Politics*, Vol. X, No. 1, January 1948). "There are today well over 30 million Catholics in our land. By background, education, occupation, and national origin, they differ profoundly from one another. There is probably a greater pluralism of attitudes among American Catholics than exists within any comparable group in the world" (editorial, *America*, March 10, 1956).

46. For the story of two Catholic big-city machine bosses, see Reinhard H. Luthin, *American Demagogues, Twentieth Century* (Beacon, 1954), chap. ii (James M. Curley) and chap. vi (Frank Hague). For a non-Catholic estimate of Catholic liberalism, see James Loeb, Jr., "Liberals and Catholics," *The Commonweal*, June 16, 1950.

47. The writings of John Courtney Murray, S.J., have already been referred to. A penetrating interpretation of some of the major problems of "faith and world order in current society" is presented in Gustave Weigel, S.J., *Faith and Understanding in America* (Macmillan, 1959). The best work of lay Catholic intellectuals will be found in such journals as *Thought*, *The Commonweal*, and *America*.

48. See Ellis, *The Life of James Cardinal Gibbons*, Vol. I, chap. xii, pp. 486–546; Allen S. Will, *Life of Cardinal Gibbons* (Dutton, 1922), Vol. I, pp. 335 ff.

49. For a survey of Catholic attitudes to labor and social questions, see Aaron I. Abell, "The Catholic Church and the American Social Question," in Waldemar Gurian and M. A.

Fitzsimons, eds., *The Catholic Church in World Affairs*, pp. 377–99.

50. Sugrue, *A Catholic Speaks His Mind*, p. 48.

51. Thus, François Houtart, a Belgian Catholic specialist in religious sociology, is reported to attribute the "dechristianization" of many American Catholics to "the progressive breakup of the national groups which have formed the basic structure of the church in the United States" ("Belgian Scholar on Church in U.S.," *America*, December 4, 1954). See François Houtart, "A Sociological Study of the Evolution of American Catholics," *Social Compass* (The Hague), Vol. 2, No. 5/6.

52. Not all Catholic ethnic stocks in the United States manifest the same proclivity toward priestly vocations. Irish and French-Canadian Catholics, for example, seem to show a considerably more pronounced tendency than do German or Italian Catholics, though in no case is the supply sufficient to meet the need of the expanding Catholic community. These differences may well become equalized with the emergence of an American third generation.

53. Waugh, "The American Epoch in the Catholic Church," *Life*, September 19, 1949.

54. For a sober estimate of Catholic mobility, see John J. Kane, "The Social Structure of American Catholics," *The American Catholic Sociological Review*, Vol. XVI, No. 1, March 1955.

55. See John L. Thomas, "Mixed Marriages—So What?", *Social Order*, Vol. II, No. 4, April 1952. See also John L. Thomas, *The American Catholic Family* (Prentice-Hall, 1956).

56. For an excellent discussion of the problem, see Thomas F. O'Dea, *American Catholic Dilemma: An Inquiry into the Intellectual Life* (Sheed and Ward, 1958), in which there is a thorough presentation and documentation of the "state of the questions."

57. *Yearbook of American Churches*, edition for 1960, pp. 261–62. The major part of the Catholic gain reflected in this table seems to come from the advance reported for the last year (1958). For comparative figures covering 1916–52 see "Trends in Church Membership," *Information Service* (National Council of Churches of Christ), April 9, 1955. From 1916 to 1952 the membership of 128 Protestant bodies increased 94.2 per cent; the membership of the Roman Catholic Church increased 92.4 per cent; population increased some 55 per cent.

58. The Catholic Church reports conversions during 1957 amounting to 140,414 (*The 1959 National Catholic Almanac*, p. 407). There are no official Protestant figures, though some extravagant estimates have been made. For a sober Catholic appraisal of the situation, see Thomas J. M. Burke, "Did Four Million Catholics Become Protestants?", *America*, April 10,

1954. A survey conducted by the American Institute of Public Opinion (Gallup poll) in 1955 indicated that of an adult population of 96,000,000, only about 4 per cent no longer belonged to the religious community of their birth; of these 1,400,000 were Protestants who had originally been Catholics, and 1,400,-000 were Catholics who had originally been Protestants; about 1,000,000 had made changes of some other kind. The number of Protestants who had become Catholics was thus balanced by the number of Catholics who had become Protestants (see *Public Opinion News Service*, March 20, 1955). See also John A. O'Brien, *You Too Can Win Souls* (Macmillan, 1955).

59. See, e.g., the statement of the administrative board of the NCWC, speaking for the American hierarchy, on "Victory—Our Faith," *The New York Times*, November 21, 1954.

60. A survey conducted by the Rev. Timothy J. Flynn, director of radio and TV work for the Archdiocese of New York, revealed that 65 per cent of TV viewers could not identify the "denominational" (Protestant or Catholic) character of the religious programs they saw (*America*, July 6, 1957).

VIII. *Judaism in America*

American Jewry first established itself in this country as an
ethnic-immigrant group. In its earlier phases it seemed but
little different from the other immigrant groups with whom
it had made the overseas journey to the New World. But
unlike the rest, it somehow did not lose its corporate identity
with advancing Americanization; instead—largely within
the last quarter of a century—it underwent a change of
character and turned into an American religious community, retaining, even enhancing, its Jewishness in the
process. It has thus in its own history exemplified with exceptional clarity the fundamental restructuring of American
society which transformed the "land of immigrants" into
the "triple melting pot." Nothing is more characteristically
American than the historical evolution of American Jewry,[1]
revealing, as it does, the inner patterns of American social
development.

I

Though in 1954 American Jewry celebrated its tercentenary, the American Jewish community of today is predominantly the product of the great wave of immigration
from eastern Europe that set in some three quarters of a
century ago. Yet the earlier history of American Jewry is
not without its significance. The early Jews in this country,
including the twenty-three who landed in New Amsterdam
in 1654, were largely Sephardic, Spanish and Portuguese
Jews seeking some place to settle after their expulsion from
the Iberian peninsula and their wanderings through Europe
and Latin America. With them came a few Ashkenazic
Jews from central Europe and Poland. The immigration
was slow—by 1776 there were perhaps 2,500 Jews in
British America—but their acculturation was rapid. They

settled along the coast—in New York, Newport, Philadelphia, the Carolinas, Georgia—and engaged in trade and finance, which sometimes reached considerable proportions. As quickly as possible they established their synagogues according to the Sephardic rite, and more slowly added the various auxiliary institutions. These Jews were, of course, orthodox, and it was their desire to re-establish the orthodox pattern as they knew it. Nevertheless, as they soon discovered, the old patterns could not be simply reproduced, and adaptation began with their first accommodations to American life.

These adaptations were at first imperceptible, but by 1825, when Jews in this country numbered some 5,000, the demand for readjustment became explicit. Partly under the influence of early German Reform, but largely under pressure of their own circumstances, a group of younger people in the Jewish community in Charleston that year organized themselves as the Reformed Society of Israelites. The year before they had petitioned the established congregation for certain reforms and modifications—greater decorum in the services, elimination of Spanish from the ritual, sermons in English—but their petition had been rejected, and so they seceded. They could not make their bold act good and were soon forced to return to the older congregation, but the future was obviously with them.

By the 1820s the handful of Jews in the United States, some 5,000 out of a population of 13,000,000, had established their way of life as Americans and as Jews, a way recognizably Jewish though also characteristically American. In that decade, however, began the wave of German immigration, which was to last half a century and was to remake Jewish life in America. From 1820 to 1870 between 200,000 and 400,000 Jews came to the United States, mostly from central Europe.[2] These "Germans" did not by any means immediately fuse with the native Jews, any more than the German Catholics who came in the same migration fused with the native Catholics they found in this country. The German Jews were foreigners, of different ways and cultural background; and they were Ashkenazim, whereas the native Jews, actually descended from immigrants of many different strains including East Europeans, regarded themselves as Sephardim and therefore superior. Decades were to pass before the social and institutional distinctions were overcome.

Americans tended to regard the newcomers as primarily Germans rather than Jews, one with the German Catholics and Lutherans who had migrated with them. On their part, the German Jews also identified themselves as Germans and joined cultural and mutual benefit societies set up by Germans without regard to religious lines. But their identification was actually double, and before long, where the German Jews were numerous enough, they established specifically Jewish institutions and movements, often existing side by side with their all-German counterparts. Only gradually, with increasing Americanization, did the German Jews cease to feel themselves part of the German community in the United States.[3]

The Jews who came in this German migration took up occupations that dispersed them throughout the land with the advancing frontier. They became peddlers, retail merchants, ultimately even bankers and large-scale businessmen. The high degree of dispersal and the relative prosperity which they achieved made their accommodation to American life remarkably easy. Before mid-century they were already busily erecting a network of community institutions that "were reflections of their conditions of settlement and not simply traditions carried over from the past or from abroad."[4] Synagogues were established, charitable and philanthropic efforts were launched, cultural activities were set going, and education became a serious concern. In the two decades before the Civil War, Hebrew Benevolent Societies made their appearance in New York, Philadelphia, and other cities; in Cincinnati, New York, and Chicago, Jewish hospitals were built. Literary and cultural societies prepared the way for the establishment of the first Young Men's Hebrew Association in 1854 in New York "for the purpose of cultivating and fostering a better knowledge of the history, literature, and doctrines of Judaism . . ." Attempts were made to set up full-time religious schools, but with the expansion of the public school system, the effort failed and was replaced by various schemes of supplementary education. By 1860, also, American Jews had already established five national orders of their own, including the B'nai B'rith (Sons of the Covenant), which then had some fifty lodges. Settlements of American Jews were to be found in all inhabited parts of the land.[5]

Reflecting the dispersal and the speed of acculturation of the German Jews under mid-nineteenth century conditions, intermarriage and defection from the Jewish community reached considerable proportions. "As the second generation grew to maturity, there was a strong likelihood that, eager to be Americanized, it would discard everything associated with the immigrant heritage of its fathers, including religion."[6] To stem the tide of dissolution, leaders of the German-Jewish community in America made strenuous efforts to hasten the adaptation of Jewish religious patterns to American conditions. Unless the synagogue adjusted itself to the new way of life, warned the *American Israelite* in 1854, "we will have no Jews in this country in less than half a century."[7]

The new venture at reform was more directly influenced by the outlook and program of the German Reform movement, by this time some fifty years old. Yet the first attempts related not to theology but to synagogue procedures and forms of worship. Again there was a call for more decorum, for the revisions of the liturgy to permit shorter and more intelligible services, for the replacement of "German and Slavonic dialects" by English, for family pews to eliminate the segregation of women, for sermons in the American style, for mixed choirs and organs. Later, demands for the "simplification" of *kashrut* (dietary) and Sabbath prohibitions were heard. At Emanu-El in New York, Har Sinai in Baltimore, and other of the German synagogues, the reforms were introduced all at once; elsewhere, they came gradually. There was a great deal of conflict, but on the whole, at least so far as the synagogal reforms were concerned, the new order spread rapidly.

A great power in the movement was Isaac Mayer Wise. He came to this country from Bohemia in 1846 when still under thirty. He served as rabbi in Albany, but in 1854 went to Cincinnati, which he succeeded in making the Mecca of Reform Judaism in America. One of his first ventures was to compile a new prayer book and order of service according to the *Minhag America* (American custom). In 1873 he promoted the formation of the Union of American Hebrew Congregations, and in 1875 he effected the establishment of a theological seminary, the Hebrew Union College in Cincinnati. Finally, in 1889, he launched a rabbinical association under the name of the Central Conference of American Rabbis. These institutions were intended by him to be all-inclusive, and indeed for a time they did include synagogues and community leaders of many shades of belief and practice, Sephardic as well as Ashkenazic, East European as well as German. The promise of unity along American Reform lines, however, was gravely jeopardized when the Reform movement made the attempt to define itself theologically; it was altogether shattered by the flood of East European orthodox immigrants that began in the 1880s.

In 1885 the rabbis of some dozen congregations, meeting in Pittsburgh, adopted what came to be known as the Pittsburgh Platform. It represented a drastic revision of traditional Jewish teaching along lines of German idealism and American Protestant liberalism. It substantially sanctioned the various Reform practices that had already established themselves and foreshadowed others. It relegated the Talmud and Talmudic tradition to the margin of Jewish life. It converted the messianic hope and expectation into an affirmation of the nineteenth century doctrine of progress, and eliminated Zion (Palestine) from the Jewish vision of fulfillment.[8] While many of the more conservative synagogues had been quite ready to go along with the reforms in practice, they rose against the radical theological innovations contained in the Pittsburgh Platform. A substantial group, primarily Sephardic, under the leadership of Sabato Morais, withdrew, and the Cincinnati institutions and movement very soon became the expressions of a "party" in American Judaism, Reform in the specific and narrower sense. Nevertheless, Reform continued to grow and seems unquestiona bly to have dominated American Jewish religious life before the new wave of immigration from eastern Europe.

The dissidents who rejected the Pittsburgh Platform regarded themselves as orthodox, but they were very far from being orthodox in the East European sense. Their differences with Reform were largely matters of temper and degree; they accepted almost wholly the emerging pattern of accommodation, though they shied away from some of its extreme manifestations (for example, replacing Saturday by Sunday for Sabbath worship) and objected to the radical theological revisionism of Reform. In defense of what they felt to be the enduring tradition of Judaism, to be made viable under American conditions, they proceeded to set up a parallel set of institutions under the banner of "historical Judaism," later to become the Conservative movement.[9] With Sabato Morais were such men as Benjamin Szold and Alexander Kohut; but the man who really made the new movement was Solomon Schechter. That, however, was the work of a new time.

The second epoch in the history of American Jewry, the "German" period roughly from 1820 to 1880, thus ended with two forms of an Americanized Judaism substantially similar in pattern though different in temper and ideology. Sporadic attempts had been made to unite the Jewish community in an over-all organization and to establish a central authority for American Jews, but they failed: American Jews remained loosely and autonomously organized, unwilling, or unable, not merely to transplant the traditional *kahal*-type of all-inclusive community, but equally reluctant to follow the British Jews in the establishment of an authoritative Board of Deputies. In this respect, too, they were American, following closely the Protestant-American pattern of decentralization and voluntarism.

II

Some East European Jews had come to America in colonial times, and by 1852 immigrants from Russia and Poland were sufficiently numerous to set up a congregation in New

York. But the great deluge of East European immigration
did not begin till the 1870s. Between 1870 and 1914 some
2,000,000 Jews migrated to America, 60 per cent from Russia and 20 per cent from the Austro-Hungarian Empire.
During the years of World War I, some 100,000 more, and
from 1920 to 1924, when immigration restrictions were finally clamped down, an additional 250,000 entered the
country. All in all, therefore, nearly 2,500,000 Jews arrived
in the five and a half decades after 1870.[10] The sudden
mass deluge of East European Jews completely upset the
settled pattern of American Judaism that had begun to
emerge in the third quarter of the nineteenth century.

This time the Jews came not as part of a larger migration
from their countries of birth; "in eastern Europe, the Jews
were almost alone as emigrants, and were the first to take
the move, peasants from that part of the continent . . .
[arriving] in large numbers . . . not until after 1890."[11]
This time, too, there was much less dispersal; the great bulk
of the immigrants settled in a few large cities and established urban ghettos as areas of primary settlement. They
came as petty merchants, artisans, or men without occupation, and went into small retailing and light manufacturing,
particularly the garment trades. For the first time in the
United States, and indeed in the Western world, there
emerged a large Jewish proletariat, making a living by
working for wages in industry. There is, indeed, reason
to believe that at the turn of the century the Jews were the
most industrialized ethnic group in the city of New York.[12]
But side by side with the Jewish factory operative there
soon appeared the Jewish businessman, the Jewish white-
collar worker, and somewhat later, the Jewish professional
man. The "deproletarianization" of the Jewish immigrant
began almost as soon as he became proletarianized; it proceeded apace with the second generation.[13]

Like the German Jews before them, many of the early
East European Jewish immigrants were identified with the
nation and culture from which they came, and some of them
indeed so identified themselves.[14] But the fact that the
great bulk of East European Jewry derived from Yiddish-
speaking communities but little associated with the national

culture of the land of their birth soon changed their context of identification. With the vast influx of East European Jews in the first years of the new century, a well-defined Yiddish-speaking Jewish ethnic group emerged, very different indeed in self-understanding and social conformation from the Jews of Sephardic and German origin who had preceded them.

At the opening of the new century, and for some two decades thereafter, the Jews in this country, and particularly in New York City (where, in 1909, half of the American Jews were to be found), constituted in effect two distinct communities, German and East European, each with its own characteristic outlook and pattern of behavior, each busily engaged in building and developing its own network of institutions. "These newcomers [from eastern Europe] were strangers . . . not much less strangers to the Jews already settled than to other Americans."[15] They felt themselves to be strangers and were treated as strangers, and they proceeded to make their own adjustment to American reality.

East European Jewry came in two ideological streams, thoroughly mingled in the migration. The great majority were religious Jews in the age-old tradition of the East European ghetto; a significant minority, however, had broken with Orthodoxy and with Jewish religion and were caught up in one or another of the secularist ideologies of the time, usually labor radicalism. This group was small at first but grew appreciably after 1905; it wielded a very considerable influence among American Jews in the decade before World War I. Both Orthodoxy and secular Judaism flourished in the first quarter of the century, each working to extend its institutions and to establish its ascendancy among the new arrivals.

Orthodoxy attempted persistently to transplant the old religious and community institutions, but without success; it, too, had to make its adjustments, though it frequently did not recognize how far-reaching they were.[16] The old unity of the *kahal* was gone; Jewish life was fragmented in many parts, under many and often conflicting authorities.

In the crucial field of the education of the young the East
European Jews tried to fall back on the *heder* and *yeshivah*,
as these had functioned "at home," but of course they could
hardly be made to serve the old purpose in the new environment. Part-time Hebrew and religious instruction in
Talmud Torah schools unattached to synagogues in the area
was attempted, with somewhat better success. But in 1908,
Samuel Benderly, after an extensive survey, found that
"only 28 per cent of the Jewish children in New York between the ages of six and sixteen received even the scantiest
Jewish education."[17]

The record was better in the field of charitable and social
organization. The newer immigrants did not, like the older
and wealthier Jews, establish large-scale organized charities, but they did set up countless informal agencies of mutual aid and comfort, as well as a great variety of *lantsmanshaftn.* The Yiddish press and theater were vital expressions
of the expanding community life of East European Jewry.
All of these enterprises, it should be noted, were essentially
American, however foreign their appearance. They were
the normal forms of expression of the ethnic-immigrant
group as that came into being in this country in the period
of the great immigration.

The labor-radical element among the East European immigrants was ethnically and culturally identical with the
Orthodox, but the ideological differences were so great that
coexistence within the same community institutions was
hardly possible. The Jewish labor movement, when it
emerged toward the end of the nineteenth century, became,
in effect, the core of a dual community within the East European immigration. It set up its own secular Yiddish
schools, its own *lantsmanshaftn,* its own press, its own welfare agencies, even its own national fraternal order (Workmen's Circle).[18] Thus, in the half century from about 1870
to the end of World War I, there were not only two communities of American Jews in this country, different ethnically and culturally—the "Germans," with whom all the
older elements were now identified, and the "Russians," as
the Yiddish-speaking newcomers were known[19]—but the
East European community was itself deeply divided be-

tween the religious Jews and the labor-radical secularists. It was a period of turmoil and conflict, dissension and disorder; but it was also a period of new creativity.

With the turn of the century, unitive forces and processes began to make themselves felt. As the newcomers advanced in Americanization, prospered, and improved their social status, the cultural divergence between the two communities was narrowed and ethnic amalgamation encouraged through intermarriage of "Germans" and "Russians." Common enterprises and concerns also helped to bridge the chasm. Mounting persecution of Jews abroad—the Dreyfus case, the Russian and Rumanian pogroms, the Beilis blood libel—roused American Jewry to united protest. Philanthropy at home and abroad established contacts that improved with time.[20] The European "minority" problems in the Versailles settlements as they affected the Jews called for united American Jewish intervention. "Defense" against manifestations of anti-Semitism at home also stimulated a "German-Russian" rapprochement. The labor-radical secession, however, was not to be overcome till almost the fourth decade of the new century.

Interpenetration and amalgamation of the two communities were reflected in institutional development. In 1899 a National Conference of Jewish Charities was established in which all elements of American Jewry were somehow represented. The American Jewish Committee, formed in 1906 to champion the common interests of American Jewry, was originally "uptown" and "German" in composition, but before long prominent "Russian" Jews were to be found in its ranks. The Reform movement itself was no longer "German" in an exclusive sense; more and more, East European Jews were making their way into the temples.[21] The B'nai B'rith, formed in 1843, remained predominantly "German" until well into the twentieth century, but the new immigrants found entry as their numbers increased and their position improved. The short-lived *kehillah* (over-all community organization), set up in New York in 1909 under Judah L. Magnes, embraced and was supported by almost all segments of the Jewish population except the ex-

treme radicals. Even the American Jewish Congress, which
emerged immediately after World War I as a pro-Zionist
and "democratically representative" movement of American
Jewry, neither desired to become, nor actually became, an
institutional instrument of the "Russians" against the "Germans." By that time the conflict was virtually over. Only
in patterns of education did notable differences remain, but
even there the establishment of the Bureau of Jewish Education as part of the New York *kehillah,* which it survived
as the Jewish Education Committee, tended to narrow the
cleavage. By 1924 American Jewry, despite all internal
divisions, already constituted a well-defined ethnic group.

By that time, however, all of the ethnic groups in America were entering upon a new phase of development that
could only end with their dissolution, or radical transformation, into a new structure of American society.

III

Like the earlier Sephardic settlers, the German Jews of the
nineteenth century, once they had become American and
produced one, perhaps two, native-born generations, came
increasingly to lose their sense of ethnic and cultural distinctiveness and to see themselves as essentially a religious
grouping. By the end of the century the older community
had stabilized itself as a community of Americans differing
from other Americans in little but religion. They had ceased
to be Spaniards, or Portuguese, or Germans, or whatever
else their forebears had been at the time of migration; they
were now Americans who remained Jews by virtue of their
religious affiliation. Such was their understanding of their
Jewishness.

Very different was the conception of the East European
Jews who were arriving by the hundreds of thousands. They
understood their Jewishness in terms of the religio-cultural
complex that had developed in the East European Jewish
communities through the previous centuries. Yiddish was
both the vehicle and expression of this culture, and Yiddish
they virtually identified with their Jewishness. Their predecessors, too, had tended to associate their religion with their

immigrant native language and culture, but that language and culture—Spanish, German, or whatever it may have been—was something shared with a vastly larger number of non-Jews, and so could hardly be equated with Jewishness. But Yiddish was the peculiar possession of Jews, the cultural mark of their Jewishness; indeed, in the Yiddish language "Yiddish" meant "Jewish" and could not be distinguished from it. In the eyes of the immigrants they were substantially identical.[22] Religion and the cultural matrix in which it happened to be embedded were fused into a single religio-cultural entity known as *Yiddishkait* (Jewishness). The secularists merely replaced the element of traditional religion in this complex with their particular radical gospel; for them, too, their Jewishness was *Yiddishkait*, virtually inconceivable apart from the Yiddish language and culture.

Both the religious and the secularist Jews in the new immigration were "cultural pluralists" insofar as they had any views on their future in their new home. They looked forward to the perpetuation of their Yiddish cultural community, with its language, literature, and ways of life, in the New World, and all their institutions were designed to achieve this end. This was not, in their minds at least, a rejection of America, but their way of adaptation to it without losing their Jewishness. When the Russian Jew undertook to teach Yiddish to the Turkish Jews on the East Side, he did so in order to make them both "real" Jews and better Americans.[23] How could one be a "real" Jew without knowing Yiddish?—while for a Jew to live on the East Side without knowing Yiddish was obviously to be some kind of foreigner.

Because religion and immigrant culture were so thoroughly fused as to seem almost indistinguishable, the East European immigrants came up against a shattering crisis as they confronted the second generation, their American sons and daughters. The second generation, desperately anxious to become unequivocally American, was resentful of the immigrant culture which the older generation seemed so eager to transmit to it. "The whole process of its upbringing had emphasized the contrast between 'American' and 'foreign'; for the children, Judaism was still associated with the foreign,"[24] because the Judaism they knew was indeed a foreign immigrant culture. Rejection of foreignness meant rejection of Jewishness and Judaism. The second generation, for the East European Jews even more than for their German and Sephardic predecessors, became indeed the "weakest link in the chain of Jewish continuity," an "in-between layer . . . which [had] broken with the Jewish past and [had] lost faith in a Jewish future."[25]

Reform leaders had anticipated this development and had expected that as the second generation turned away from its East European foreignness it would embrace the pattern of Judaism worked out under Reform auspices; had not Isaac Mayer Wise in 1897 insisted that Reform represented "the sentiment of American Judaism minus the idiosyncrasies . . . of late immigrants"?[26] The new Conservative movement, more traditional but equally American, also felt that this was its opportunity. The Jewish Theological Seminary was reorganized in 1902, with Solomon Schechter, himself an East European Jew who had become reader in rabbinics at Cambridge, as head. Schechter, despite his own origin, clearly saw the lines of development American Jewry would take; he predicted the ultimate dissolution of the transplanted Yiddish culture and urged American Jews to make themselves at home in America, master English, and learn Hebrew.[27] Under his guidance the association of Conservative rabbis (Rabbinical Assembly), which had been formed in 1900, was reinvigorated and the United Synagogue, a federation of Conservative congregations, was established in 1913. Even in Orthodoxy there were stirrings, which, however, did not receive institutional implementation until the 1920s, when an "American Orthodoxy" emerged with its seminary (Yeshiva College, later University, in New York), its rabbinical association (Rabbinical Council), and its synagogal federation (Union of Orthodox Jewish Congregations).[28]

But perhaps the most earnest effort to win the second generation was made by Reconstructionism, a movement within Conservatism created by Mordecai M. Kaplan. Reconstructionism strove to combine an extremely "liberal quasi-naturalistic theology with a conception of Judaism which saw the Jews in America as living in two "civilizations," one American and the other Jewish. Since the second generation did in fact live in two worlds, it was felt that this conception would find a favorable response in its ranks.

To some degree, Reform, Conservatism, American Orthodoxy, and Reconstructionism did make an impression on a certain segment of the second generation, but, by and large, this generation remained untouched and unaffected by any of the religious "parties" in American Jewry. For the young people who were breaking with the foreign religio-cultural heritage of their group were only too inclined to feel that no substitute was necessary; the age was one of militant secularism, and a clean break with religion seemed the best and surest way of becoming an American. Even Reconstructionism had little appeal for those who were not already somehow committed to Judaism; the second generation did indeed find itself in two "civilizations," but this duality was precisely what it was so eager to get rid of, and it was hardly to be attracted by a philosophy that desired to normalize and perpetuate it.

The characteristic response of the second generation was secularism. Yet it was secularism with a difference, for even in their secularism the young people of the second generation often showed the impress of the religion they were abandoning. Many of them became radicals and "internationalists," but their radicalism was usually quite different culturally from the radicalism of the immigrants, with whom they had little real contact. Others, in a reaction against devaluation, became Zionists; their "nationalism" was paradoxically also an effort to adjust themselves to America, where ethnic nationalism was a recognized feature of acculturation.[29] Both radicalism and Zionism were second-generation phenomena;[30] yet both were also somehow strangely "Jewish," for was not internationalist socialism a secularized version of the "universalist" aspect of Jewish messianism and Zionist nationalism a secularized version of the "particularist" aspect? Both grew in the 1920s and 1930s, strengthened by world developments; both began to wane in the next two decades, when the world situation changed and the third generation emerged.

IV

The emergence of the third generation changed the entire picture of American Jewry and Judaism in America. Each of the earlier immigrations, the Sephardic and the German, had had its third generation, but in both cases the emergence of the third generation had fallen in with a new and overwhelming wave of immigration, so that it was not this generation but the newcomers who came to define the character and structure of the Jewish community. Now, however, immigration was virtually at an end—the restrictive legislation of 1924 became the settled policy of the nation—and the third generation of East European stock that began to appear in the 1930s and 1940s became increasingly the decisive element. With the appearance of this generation, the whole aspect of American Jewry began to undergo a profound transformation, perhaps the most significant in its entire history on this continent.

The third generation played a role in American Jewry that was in many ways quite unique. Among other immigrant groups the emergence of the third generation regularly meant the approaching dissolution of the ethnic group, which the first generation had formed and the second generation had perforce been identified with. True, according to "Hansen's Law,"[31] the third generation, secure in its Americanness, was not unwilling to "remember" what the second generation had been so eager to "forget." But all that the third generation of the Italian or Polish group, for example, could, as Americans, remember was the religion of the grandfather; the immigrant language and culture and way of life were, of course, irretrievably gone. And so the emergence of the third generation meant the disappearance of the "Italianness" or the "Polishness" of the group, or rather its dissolution into the religious community.[32] With the Jews, however, it was different. The first and second generations of Jews in America repeated the common immigrant pattern: immigrant foreignness followed by an anxious effort to overcome that foreignness and become American. But the third generation of American Jews, instead of somehow finally getting rid of their Jewishness, as the Italians were getting rid of their "Italianness" and the Poles of their "Polishness," actually began to *reassert* their Jewish identification and to *return* to their Jewishness. They too were striving to "remember" what their parents had so often striven to "forget," but the content and consequences of their "remembering" were strikingly different.[33]

We can account for this anomaly by recalling that the Jews came to this country not merely as an immigrant group but also as a religious community; the name "Jewish" designated both without distinction. As the immigrant Jews developed their ethnic group in the United States, the same duality—and ambiguity—persisted: the Jewish community was both ethnic and religious, and was so understood by all except a few hard-bitten secularists, who tried to replace its religious character by a secular nationalism or culturalism. When the second generation rejected its Jewishness, it generally, though not universally, rejected both aspects at once. With the third generation, the foreign-immigrant basis of the ethnic group began to disappear and the ethnic group as such began to give way. Among the Jews, as among other immigrants, the advancing dissolution of the old ethnic group meant the returning identification of the third generation with the religious community of its forebears, but among the Jews alone this religious community bore the same name as the old ethnic group and was virtually coterminous with it. The young Jew for whom the Jewish immigrant-ethnic group had lost all meaning, because he was an American and not a foreigner, could still think of himself as a Jew, because to him being a Jew now meant identification with the Jewish religious community.[34] What the Jewish third generation "returned" to was, of course, that which, as American, it could "remember" of the heritage of its forebears—in other words, their religion —but in returning to the religion it was also returning to Jewishness, in a sense in which the Italian or Polish third generation, in returning to Catholicism, was *not* returning to "Italianness" or "Polishness." The dual meaning of "Jewish" as covering both ethnic group and religion made the "return" movement of the third generation into a source of renewed strength and vigor for the American Jewish community.[35]

The American Jewish community, under the sign of the third generation, was in many ways significantly different from what it had been in earlier decades. Many of the earlier tendencies were being carried to completion. Ethnic amalgamation of the many stocks and strains that had gone into American Jewry was now virtually accomplished. The Jews who had come to this country neither spoke the same language nor felt particularly eager to mix with other Jews of different origins; intermarriage had often been "opposed not simply on religious grounds, but also because it disrupted the continuity of the particular group—Lithuanian Jews objected to a German or Galician or Syrian daughter-in-law almost as violently as to a gentile, and to the latter even were she converted."[36] These bars had already begun to crumble with the second generation; by the time the third appeared, they had ceased to have any meaning whatsoever. Intermarriage within the Jewish community was rapid and unhampered, and a new American type of Jew, a mixture of many strains with the East European predominant, came into being.[37] Wide ethnic amalgamation within the Jewish group was accompanied by a somewhat reduced rate of outside intermarriage,[38] which now came to mean not ethnic but religious mixing.

In the same way, the earlier tendencies towards "bourgeoisification" were carried further with the third generation. "The evolving style of life of the group fell imperceptibly into the molds of American middle-class culture, although retaining distinctive features derived from the past."[39] The Jewish proletarian in the United States was, indeed, a man of one generation; it was his ambition that neither his son nor his daughter should follow him into the factory, and to make sure that this would be so he strained every effort to give them an education. Proportionately three times as many Jewish young people were going to college in 1950 as young Americans of their age generally.[40]

Jews were to be found increasingly in business, white-collar occupations, professions, government service, decreasingly in shops and factories. This trend was one characteristic of all immigrant groups as they became acculturated and acquired American goals and standards. "The difference between the Jew and the non-Jew in this area was one of degree rather than of kind. Both moved in the same direction; only the Jew moved at a faster pace. And for obvious reasons: the drift entailed a greater measure of urbanization and a higher education, and Jews had both."[41] With the new American and middle-class style of life came the dispersion of the older ethnic "ghettos" in the large cities. Jews had begun to move away from the areas of first settlement with the second generation or even earlier, but they still gathered in "Jewish" neighborhoods. Now they were leaving these "Jewish" neighborhoods and spreading out into the suburbs and other areas of third settlement, in line with the trend of the social and cultural strata to which they belonged. This change involved not merely an alteration in place of residence; it involved a certain transformation in the entire outlook and mode of life of the Jews making the shift.[42]

The third generation, as we have seen, felt secure in its Americanness and therefore no longer saw any reason for the attitude of rejection so characteristic of its predecessors. It therefore felt no reluctance about identifying itself as Jewish and affirming its Jewishness; on the contrary, such identification became virtually compelling since it was the only way in which the American Jew could now locate himself in the larger community. Third-generation attitudes became prevalent among all but the most "old-fashioned" elements in American Jewry. A recent survey of an eastern seaboard city of 127,000, with a Jewish community of some 8,500, found that "overwhelmingly those whom we interviewed, both young and old, wished to retain their Jewish identity. . . . This desire . . . was so strong as to constitute a firm obstacle to either assimilation or intermarriage."[43] The survey also found—and this is of major significance for our story—that "fully 97 per cent of the adolescents [teenagers from 13 to 20, all of the third generation], when

asked, 'What is a Jew?', replied in terms of religion," as
against 80 per cent of the parents (mostly of the second
generation). "The stressing of this fact by the teen-agers,"
it is cogently noted, "may well be considered indicative of
the fact that they were more thoroughly acculturated than
were their parents." With self-identification in religious
terms almost universal among American Jews, especially
the native-born, synagogue affiliation grew markedly in the
decade after World War II. The expansion of the synagogue is, indeed, one of the most striking features of
our time.[44] In the smaller towns and in the suburbs, as
distinct from New York and other metropolitan centers of
old Jewish settlement, the synagogue came to play a particularly salient role;[45] a very large proportion of the Jewish families belonged to it, and it was the center of community life.[46] Even many of the older people, after years of
indifference or hostility, renewed their association with it.

As the third generation began to "remember" the religion
of its ancestors, to the degree at least of affirming itself Jewish "in a religious sense," it also began to lose interest in
the ideologies and "causes" which had been so characteristic
of Jewish youth in earlier decades. Social radicalism virtually disappeared, and the passionate, militant Zionism
espoused by groups of American Jews until 1948 became
diffused into a vague, though by no means insincere, friendliness to the State of Israel.[47] The retreat from radicalism
and Zionism fell in with certain larger trends in American
life and was reinforced by historical developments, but the
surmounting of the anxieties and insecurities of the marginal
second generation undoubtedly played a major part.

Over and above, and within, the general movement for
religious identification, there could be discerned, in certain
sections of the third generation, a deeper religious concern,
motivated by a new need for self-understanding and authenticity. Serious works dealing with Jewish faith and destiny began to find interested readers precisely among the
most American segments of the Jewish community,[48] and
the response of Jewish students on the campuses and of the
younger married people in their communities to the new

religious thinking was markedly different from what had been customary in earlier decades.

What was the shape and form of the religion of the Jewish community in mid-twentieth century America? It was characterized by a far-reaching accommodation to the American pattern of religious life which affected all "denominations" in the American synagogue. The institutional system was virtually the same as in the major Protestant churches—the same corporate structure, the same proliferation of men's clubs, sisterhoods, junior congregations, youth groups, "young marrieds," Sunday school classes, discussion circles, adult education projects, breakfasts, "brunches," dinners, and suppers. With minor variations, "the arrangement of the synagogue, the traditional appurtenances of worship, and the religious ceremonies showed the effects of change wrought by the American environment."[49] The central place of the sermon, congregational singing, mixed choirs, organs, responsive readings, abbreviated services, the concluding benediction, and many other commonly accepted features obviously reflected the influence of familiar Protestant practice.

The pattern of holidays and ceremonials had also undergone considerable modification. There was weekly worship on Friday night (sometimes Saturday morning), usually poorly attended. There were the High Holy Days—Rosh Hashanah (New Year) and Yom Kippur (Day of Atonement)—at which attendance was at its maximum. Hanukkah, traditionally of minor importance, was much emphasized because of its seasonal coincidence with Christmas, and many "Christmas" customs (Hanukkah cards, massive gift-giving, "Uncle Max the Hanukkah Man" as the "Jewish Santa Claus") were associated with it. Passover, coming at Easter time and made into the occasion of family reunions, retained its traditional importance, though with changed significance. Novel, too, was the extraordinary prominence given to the boy's Bar Mitzvah (religious "coming of age" at thirteen); lavish Bar Mitzvah parties were the rule. For girls, there was "confirmation," though often a parallel Bas Mitzvah was introduced. Weddings and funerals were almost always religious affairs, with traditional procedures drastically modified along American lines.[50] Practices relating to memorials for the dead—*kaddish*, *yortsait*, and *yizkor*—were widespread and much stressed.

Of the elaborate and comprehensive system of ritual observance in traditional Judaism what remained was primarily circumcision, universally practiced, though not always in the proper ritual form; synagogue services, lighting candles, and occasionally making *kiddush* on Sabbath eve (Friday night); and a token *kashrut* (dietary law), primarily the avoidance of ham, pork, and similar forbidden foods.[51] "The rituals which had special appeal," the Sklare report concludes, "were those which were joyous, which marked the transition from one stage of life to another, which did not require a high degree of isolation from non-Jews, which did not demand rigorous devotion and daily attention, which were capable of acceptance to the larger community, and which this larger community had itself reserved for the sacred order." In Orthodox and Conservative, even in some Reform communities, there developed a curious form of vicarious observance by the rabbi, who was expected to live up more or less to the traditional standards which were no longer operative among the members of his congregation.[52]

The pattern of Jewish education showed the same thoroughgoing adaptation to familiar American practice, both in structure and methods. There were part-time afternoon classes, one-day (Sunday) schools, and full-time day schools. Almost all were avowedly religious—the secular Jewish school was virtually obsolete—and they were largely associated with the synagogue. A census of Jewish school enrollment in New York City and three suburban counties, taken in 1953–54, showed that about 32 per cent of Jewish children of elementary school age were receiving some kind of Jewish education; in the city the figure was only 28.3 per cent, while in the suburbs it was very much higher, 59.4 per cent. In both cases there was an increase over 1951–52. In other parts of the country the figures in many cases went beyond even those of suburban New York.[53]

In general, the religious pattern that emerged with the

new third-generation Jewish community was characteristically American, reflecting a far-reaching and systematic accommodation of the East European tradition to American reality.[54] The accommodation was not limited to one or another group in American Jewry; it was pervasive and affected all segments of the community, Orthodox as well as Conservative and Reform—whatever differences still remained were altogether secondary.[55] There was, in fact, under way a notable convergence between the three groups, or "denominations," in American Judaism, in everything at least except their institutional affiliations and loyalties. All were becoming American and therefore more and more like each other.

Reform Judaism had drastically modified the old Pittsburgh Platform at Columbus in 1937; the new Columbus Platform toned down much of the exuberant optimism of the earlier document, took a much more friendly attitude toward Zionism and Palestine, and placed a new emphasis on religious rituals and practices.[56] American Orthodoxy, as distinct from the immigrant Orthodoxy that still remained, adopted American ways and procedures which inevitably involved extensive changes in the traditional pattern. Thus, while Reform moved to the "right," American Orthodoxy moved substantially to the "left." In between stood Conservatism, particularly suited to the new temper and therefore apparently growing faster than either of its rivals. The Sklare report reveals that whereas over 80 per cent of the grandparents in the Jewish community under survey had been Orthodox, less than 20 per cent of the parents were, most of them having become Conservative (40 per cent) or Reform (30 per cent). Less than a fifth of the teen-agers in Orthodox homes declared their intention of remaining Orthodox; the great majority said they would become Conservative. Both Conservatism and Reform appeared to be holding their own in that community. "The Orthodox adults were primary immigrants," the report continues; "the Reform and Conservative people were overwhelmingly native born. . . . The pattern as it emerges is that of an adult group coming originally from an Orthodox background, but which now considers itself largely Con-

servative or Reform. . . . The Conservative synagogue
seems to be keeping most of its older congregants, as well
as gaining new adherents from the offspring of the Orthodox
families, and even from the scions of *fin de siècle* Bundists
(secular-minded Jewish socialists)." While these results
cannot be generalized without further ado, they would
seem to be indicative of what is going on among American
Jews in most parts of the United States.

As the new religious pattern of American Jewry began to
define itself, it became increasingly clear that, with certain
qualifications (discarding of Sunday services, a more positive attitude to Zionism), what was emerging resembled
very closely the original moderate Reform program. Samuel S. Cohon was quite justified in asserting: "The Conservative and Reconstructionist movements have been following in the footsteps of Reform";[57] indeed, he might
almost have included American Orthodoxy as well. And yet,
while the Reform program was thus triumphing, the Reform
movement did not seem to be making any comparable headway. Reform, which in the 1870s seemed to be destined
to carry everything before it, was overwhelmed by the deluge of East European immigration. To the East European
Jew, whether religious or secular, the kind of Judaism
championed by Reform appeared ridiculous, even abhor-
rent. Reform, therefore, was driven into retreat, and Orthodoxy became dominant. With advancing Americanization,
however, the East European Jews themselves began to
make their adaptations and adjustments to American life,
in the field of religion as in every other field. Orthodoxy
began to change, and Conservatism came to the fore as the
characteristic expression of the acculturated East European
Jew. What resulted was substantially similar to moderate
Reform, but since it had not come about through direct
Reform influence, but rather through the continuing pressure of the American environment, it was not recognized as
having any relation to the older Reform idea. Not Reform
but Conservatism thus became the prime beneficiary of the
Americanization of Judaism in this country. But this was
only a matter of degree; by the mid-century all three of

the "denominations" were substantially similar expressions of the new American Jewish religious pattern, differing only in background, stage of development, and institutional affiliation.

V

There would seem to be about 5,500,000 Jews in the United States today—rather more perhaps, though some say less—making up about 3.2 per cent of the American people. There is every evidence that the American Jewish population has in recent years not been keeping pace with population growth in the country as a whole, though here again there is no assurance as to future trends. American Jews are predominantly middle-class in economic and social structure, in culture and outlook. They are a highly urbanized group; about 40 per cent of all American Jews are to be found in New York, and about 75 per cent in five metropolitan communities. They are very well represented in the contemporary movement to the suburbs; the suburban Jewish community is becoming an important element in American Jewry.[58]

It is hard to say with any accuracy how many American Jews are affiliated with the synagogue. A recent poll showed 50 per cent of American Jews replying affirmatively to the question, "Do you happen at the present time to be an active member of a church or of a religious group?"[59] Estimates of synagogue membership vary all the way from 2,000,000 to 3,750,000. But all agree that membership is increasing, particularly in the growing suburban communities. Many more presumably feel themselves associated with the synagogue, and attend High Holy Day services, than are actually enrolled.

Figures for the three "denominations" in American Jewry are no more precise. In 1953–54 Reform claimed 461 congregations, Conservatives 473, and American Orthodoxy 720, with an uncertain number, mostly of the older Orthodoxy, unaffiliated.[60] Though in their patterns of religious thought and practice the three groups have been converging, their antagonisms and rivalries have by no means diminished; precisely because they are, increasingly, making very much the same kind of appeal to very much the same kind of people, their institutional competition has been growing sharper, if anything, and the possibilities of unity, or even united action in the religious sphere, more remote.[61] There are, it is true, a number of all-inclusive bodies, such as the Jewish Welfare Board, which was formed in 1917 to minister to the religious and social needs of Jewish soldiers and has since been performing a variety of other functions; the Synagogue Council of America, set up in 1926 as a delegate body of the three "parties" for their common interests; and local joint rabbinical associations. But these are all agencies for specific purposes and are vested with very limited powers; they do not bring American Jewry much nearer to the religious unity that all profess to desire. The situation is particularly anomalous since among the armed forces in World War II, where official "party" lines could not be preserved and Jewish chaplains had to serve their people simply as Jews, a common pattern—essentially Conservative—quickly developed that overrode the rivalries that loom so large in civilian life.[62]

Whatever may be the institutional situation at the moment, it is incontrovertible that the Jewish community in the United States has become a religious community in its own understanding, as well as in the understanding of the non-Jew. Old-line secular Judaism is obsolescent. "The type of secular Jewish organizations which existed around the turn of the century, and for some years thereafter," the Sklare report finds, "are hardly a force today." But while Jewish community life has become more religious in this sense, it has also become more secularist in another. Virtually all Jewish children become Bar Mitzvah today,[63] as was not the case twenty, thirty, or forty years ago, but the Bar Mitzvah is usually nothing but a lavish and expensive party, with the religious aspect reduced to insignificance, if not altogether ignored.[64] Much of the institutional life of the synagogue has become thus secularized and drained of religious content precisely at the time when religion is becoming more and more acknowledged as the meaning of Jewishness.[65]

The Jewish community in the United States presents an anomalous picture in other ways as well. It has no over-all organization, and every attempt to give it one so as to eliminate "overlapping" and "conflict" has failed.[66] It has, therefore, all along given the appearance of hopeless chaos and confusion. And yet this community without central control is capable of great communal efforts;[67] without over-all organization, it yet embraces the vast majority of American Jews.[68] In the last analysis, it is, as we have had occasion to note, based on a voluntarism that is characteristically American.[69]

But perhaps it is not correct to say that the American Jewish community possesses no over-all organization. It does possess what comes close to being a single hierarchical structure embracing the entire community, and that is the machinery of fund raising and fund allocation.[70] Not the synagogal bodies but the fund-raising agencies, combined in the Council of Jewish Federations and Welfare Funds (1932), and operating mainly through the United Jewish Appeal (1940), reach into every nook and cranny of the land to establish connections with the tiniest of Jewish groups.[71] "Fund raising [among American Jews] has reached an exceptionally high level of efficiency. The Jews contribute considerably more per capita than any comparable group in the United States . . ." But fund raising is not simply a financial operation. "The initial efforts to establish welfare funds and federations soon disclosed that it was not possible to restrict the new organizations to problems connected with the collection of funds. Relatively early in the development of these welfare funds, it became clear that there was a close relationship—an inevitable one—between unified efforts at fund raising and unified control over allocations."[72] Since all Jewish institutions raise funds under centralized control and virtually all are in some way dependent on allocations, it is by no means far-fetched to think of the vast and complex machinery of fund raising and allocation as in fact the organizational armature of the American Jewish community.

From the very beginning, from the first settlements in New York, Newport, Philadelphia, and Charleston, the Jews in America strove to become American and establish themselves as an American community. Twice in the nineteenth century the measure of stability they had achieved was upset by new waves of immigration, which vastly increased their numbers and enriched their heritage, but also threw into confusion the patterns of accommodation they had developed in their adjustment to American life. Finally, as America approached mid-twentieth century, the confusion began to subside and the shape and form of Judaism in America, reflecting the rise of a secure and confident third generation, began to emerge. The American Jewish community became integrally part of American society; the American Jew was now in the position where he could establish his Jewishness not apart from, nor in spite of, his Americanness, but precisely through and by virtue of it. Judaism had achieved its status in the American Way of Life as one of the three "religions of democracy."

And yet among some American Jews there was perplexity and restlessness. Was this all there was to Judaism after all? Had it no higher purpose or destiny? What was it, in the last analysis, that made the Jew a Jew, and kept him a Jew? A young Jewish sociologist, at mid-century point, formulated his perplexity in a way that was bound to find an echo in many of the third generation: "A social group with clearly marked boundaries exists, but the source of the energies that hold [it] separate, and of the ties that bind it together, has become completely mysterious."[73]

FOOTNOTES

1. No adequate history of American Jewry to the present day exists. Three recent studies, from very different standpoints, are: Oscar Handlin, *Adventure in Freedom: Three Hundred Years of Jewish Life in America* (McGraw-Hill, 1954), Rufus Learsi, *The Jews in America: A History* (World, 1954), and Nathan Glazer, *American Judaism* (Chicago, 1957). Older works include Lee J. Levinger, *History of the Jews in the United States* (Union of American Hebrew Congregations, Cincinnati, 1932) and Peter Wiernick, *History of the Jews in America* (Jewish

History Publishing Company, New York, 1912). Moses Rischin, *An Inventory of American Jewish History* (Harvard, 1954) is very useful. Charles B. Sherman, *Jews and Other Ethnic Groups in the United States* (in Yiddish; Ferlag Unzer Veg, 1945) is a valuable study. Oscar Janowsky, ed., *The American Jew: A Composite Portrait* (Harper, 1942) and Theodore Friedman and Robert Gordis, eds., *Jewish Life in America* (Horizon, 1955) include a number of significant essays on aspects of Judaism in America. Isacque Graeber, Steuart Henderson Britt, and others, *Jews in a Gentile World* (Macmillan, 1941) includes much relevant material on American Jews. Elliot E. Cohen, ed., *Commentary on the American Scene: Portraits of Jewish Life in America* (Knopf, 1953) contains many significant insights. The Tercentenary Issue of *Judaism* (Vol. III, No. 4, Fall 1954) features articles relevant to the development of American Jewry. Marshall Sklare, *Conservative Judaism: An American Religious Movement* (Free Press, 1955) is the first really adequate sociological study of Jewish religion in America. Two interesting community studies are to be found in Albert I. Gordon, *Jews in Transition* (University of Minnesota Press, 1949), and Stanley K. Bigman, *The Jewish Population of Greater Washington in 1956* (Jewish Community Council of Greater Washington, 1957). Moshe Davis, *The Shaping of American Judaism* (in Hebrew; Jewish Theological Seminary, New York, 1951) deals primarily with the development of Jewish religion in America. Louis Finkelstein, ed., *The Jews: Their History, Culture, and Religion*, 4 vols. (Jewish Publication Society, 1949) contains a number of relevant essays. Marshall Sklare, ed., *The Jews: Social Patterns of an American Group* (Free Press, 1958) is a valuable collection. Volume 56 (1955) of the *American Jewish Year Book* contains three special articles: Nathan Glazer, "Social Characteristics of American Jews, 1654–1954"; Oscar and Mary F. Handlin, "The Acquisition of Political and Social Rights by Jews in the United States"; and Joseph L. Blau, "The Spiritual Life of American Jewry, 1654–1954." Glazer's excellent study is particularly relevant to this and earlier chapters. See also: "Jewish Religious Life in America," *Information Service*, February 11, 1956, and "Report on American Rabbis," *Information Service*, November 30, 1957. Albert I. Gordon's *Jews in Suburbia* (Beacon, 1959) is a valuable survey.

2. Oscar and Mary Handlin, "A Century of Jewish Immigration to the United States," *American Jewish Year Book*, Vol. 50 (American Jewish Committee, 1949), p. 11.

3. See Rudolf Glanz, "Jews in Relation to the Cultural Milieu of the Germans in America up to the Eighteen Eighties" (in Yiddish), *Yivo Bleter*, Vol. XXV, Nos. 1 and 2.

4. Handlin, *Adventure in Freedom*, pp. 71–72.

5. A survey of Jewish communities in the United States in

1860 is to be found in Learsi, *The Jews in America*, pp. 66–75.

6. Handlin, *Adventure in Freedom*, p. 76. Handlin adds: "To the well-established native American Jews, this was no danger. Judaism was not 'foreign' to their children, as it was to the children of Germans and Poles."

7. Quoted by Handlin, *Adventure in Freedom*, p. 76.

8. On messianism: "We recognize in the modern era of universal culture of heart and intellect the approaching of the realization of Israel's great messianic hope for the establishment of the Kingdom of Truth, Justice, and Peace among men." The attitude on Palestine was not so much a rejection of modern Zionism, since Zionism was of little significance in America in the 1880s; it was primarily a repudiation of biblical-rabbinic "particularism" and an affirmation of the fulfillment of Jewish destiny in the context of Western civilization. For the Pittsburgh Platform, see *Year Book of the Central Conference of American Rabbis*, Vol. I, pp. 120–23.

9. "Historical Judaism," too, had its German inspiration. It derived from the position taken in Germany by Zecharias Frankel in his struggle against Reform. See Louis Ginzberg, *Students, Scholars, and Saints* (Jewish Publication Society, 1928), chap. viii, pp. 195–216.

10. Handlin, *Adventure in Freedom*, pp. 84–85; also Handlin, "A Century of Jewish Immigration in the United States," *American Jewish Year Book*, Vol. 50 (1949), pp. 11–13.

11. Handlin, *Adventure in Freedom*, p. 84.

12. Sherman, "Jewish Economic Adjustment in the U.S.A.," *The Reconstructionist*, December 18, 1953.

13. "Comparing the Jews with their sociological counterparts —ethnics who arrived at the same time and in about the same numbers—we find that the Jews have been more mobile than any of their fellows. . . . In contrast to other groups, social mobility in the Jewish community frequently begins with the first rather than the second generation" (Sklare, *Conservative Judaism: An American Religious Movement*, pp. 26, 48). "Statistics demonstrate that the rise in the social and economic position of the Jew has been extremely rapid, far surpassing that which can be shown for any other immigrant group, and indeed surpassing for the same period changes in the socioeconomic position of long-settled groups" (Glazer, "Social Characteristics of American Jews, 1654–1954," *American Jewish Year Book*, Vol. 56 [1955], p. 29).

14. "Romanian Jews formed the backbone of the Carmen Sylva Association in New York, a nonsectarian society named after the queen of their former homeland and dedicated to the study of its literature. Similarly, Jewish intellectuals played a

prominent role in Russian radical circles in the late nineteenth century and in the first two decades of the twentieth century" (Handlin, *Adventure in Freedom,* p. 121).

15. Handlin, *Adventure in Freedom,* p. 113. "Between 1880 and 1920, American Jewry was completely transformed. In 1880, they numbered about 250,000, approximately one-half of one per cent of the total population of some 50,000,000. In 1920, about 3,500,000 of the 106,000,000 inhabitants of the United States were Jews—nearly 3½ per cent of the population. Moreover, in 1880, the relatively small number of Jews blended with the American environment. They were members of the respectable middle class, not too concentrated in any particular locality, and at home in the language and mores of the country. However, during the last two decades, and especially after the turn of the century, as the flood of East European immigration continued, the mass of American Jewry became conspicuous as an immigrant element. In several large cities, they lived huddled together in 'ghettos,' spoke their own tongue, and perpetuated customs and ideas which appeared alien to many of their co-religionists, whose parents and grandparents had had the foresight to embark upon previous sailings and cultivate their own 'alien' habits in a previous generation" (Janowsky, *The JWB Survey* [Dial, 1948], p. 239).

16. For an account of "Orthodoxy in Transition" in Chicago, see Sklare, *Conservative Judaism: An American Religious Movement,* chap. ii, pp. 43–65.

17. Handlin, *Adventure in Freedom,* p. 119.

18. See Will Herberg, "The Jewish Labor Movement in the United States," *American Jewish Year Book,* Vol. 53 (1952), esp. pp. 29–30. For a valuable study of the Jewish labor movement, see Melech Epstein, *Jewish Labor in the U.S.A.,* 2 vols. (Trade Union Sponsoring Committee, New York, 1950, 1953).

19. "The way of the East European Jew in these years parted company on so many counts with the 'German' Jew, the product of an earlier migration. The necessities of each group had led it, since 1870, to create its own institutional life. The newcomer could no sooner worship on Sunday to the accompaniment of the temple's organ, than the native would be found downtown on his way to the Yiddish theater. They seemed almost to inhabit two distinct communities" (Handlin, *Adventure in Freedom,* p. 142). As indicative both of economic and social status and of place of residence, the two communities were referred to respectively as "Uptown" and "East Side."

20. "The marked degree of heterogeneity which long characterized American Jewry—largely a reflection of successive and continuing waves of immigrants from different parts of Europe —placed almost insuperable hurdles in the path of group action;

for a long time, the only meeting ground was 'charity.' Irrespective of one's social or economic status, or political or religious beliefs, it was possible to join with others to raise funds for the Jewish needy at home and abroad" (Eli Ginzberg, *Agenda for American Jews* [King's Crown, 1950], p. 17).

21. A study made between 1928 and 1930 of forty-nine Reform temples in the eleven cities whose Jewish population was then over 50,000 showed that: "About equal proportions of Temple members are of German parentage and of East European parentage. However, considering the foreign-born responders by themselves, the proportion of those born in Germany proves to be considerably less than those born in East European countries (33 per cent of foreign-born responders were born in Germany; 57 per cent were born in East European countries). This is indicative of a marked increase in the enrollment of Jews of East European origin in the ranks of Reform within the space of one generation" (*Reform Judaism in the Large Cities: A Survey* [Union of American Hebrew Congregations, Cincinnati, 1931], p. 10).

22. I remember once speaking to a group of East European immigrants long resident in this country, but still retaining their Yiddish cultural identification. I happened to mention that Maimonides, the great Jewish sage, was Arabic-speaking and could not possibly have known any Yiddish. One of the audience, an elderly man, listened intently, and then broke out sarcastically in Yiddish: *"Eikh mir a Yid!"* ("You call that a Jew!"). In his eyes, even Maimonides could not rate as a "real" Jew because he did not know any Yiddish.

23. See Handlin, *Adventure in Freedom*, p. 162.

24. Handlin, *Adventure in Freedom*, pp. 162–63.

25. Sherman, "Three Generations," *Jewish Frontier*, Vol. XXI, No. 7 (229), July 1954.

26. Quoted in Handlin, *Adventure in Freedom*, p. 157.

27. See Norman Bentwich, *Solomon Schechter* (Jewish Publication Society, 1938), pp. 213–14.

28. Some of these institutions had been launched considerably earlier, but were transformed when American Orthodoxy emerged. The Yeshiva Rabbi Isaac Elchanan was established along older lines in 1896–97, but was reorganized when Yeshiva College was set up in 1927–28; the college was expanded into a university in 1945.

29. See above, chap. ii, pp. 17–18.

30. "Zionism was the outlet, particularly for the second generation. This group was especially perplexed, as all second generations were, by the question of their place in American culture, confused by specific problems of social and economic adjust-

ment, and anxious over the meaning of anti-Semitism. Americans tended to be extremists in the world Zionist movement, in no small measure because they carried into it the whole burden of their worries and fears as American Jews" (Handlin, *Adventure in Freedom*, p. 217). For the meaning of second-generation radicalism, see Sherman, "Three Generations," *Jewish Frontier*, Vol. XXI, No. 7 (229), July 1954.

31. "Hansen's Law": "What the son wishes to forget, the grandson wishes to remember." (See above, chap. iii, p. 30.)

32. See above, chap. iii, pp. 30–31.

33. For some comments on the Jewish third generation, see Herberg, "Religious Trends in American Jewry," *Judaism*, Vol. III, No. 3, Summer 1954; and Sherman, "Three Generations," *Jewish Frontier*, Vol. XXI, No. 7 (229), July 1954.

34. "As their immigrant antecedents receded, their identification remained most meaningful in the area of diversity which America most clearly recognized—that of religion" (Handlin, *Adventure in Freedom*, p. 250).

35. "The differences that distinguished the development of the Jewish community in the United States from that of all other white ethnic groups stand out in bold relief when the role played in their communal affairs by the native generations they have produced is compared. Insofar as the non-Jewish settlements constitute centers of ethnic, social, and cultural activities, they represent immigrant colonies. Rarely do American-born children of these immigrants engage in those activities, and their children's children hardly ever. As for the great-grandchildren, they have no organized affiliation whatsoever with the ethnic groups of their origin. It is not so in the case of the Jews. They were a disjointed and fragmentized community during their early sojourn in this country, and became a consolidated community precisely when they ceased to be an immigrant settlement" (Sherman, "Three Generations," *Jewish Frontier*, Vol. XXI, No. 7 [229], July 1954). In other words, thorough acculturation of American Jews has led not to assimilation but to a stronger affirmation of Jewishness; see also Sklare, *Conservative Judaism: An American Religious Movement*, p. 34. See also Nathan Glazer, "The Jewish Revival in America," *Commentary*, December 1955, January 1956.

36. Handlin, *Adventure in Freedom*, p. 164.

37. "Not only is the Jewish community greatly influenced by the American cultural melting pot; it is also going through a process of miniature melting pot fusion of its own, with its subethnic ingredients rapidly combining to produce the pattern of the native American Jew. The overwhelming majority of American Jews are East European in origin. It is this group and its descendants that is in the process of absorbing all others in a

miniature internal Jewish melting pot, with a resultant cultural
pattern where the Jewish residues are distinctly of East European origin, but not without contributions from other groups.
. . . The East European majority slowly but surely manages to
absorb, by marriage and influence, groups that are less related
culturally, such as the Sephardic and even Yemenite" (Abraham G. Duker, "Emerging Culture Patterns in American Jewish
Life," *Publications of the American Jewish Historical Society*,
No. xxxix, part 4, June 1950).

38. "All rates of Jewish intermarriage are found to be low,
most of them ranging from one per cent to ten per cent" (Mil-
ton L. Barron, *People Who Intermarry* [Syracuse, 1946], p.
341). For other information on intermarriage, see Nathan Glazer,
"What Sociology Knows About American Jews," *Commentary*,
Vol. IX, No. 3, March 1950; also Hershel Shanks, "Jewish-
Gentile Intermarriage: Facts and Trends," *Commentary*, Vol.
XVI. No. 4, October 1953.

39. Handlin, *Adventure in Freedom*, p. 254.

40. See Robert Shosteck, "Jewish Students in American Universities," *American Jewish Year Book*, Vol. 50 (1949), pp.
767–74.

41. Sherman, "Jewish Economic Adjustment in the U.S.A.,"
The Reconstructionist, December 18, 1953. "In many ways, the
Jewish group became more rapidly and successfully adjusted to
life in America than the other immigrant groups. This has been
true with reference to participation in civic life, and educational
achievement" (Charles F. Marden, *Minorities in American Society* [American Book Company, 1952], p. 415).

42. For a very suggestive discussion of what is implied in the
shift from areas of second to areas of third settlement, see Sklare,
Conservative Judaism: An American Religious Movement, pp.
47–48, 67–72.

43. Marshall Sklare, *Forms and Expressions of Jewish Identification*, unpublished report presented at the Tercentenary Conference on American Jewish Sociology, convened by the Conference on Jewish Relations, New York, November 27–28, 1954;
all future references to the Sklare survey are to this report. A
good deal of the material of this report is presented in: Marshall
Sklare and Mark Vosk, *The Riverton Study: How Jews Look at
Themselves and Their Neighbors* (American Jewish Committee,
1957).

44. See Herberg, "The Postwar Revival of the Synagogue,"
Commentary, Vol. IX, No. 4, April 1950.

45. "The synagogue symbolizes the most important change in
the move to Suburbia—a change in our concept of ourselves as
Jews. In the rest of the country, the leaders of the Jewish community can argue about who represents The Jews. . . . In Sub-

urbia, there is no question about who speaks for us. . . . The closest thing to a Jewish community in the United States is the suburban synagogue. . . . The Jew is perforce a member of his religious community. Even if he refuses to accept formal membership, he does not openly dispute the synagogue's right to speak for him" (Harry Gersh, "The New Suburbanites of the 50's," *Commentary*, Vol. XVII, No. 3, March 1954). Mr. Gersh suggests a reason: ". . . in the city . . . we found it unnecessary to think seriously of ourselves as Jews." In the city, living in a "Jewish" neighborhood, one may unconsciously continue to accept one's Jewishness in residual terms of ethnic "belonging"; in the suburbs and in most smaller towns this is no longer possible: one must begin to think "seriously" of his Jewishness, and the only possible outcome of such thinking in present-day America is identification with the Jewish religious community, frequently leading to affiliation with the synagogue. See also the very interesting survey article by John Wicklein in the *New York Times* for April 5, 1959, headed "Judaism on Rise in the Suburbs."

46. See Max Arzt, "The Synagogue and the Center in Contemporary Jewish Life," *Judaism*, Vol. III, No. 4, Fall 1954.

47. From the Sklare report: "We find that the answers to 'How do you feel about the State of Israel?' indicate that almost unanimously both parents and teen-agers possess positive feelings about the State of Israel. . . . Answers to the other important question, 'Would you like to live in Israel?' [show that] almost nine out of ten respondents, both among the teen-agers and the parents, answer in the negative." "With the establishment of the State of Israel, the zeal of American Zionism was spent and the movement is presently being slowly deflated to minor proportions" (Jacob B. Agus, *Guideposts in Modern Judaism: An Analysis of Current Trends* [Bloch, 1954], p. 13). A number of Zionists, however, maintain that American Zionism was never very real. Thus Eliezer Livneh writes: "The truth is that there never existed in America a Zionist movement in the accepted (European) sense of the term. Zionist organizations in America *always* have had a purely pro-Israel character and no more" (*State and Diaspora* [Jewish Agency, Jerusalem, 1953], p. 15).

48. Among recently published works in the new spirit may be mentioned: Ludwig Lewisohn, *The American Jew: Character and Destiny* (Farrar, Straus, 1950); Abraham J. Heschel, *Man Is Not Alone: A Philosophy of Religion* (Farrar, Straus, 1951); *Man's Quest for God* (Scribner's, 1954); *God in Search of Man: A Philosophy of Judaism* (Farrar, Straus, 1955); Herberg, *Judaism and Modern Man: An Interpretation of Jewish Religion* (Farrar, Straus, 1951). Translations and interpretations of Martin Buber's works, and *Franz Rosenzweig: His Life and Thought*,

presented by Nahum N. Glatzer (Schocken, 1953), have exerted significant influence.

49. Handlin, *Adventure in Freedom*, p. 255.

50. For an interesting account, with many details, see Duker, "Emerging Culture Patterns in American Jewish Life," *Publications of the American Jewish Historical Society*, No. xxxix, part 4, June 1950.

51. Despite the relatively slight observance of *kashrut*, there has developed a very considerable "kosher" and "kosher-style" food industry, with an appeal by no means limited to observant Jews, or to Jews only. Use of these foods does not by any means imply observance of *kashrut*.

52. "There has developed," notes Eli Ginzberg, "especially among the large sector of American Jewry which is affiliated with Conservative congregations, a marked dichotomy between the behavior of the vast majority of the congregants, which is largely non-observant, and the expected and required behavior of the rabbi" (*Agenda for American Jews*, p. 16). That this "dichotomy" is not limited to Conservatives is indicated by the following statement of an Orthodox publicist, who quotes a member of an Orthodox synagogue as saying: "There is no difference in ritual observance [between the Orthodox and the non-Orthodox], except that they don't care if their rabbi, too, isn't observant, whereas we want the rabbi to eat kosher and keep Shabbes" (Trude Weiss-Rosmarin, "From a Lecturer's Notebook," *Jewish Spectator*, April 1945).

53. For New York and suburban counties, Israel S. Chipkin, "Census of Jewish School Enrollment (1953–54)," *JEC Bulletin*, No. 92, December 1954. For the country as a whole, see Uriah Zevi Engelman, "Jewish School Enrollment," *American Jewish Year Book*, Vol. 56 (1955), pp. 247–51. A comprehensive survey of Jewish education in this country is to be found in Alexander M. Dushkin and Uriah Z. Engelman, *Jewish Education in the United States: Report of the Commission for the Study of Jewish Education in the United States*, Vol. I (American Association for Jewish Education, 1959); see especially Chap. III, "Is Jewish Education Wanted—How Much and What Kind" (pp. 39–68).

54. An extensive syncretism of practice has developed among many Jews in which, for example, Christmas and Hanukkah are both celebrated, sometimes together. This, indeed, has become so common that the Jerusalem Bible Publishing Company, advertising the "first complete Bible in English and Hebrew ever to be printed in the Holy Land," a publication "hailed by religious and lay leaders and sanctioned by the Chief Rabbinate," recommends it as the "most appropriate and everlasting gift for

Christmas and Chanukah" (*New York Post,* December 12, 1954).

55. "Reform Judaism [is] retracing its steps to the middle ground in Judaism, so much so that it is difficult to distinguish between some Conservative synagogues and Reform temples. . . . [It is also] frequently difficult to distinguish between an Orthodox and a 'right-wing' Conservative synagogue, services, and functionaries" (Duker, "On Religious Trends in American Jewish Life," *Yivo Annual of Jewish Social Science,* Vol. IV [1949], pp. 58–59, 60.) The newer tendencies in the Reform movement have met with strong protest from the remaining representatives of old-line "classical" Reform. "Reform [in the United States] has been faithless to its own spirit," Rabbi Morris S. Lazaron charged recently. "Reform has accomplished many good things and has grown in numbers, but it has lost its soul! It has been swept from its ancient moorings" ("Reform Judaism in Europe and in the U.S.A.," *Jewish Newsletter,* Vol. XI, No. 11, May 30, 1955).

56. See Samuel S. Cohon, "The Contemporary Mood in Reform Judaism," *The Journal of Bible and Religion,* Vol. XVIII, No. 3, July 1950. For the Columbus Platform, see *Yearbook of the Central Conference of American Rabbis,* Vol. LXVII, pp. 94–100.

57. Cohon, "The Contemporary Mood in Reform Judaism," *The Journal of Bible and Religion,* Vol. XVIII, No. 3, July 1950. Actually, a curious double shift has taken place: (a) Schechter's original program—English sermons, decorum at services, modern pedagogical methods (see Sklare, *Conservative Judaism: An American Religious Movement,* p. 235)—has become the avowed program of so-called "modern Orthodoxy," while Conservatism has taken over substantially the earlier Reform program (with the exceptions noted). In both cases, the development has been brought about by the force of circumstances rather than conscious influence; the two types of adaptation, moreover, constitute phases in the same pattern, rather than divergent paths.

58. For demographical information on American Jewry, see: Alvin Chenkin and Ben B. Seligman, "Jewish Population of the United States, 1953," *American Jewish Year Book,* Vol. 55 (1954), pp. 3–12; Nathan Goldberg, "The Jewish Population of the United States," *The Jewish People, Past and Present* (Central Yiddish Culture Organization, New York, 1948), Vol. II, pp. 25–34; Sophia M. Robison, "How Many Jews in America?", *Commentary,* Vol. VIII, No. 2, August 1949; Ben B. Seligman, "The American Jew: Some Demographic Features," *American Jewish Year Book,* Vol. 51 (1950), pp. 3–52; Erich Rosenthal, "Five Million American Jews: Progress in Demography," *Commentary,* December 1958. The latest estimate of Jews in America, made by the U. S. Census Bureau in 1957, gives 5,900,000 Jews, or

3.2 per cent of the population (see above, chap. iv, pp. 64–65, note 2). The *American Jewish Year Book*, 1959 edition, reports 5,260,000 Jews in the United States (p. 3).

59. "Who Belongs to What Church?", *The Catholic Digest*, January 1953. The corresponding figures for Catholics and Protestants were 87 per cent and 75 per cent; for the nation as a whole it was 73 per cent. The impossible figure 5,000,000 (the entire body of American Jews) for synagogue membership in the United States seems to have arisen because "the Jewish agent [of the U. S. Census of Religious Bodies] decided that he would get estimates of the total number of Jews in each city or town, on the theory that, in an ideological sense, all Jews are members of the congregation" (Robison, "How Many Jews in America?", *Commentary*, Vol. VIII, No. 2, August 1949).

60. See Learsi, *The Jews in America: A History*, p. 352. Sklare is of the opinion that "probably the number of adherents of Reform, Conservative, and Orthodoxy is roughly similar at present" (*Conservative Judaism: An American Religious Movement*, p. 25). See also Herbert Parzen, "Religion," *American Jewish Year Book*, Vol. 52 (1951), pp. 86–87, and "Jewish Religious Life in America," *Information Service*, February 11, 1956.

61. Many of the Orthodox refuse even to recognize Reform and Conservative rabbis as rabbis, and refrain from calling them by that title, since Reform and Conservative rabbis do not have Orthodox ordination; they employ instead such terms as "clergyman," "minister," "spiritual leader," or even "Reverend." On the other hand, there are cases, as in Cambridge, Massachusetts, where a single rabbi (Orthodox) serves two congregations, one Orthodox, the other Conservative (*Boston Daily Herald*, September 18, 1954).

62. See Philip Bernstein, "Jewish Chaplains in World War II," *American Jewish Year Book*, Vol. 47 (1946), pp. 173–200; also Isaac Klein, "Experiences of a Jewish Chaplain," *Yivo Bleter* (Yiddish), Vol. XXVII, 1946.

63. Even the secularist Workmen's Circle schools now conduct "special Bar Mitzvah classes."

64. A typical Bar Mitzvah invitation announces a "Bar Mitzvah Reception" at a big hall in Brooklyn for six o'clock Saturday evening, and then adds in tiny type in the corner: "Religious Services at 10:30 A.M. . . ."

65. See Herberg, "The Postwar Revival of the Synagogue," *Commentary*, Vol. IX, No. 4, April 1950, esp. pp. 321–25. A striking expression of this thoroughgoing secularization of Jewish religious life may be found in the statements issued by Jewish leaders on the occasion of Passover. Neither God nor his gracious act of redemption in the Exodus—the authentic and traditional content of Passover—is ever mentioned; instead, Passover is pre-

sented as a "festival of freedom," an example of democracy, a symbol of "spiritual values," a "folk holiday" and family reunion, an occasion for urging support of the various funds and philanthropic causes. The *religious* significance of Passover has entirely disappeared. A penetrating criticism of the secularization of American Jewish religious life, particularly in regard to prayer and synagogal liturgy, will be found in Abraham Joshua Heschel, *Man's Quest for God* (Scribner's, 1954), pp. 21–114. The pervasive secularism of American Jewish life has lately been challenged by groups of ultra-Orthodox refugees from eastern Europe. Largely Hasidic in background, these groups have displayed remarkable activity, especially in education (the religious "day school" movement owes much to them). Their unwillingness or inability to separate their Jewishness from the alien East European culture in which it was embedded has, however, virtually isolated them from the mass of American Jews, who, insofar as they are aware of them at all, regard them as a "quaint" survival of a vanished world. In any case, there would seem to be little chance that this Orthodoxy will survive the process of acculturation, or succeed in escaping it, any better than did its predecessors. For an interesting and informative report on what is probably the most important of these groups, see: Herbert Weiner, "The Lubovitcher Movement," *Commentary*, March, April 1957.

66. For the latest of these efforts, the so-called MacIver Report program, see Robert M. MacIver, *Report on the Jewish Community Relations Agencies* (National Community Relations Advisory Council, New York, 1951). For a brief survey of the American Jewish community as an institutional system, see Duker, "Structure of the Jewish Community," in Janowsky, ed., *The American Jew: A Composite Portrait*, pp. 134–60; also Samuel C. Kohs, "The Jewish Community," in Louis Finkelstein, ed., *The Jews: Their History, Culture, and Religion*, Vol. IV, pp. 1267–1324. For a list of national Jewish organizations, see *American Jewish Year Book*, Vol. 55 (1954), pp. 397–418.

67. "In 1947, the [United Jewish] Appeal raised a total of about $170,000,000, about half of it being allotted to Palestine . . . In the five years that followed, the new State of Israel received $416,000,000 from American Jews, of which two thirds came from the proceeds of the United Jewish Appeal" (Learsi, *The Jews in America*, p. 314 and note).

68. "Every effort to bring a coherent, unified community into being came to naught; yet the Jews were more conscious of their identity at mid-century than they had been for many decades before" (Handlin, *Adventure in Freedom*, pp. 229–30).

69. The same principle permeates Jewish religious life. Jewish religious polity is ultra-congregational, and this is equally true of all three "denominations." "Within the local congrega-

tion, there is full independence. There are no synods, assemblies, or hierarchies of leaders to control anything whatsoever in the synagogue" (Frank S. Mead, *Handbook of Denominations in the United States* [Abingdon-Cokesbury, 1951], p. 103). The various rabbinical and synagogal associations have no formal power over their constituents and can make no decisions binding on the individual congregations.

70. "By then [the 1940s], the logic of federation had, in many cities, been pushed to its extreme: each Jew made a single donation allocated for him by a hierarchy of intermediaries to the constituent agencies of whose existence the donor was hardly conscious" (Handlin, *Adventure in Freedom*, pp. 223–24).

71. "In 1941, federations, welfare bodies, or community councils functioned in 266 urban centers, embracing no less than 97 per cent of the Jewish population of the United States" (Duker, "Structure of the Jewish Community," in Janowsky, ed., *The American Jew: A Composite Portrait*, p. 153 note).

72. Ginzberg, *Agenda for American Jews*, pp. 48, 50.

73. Glazer, "What Sociology Knows About American Jews," *Commentary*, Vol. IX, No. 3, March 1950. For an account of the perplexed and disturbed reaction of many young people to the externalism and secularization of Jewish religious life in America today, see Herberg, "Religious Trends in American Jewry," *Judaism*, Vol. III, No. 3, Summer 1954. For divergent forecasts as to the future of American Jewry, see: Jacob R. Marcus and Oscar Handlin, "The Goals of Survival: What Will U. S. Jewry Be Like in 2000?—Two Views," *The National Jewish Monthly*, May 1957.

IX. *The Three Religious Communities: Comparisons and Contrasts*

The three religious communities—Protestant, Catholic, Jewish—are America. Together, they embrace almost the entire population of this country. In the scheme of things defined by the American Way of Life, they constitute the three faces of American religion, the three "pools" or "melting pots" in and through which the American people is emerging as a national entity after a century of mass immigration. In one sense these three communities stand on the same level, recognized as equi-legitimate subdivisions of the American people. In another sense, however, they are markedly different—in their historical background, their social and cultural structure, their place in the totality of American life. An examination of the three communities from this standpoint will serve to bring this phase of our study to its close.

I

America was once almost entirely Protestant; the transformation of Protestant America into the tripartite America of the "triple melting pot" has taken place, in a measure, through its union with two minority communities very different in ethnic and social composition. Present-day America reflects, at almost every point, this basic fact of its history.

In terms of self-identification, the American people today are roughly about 66 per cent Protestant, 26 per cent Catholic, and 3.5 per cent Jewish.[1] Each of these groups reveals its own characteristic conformation. A breakdown of four surveys made in 1945–46 for the Federal Council of Churches by the Office of Public Opinion Research at Princeton presents us with an illuminating picture of the comparative structure of the three communities.[2] In terms of a scheme of social stratification in which people were grouped according to such criteria as dress, home, furnishings, neighborhood, and occupation, it was found that of the national sample about 13.1 per cent fell into the "upper" class, 30.7 per cent into the "middle" class, and 56.2 per cent into the "lower" class. Protestants reflected this pattern—13.8 per cent, 32.6 per cent, and 53.6 per cent respectively. Catholics, however, were found to be underrepresented at the upper end and Jews at the lower: for Catholics the figures were 8.7 per cent, 24.7 per cent, and 66.6 per cent respectively; for Jews they were 21.8 per cent, 32.0 per cent, and 46.2 per cent in the same order.[3] In other words, the Protestant group agreed very closely in structure with the general community, of which it made up nearly 70 per cent; the Jews, however, had a considerably larger upper class, and the Catholics a considerably larger lower class than indicated in the national sample.

It will be seen that the popular notion that American Protestantism is primarily a middle-class group is not borne out by the available facts; the class structure of Protestantism follows very nearly the class structure of the nation as a whole, at least as that was measured in the survey we are considering. Whatever significant social-class differentiation there is, is to be found *within* the Protestant community, among the denominations that compose it. "Protestant denominations in their total outreach touch nearly all sections of the population. But each denomination tends also to be associated with a particular social status. . . . Individual Protestant churches tend to be 'class churches,' with members drawn principally from one class group."[4] Thus, Baptists, in the Federal Council study, had an exceptionally large lower class in close parallel to Catholic stratification (except that the Baptist lower class was largely rural, while its Catholic counterpart was mainly urban). The distribution of Episcopalians, on the other hand, was

very much like that of the Jews, a good majority coming
from the upper and middle classes; this was even more so
for the Presbyterians and the Congregationalists. But Protestantism as a whole hewed remarkably close to the national profile.

In the matter of education, it was found that 51.9 per
cent of the national sample had not graduated from high
school, while 48.1 per cent were high school graduates or
better. Again, the Protestant figures were very close, 50.9
per cent and 49.1 per cent respectively. Jews, however,
showed 63.1 per cent high school graduates or better,
Catholics only 43.0 per cent.[5] Educational level, as might
be expected, seemed to be closely linked with social-class
structure.[6] Here, too, the differences among Protestant
denominations were significant. Lutherans, with 56.3 per
cent non-high school graduates were at virtually the same
level as the Catholics (57.0 per cent), while the Baptists
took a place even lower on the scale (64.6 per cent);
Episcopalians, on the other hand, with only 35.3 per cent
non-high school graduates, and Presbyterians with 37.1 per
cent, closely paralleled the Jews (36.9 per cent) at the upper end.

Urbanization was discovered to be highest among Jews
and Catholics. Jews were almost entirely metropolitan, with
over 75 per cent living in cities of half a million or more.
Catholics, however, had some 43 per cent of their people
in cities between 10,000 and 500,000, where America's big
industries are largely located; another 28.3 per cent lived
in metropolitan centers. No Protestant group, not even the
Episcopalians, were as urban as the Catholics or the Jews,
and of course neither Catholics nor Jews were anywhere as
rural or "small town" as the Baptists, Methodists, or Lutherans. Protestantism as a whole showed a higher proportion of residents on the farm and in smaller towns, and a
lower proportion in big cities, than the national sample.[7]

These differences were, of course, related to occupational distribution. Again, Protestants reflected the national pattern, except for a somewhat higher proportion of
farmers; Catholics had proportionately fewer professionals,
businessmen, and farmers, proportionately more white-

collar workers, workers in service occupations, and skilled and semi-skilled workers; while Jews showed a much higher proportion of professionals, businessmen, and white-collar workers, a lower proportion of service workers and of skilled and semi-skilled workers in industry, and practically no unskilled workers or farmers.[8] Jews were thus disproportionately "bourgeois" (professional and business);[9] Catholics, disproportionately "working class" (service, skilled and semi-skilled); while Protestants, taken together, reflected the national distribution. But again, within the Protestant community there were wide differences. Episcopalians and Congregationalists had an even higher proportion of professionals than had the Jews; Presbyterians, Episcopalians, Congregationalists, and Reformed showed an above-average proportion of businessmen; Baptists had an above-average proportion of skilled and semi-skilled workers, though less than the Catholics; while Methodists, Baptists, and Lutherans were far above the national sample in the proportion of farmers—it was the weight of these big denominations that raised the Protestant figure for farmers so much above that of the nation as a whole.

Some 18.9 per cent of the national sample answered affirmatively the question of union membership.[10] Of Catholics 28 per cent said they were union members, of Protestants 15.6 per cent, and of Jews 22.6 per cent. In view of the occupational distribution we have just glanced at, these figures are hardly surprising. Catholics, more urban and more involved in service and industrial occupations, are, of course, organized to a relatively high degree in labor unions, though perhaps the notably friendly attitude of the church in America to labor organization is also a factor. Jews, increasingly prominent in white-collar occupations and still retaining a considerable group of older people in light industry (particularly in the garment trades), show a higher-than-average trade union affiliation. Protestants, on the other hand, more rural, "small town," and "individualistic," fall below the national sample. Much the same picture emerges from a survey of two hundred top leaders of the American Federation of Labor and the Congress of Industrial Organizations made in 1945 by the

Bureau of Applied Social Research at Columbia. Fifty-one per cent designated their "religious preference" as Protestant, 35 per cent Catholic, and 4 per cent Jewish.[11] Protestants (in terms of "religious preference" or self-identification) constitute, it will be remembered, some 66 per cent, Catholics 26 per cent, and Jews 3.5 per cent of the American people. In the labor movement, however, though no exact figures are available, there can be little doubt that Catholics make up, and have long made up, a considerably greater proportion than they do in the population as a whole, and Protestants a considerably smaller proportion. The religious affiliation of labor leaders would seem to be consonant with this fact.

Taken as a whole, these data as to social-class composition, urbanization, education, and occupation would seem to reflect the social history of religion in America. "Almost from the very beginning," Liston Pope points out, "Protestantism tended to be the religion of the ruling and advantaged groups in the United States. . . . The great Protestant revivals during the nineteenth century broadened the social base of church affiliation immensely. So did the waves of immigration during the latter half of the century; most of the new immigrants after 1880 were Roman Catholics, and their arrival greatly increased the strength of the Catholic Church in the United States, and also gave that church close connections with the growing mass of urban industrial workers. During the same period, Protestant churches were gaining strength in the rural population, among the American Negroes, and in the middle and upper classes of the rising cities."[12] There is also some evidence that "all the major religious bodies in the United States now draw a higher percentage of their members from the lower class than they did before World War II."[13] Because the earlier Protestant America was, through the nineteenth and the first quarter of the twentieth century, overlaid, so to speak, with large numbers of Catholic and Jewish immigrants, Protestantism tended to give way at the "worker" end of the occupational scale to the former, and at the "professional" and "business" end to the latter, retaining and increasing its lead only among the farmers. Of course, since Catholics constitute about a quarter of the population and Jews only a small fraction, there are still many more Protestants who are professionals, businessmen, service employees, unskilled, skilled, and semi-skilled workers, as well as farmers, than there are Catholics or Jews, and there are likely to remain more in the foreseeable future. But the wide differences in the internal structure of the three communities are not thereby diminished, nor is the significance of these differences reduced.

The picture, however, should not be taken statically. Judging by present trends, there can be little doubt that Catholics will be producing a higher proportion of college graduates, professionals, and businessmen in coming years, and that Jews will become almost entirely businessmen, professionals, and white-collar workers. The Protestant outlook is not so clear; probably pretty much the same structure will remain, with gains among professional and white-collar suburbanites by some denominations matched by the headway among workers and the rural population made by others. For Protestantism, the social-class, cultural, and occupational differences *among* the denominations will very likely continue to be at least as significant as the over-all pattern.[14]

A close-up view of a revealing, though untypical, American community, where the social structure of American religion emerges in all its starkness, is provided in the study of "Class Denominationalism in Rural California Churches" made by Walter R. Goldschmidt in the early 1940s.[15] Goldschmidt studied a town in the San Joaquin Valley, in which "the most important single cleavage separated an upper from a lower class. . . . The privileges of the major institutions of the community—clubs, churches, official and quasi-official bodies—were the prerogative of a certain segment of the population which might be designated as the *nuclear* group. Remaining on the social peripheries was the large body of unskilled labor that had come to the community in search of work and settled there. These *outsiders* were Mexicans, Negroes, and whites."

Ten churches, it was found, served whites (including Mexicans) in the community, "the nuclear and outside populations [being], for the most part, served by separate religious bodies." The Catholic Church very nearly represented a cross-section of the churchgoing people. The Christian Science Church was small, the data for it were inadequate, and it served the "nuclear" group exclusively. "Of the eight remaining churches [Protestant], four served the nuclear population and four the outsider element." The four serving the "nuclear" upper class were the Congregational, the Methodist, the Baptist, and the Seventh-Day Adventist; the four of the "outsider" lower class were the Nazarenes, the Assembly of God, the Church of Christ, and the Pentecostals.[16] In the first four churches only a third of the members were laborers (including 6 per cent agricultural workers), whereas laborers made up three quarters (agricultural workers, 42 per cent) of the membership of the latter four. Of the four Protestant churches serving the "nuclear" population, one (Congregational) "was definitely for the élite. . . . The others served more fully the middle rungs of the social hierarchy." *Together,* however, the eight Protestant churches displayed a social composition almost the same as that of the Catholic Church and therefore very close to that of the religiously affiliated population of the town. In the Catholic Church the various classes were included in one institution, though maintaining a certain social distance; among the Protestants, however, there was a strong tendency towards class segregation in separate denominations. In this respect the picture presented by the California town was quite representative of American Protestantism as a whole.

In another respect, however, there was a significant difference. Congregationalists constitute an upper- and upper-middle-class church almost everywhere in the United States; the Methodists are not far from the average for Protestantism; but the Baptists, especially in areas not highly urbanized, are definitely a lower- and lower-middle-class church. But in the California town under study, Baptists, Methodists, and Seventh-Day Adventists took their place as upper- and upper-middle-class churches, side by

side with the Congregationalists, leaving the lower classes
to what elsewhere would be regarded as marginal, or
"fringe," groups. As a consequence, some recent immigrant
white workers, who had belonged to the Methodist and
Baptist churches back home, could not find a place for
themselves in these churches in the San Joaquin town and
therefore joined one or another of the "outsider" churches.[17]
The social hierarchy of Protestant denominations is apparently something that depends in part at least on the local
situation, although the over-all structure of the Protestant
community is everywhere relevant.

Even within the "outsider" churches there was social
differentiation. The Nazarenes had some (10 per cent) of
the top occupational group (professionals, managers, and
proprietors), a good many (22 per cent) of the next stra-
tum (farm operators and managers), and a very considerable bloc (43 per cent) of skilled laborers, with about 25
per cent unskilled. The other three "outsider" churches had
none of the top group, and proportionately larger numbers
of unskilled workers. The Pentecostal Church at the extreme
was made up almost entirely of laborers, of whom some
80 per cent were unskilled, with 18 per cent skilled workers, and 2 per cent clerks and other white-collar employees.
This Pentecostal group, significantly enough, had emerged
as a schism in the Assembly of God, which was Pentecostal
in its origin but had become religiously and socially more
respectable with time and the social advancement of its
people. "We don't call ourselves Pentecostal," the Assembly
minister explained, "because of their extremist attitudes."
The story of religion in this California town presents quite
graphically a picture of the social configuration of American Protestant denominationalism as well as of the process
by which sects become established denominations in the
American sense.

American religious communities have been profoundly
shaped by social and cultural forces. Catholics and Protestants in America differ not only in doctrine and church
polity but also in ethnic background, social structure, cultural level, occupational pattern, and way of acculturation.

American Jews constitute a group in many ways in advance of the basic trends of American life, but unique in the history of world Jewry.[18] Within the Protestant community the complex structure of denominationalism has become a way of expressing class differentiation and racial segregation. Yet all these differences remain differences *within* the over-all structure of American religious life. For all their particularities of background and development, American Protestants, Catholics, and Jews are basically Americans and reflect the common pattern of American religion.

II

Within this common religious pattern, however, there is still room for significant differences not only in ethnic background and social structure but also in what, for want of a better term, we may call religious attitudes and ideology. Any attempt to compare the three communities makes it immediately obvious that in their attitudes and beliefs Catholics come closest to the religious norm, Jews are farthest removed, with Protestants somewhere in between, in close conformity with the national picture. (By "religious norm" is here meant the beliefs and attitudes usually associated with religion, with no necessary implications as to "real" meaning or theological validity.)

Thus, in a recent quite extensive public opinion poll,[19] some 87 per cent of the American people affirmed their belief in God as "absolutely certain" (10 per cent more were "fairly sure"); the proportion of Catholics "absolutely certain" was 92 per cent, but of Jews, only 70 per cent ("fairly sure," 7 and 18 per cent respectively). The Protestant figures were identical with the national average.[20]

Again, while 18 per cent of those who identified themselves as Catholics stated that they had not attended church in the three previous months, some 56 per cent of the Jews made this confession. Of Protestants, 32 per cent said they had not been to church in that period, the same proportion as in the national sample. At the other extreme, 62 per cent of the Catholics said that they went to church at least once a week, as against 12 per cent of the Jews, 25 per cent of the Protestants, and 32 per cent of the nation as a whole.[21]

Of Americans as a whole, 75 per cent stated they regarded religion as "very important"; 83 per cent of the Catholics had this conviction, but only 47 per cent of the Jews. Protestants registered 76 per cent. On the other hand, 37 per cent of the Jews said they regarded religion as "fairly important," as against 14 per cent of the Catholics, 20 per cent of the Protestants, and 20 per cent of the national sample. The remainder—3 per cent of the Catholics, 4 per cent of the Protestants, 5 per cent of the national sample, but 15 per cent of the Jews—held religion to be "not very important" or not important at all.[22]

About 83 per cent of Americans held the Bible to be the revealed word of God in some sense, and 10 per cent regarded it as merely a "work of literature." The breakdown shows that the Bible as revelation was affirmed by 88 per cent of the Catholics and 85 per cent of the Protestants, but by only 45 per cent of the Jews—an equal 45 per cent holding it to be merely a great literary work. Even those included in the category of "Others"—those who refused to identify themselves as Protestants, Catholics, or Jews—took a higher view of the Bible; some 52 per cent of them said they regarded it as revelation.

Though 83 per cent of Americans affirmed the Bible to be the revealed word of God, 40 per cent confessed that they read it never or hardly ever; 56 per cent of the Catholics admitted as much, 32 per cent of the Protestants, and 65 per cent of the Jews.[23]

In all of these respects, the pattern is very much the same: Catholics come closest to the religious norm, to what is usually regarded as the beliefs and attitudes proper to religious people; Protestants come next, hewing close to the national average; Jews are most remote. The one exception so far, that Catholics read the Bible considerably less and Protestants considerably more than the national sample, may easily be accounted for by the special traditions of these groups.

But how are we to account for the pattern itself? The marked differences in religious attitude and behavior we have noted cannot be reduced simply to differences in education, urbanization, or social status. For while it is true, for example, that inhabitants of very large cities and college graduates seem to be somewhat less "religious" than those who reside in communities not so vast, or have had not so extensive an education, the variation is not too great, and in other respects the relation is even more tenuous.[24] Jews have a large upper class (in the Allensmith usage of the term), but upper-class people seem to rank fairly high in those religious attitudes and beliefs in which Jews rank low. Catholics are largely below college level in education, are employed predominantly as white-collar workers, service employees, and skilled and semi-skilled workers in industry, and reside mostly in large cities under a million; yet people with these characteristics generally attend church somewhat less frequently than the average, whereas Catholics certainly attend more frequently. The factors of class, education, social status, and the like are no doubt important, but they cannot fully, or even very significantly, account for the marked deviations from the Protestant-American pattern by Catholics on the one side and Jews on the other.

The over-average religiousness of American Catholics is very probably to be related to the inner cohesiveness of the Catholic community in this country, particularly since the middle of the nineteenth century; and that in turn is no doubt a result of the fact that the church, from the beginning of the great immigration, has been composed so largely of ethnic groups only gradually acculturated to American life. The skill with which the church directed this process of acculturation, combined with the relatively low mobility of many of the Catholic immigrants, enabled American Catholics to make the transition gradually and without too much demoralization and loss of religion. The extensive network of Catholic social and educational institutions helped to protect the faithful from too drastic exposure to the secularist atmosphere that was beginning to permeate American life precisely at the most critical period of American Catholic history. What will happen now that the ethnic

groups are in dissolution and American Catholics are becoming more mobile and therefore more open to outside
cultural influences, it is hard to tell; very likely Catholics
will begin to conform more closely to the national (Protestant) pattern, although the current upswing in religion will
probably check too great a decline in overt religious beliefs
and attitudes.

The widespread secularism revealed in Jewish responses
must be understood in the context of the background history of American Jewry. Most American Jews came to this
country from eastern Europe at a time when the walls of
the ghetto were crumbling and the East European Jewish
community was beginning to give way to the social and
intellectual forces of the "Enlightenment." The great mass
of Jews in eastern Europe, we should remember, had no
Renaissance as transition from medievalism; within one or
two generations they were compelled to pass directly from
the Middle Ages into the nineteenth century. Large numbers of the younger people rose in open revolt against the
"medievalist" traditionalism of the religious leaders. Considerable numbers became overtly anti-religious; many
more adopted a passively hostile attitude to everything that
was "backward" and traditional. The confusion and dis-
orientation were further accentuated by the abrupt break
with the past incident upon uprooting and resettlement in
a new world. For various reasons, the Orthodox Jewish
rabbi, the only kind of rabbi known to most East European
immigrants, seemed neither willing nor able to serve as a
link between his ethnic-immigrant group and the larger
American community in the way in which the Catholic
priest or Lutheran pastor so frequently served his group.
On the contrary, the Orthodox rabbi tended rather to shut
himself off from the new world which he found alien and
unacceptable. A more or less openly anti-religious secularism swept the American Jewish community in those years
and left its mark on many who lived to outgrow its more
overt manifestations. Not only traditional attitudes and ob-
servances but the very minimal beliefs and practices of religion were abandoned or ignored. Had anyone taken the
trouble to conduct public opinion polls in those days, not

10 or 12 per cent of American Jews would have been found to disavow any assured belief in God, as today, but perhaps twice or three times that number; not merely 15 per cent would have asserted their conviction that religion was of little or no importance, but perhaps 30 per cent or more. It is the emergence of the third generation in recent years, with its characteristic third-generation "return," that has mitigated the force of Jewish secularism, although enough of it still remains to show up so tellingly in the polls.

Though second-generation Jews, including the younger immigrants, tended to lose their religious heritage, that did not, as a general rule, turn to outright assimilation, although the trend in that direction was growing. Somehow, perhaps illogically, they felt a desire for group survival. This desire was immensely reinforced, was indeed converted into a universal presupposition, with the restructuring of American society in terms of religious community. Today, Jews, whatever their belief or unbelief, find it obvious that they are to remain Jews, and since "Jews" is today understood as referring to a religious community rather than to an ethnic group, Jewish identification and survival cannot but assume religious forms. This leads to a number of consequences which may seem strange and paradoxical at first sight.

Thus, the very same Jews who so frequently say that they do not "believe in God" and who do not attend synagogue services very largely insist that their children should receive a religious education, and, far more than Americans as a whole, desire that this education should be received in religious or parochial schools rather than at home or in Sunday school.[25] Jews, too, are most averse to religious intermarriage, or at least profess to believe that marriages are more likely to be happy if the partners are of the same religion: 75 per cent of the national sample said they believed this to be the case, 76 per cent of the Protestants, 73 per cent of the Catholics, but 80 per cent of the Jews.[26] The anomaly is removed once we recall the curious ambiguity in the meaning of Jewishness, a term held to designate belonging to a community taken to be religious,

yet somehow not involving adherence to any particular religious belief or practice.

As against both Catholic and Jewish extremes, the Protestant pattern seems to be far more "normal" in its easy
accommodation to the benign, "pro-religious" secularism so
prevalent in this country today. There are signs that the
current upswing in religion, particularly the renewal of
Reformation theology, may raise the level of American
Protestant belief; it is certainly increasing Protestant
churchgoing. However that may turn out to be, the Protestant pattern will in all probability continue to define the
American religious pattern in general, to which American
Catholic and Jew will increasingly conform, each in his own
way and from his own direction.

FOOTNOTES

1. See above, p. 65, end of note 2. This is not the same as
church membership, for which see pp. 47–48. A comprehensive
Church Distribution Study, consisting of 80 bulletins in five
series, under the general title of *Churches and Church Membership in the United States: An Enumeration and Analysis by
Counties, States, and Regions,* was published in 1956–58 by
the Bureau of Research and Survey of the National Council
of Churches. It is based on the statistics of churches and church
membership for 1952, in correlation with certain data supplied
by the 1950 United States Census of Population.

2. The study was made by Wesley Allensmith; see "Christianity and the Economic Order, No. 10, Social-Economic Status
and Outlook of Religious Groups in America," *Information
Service* (Federal Council of Churches of Christ), May 15, 1948.
This report is reproduced in large part in Herbert Wallace
Schneider, *Religion in 20th Century America* (Harvard, 1952),
Appendix, pp. 223–38, and is interpreted by Liston Pope, "Religion and the Class Structure," in Ray H. Abrams, ed., "Organized Religion in the United States," *The Annals of the American Academy of Political and Social Science,* Vol. 256, March
1948, pp. 84–91. There is good reason to believe that, in the
decade and a half since these surveys were made, there has
been a very considerable "upgrading" of the American people,
as well as some shift in the comparative structure of the three
communities. The basic conclusions, however, would probably
remain substantially unaffected. For an excellent survey of the

recent literature on class stratification in relation to religion, see "Social Class and the Churches," *Information Service*, June 14, 1958. Valuable information on income, educational attainment, and occupational composition in relation to religious preference may also be found in Daniel J. Bogue, *The Population of the United States* (Free Press, 1959), Chap. 23, Religious Affiliation.

3. This as well as the other tables in this chapter, unless otherwise indicated, are adapted from "Social-Economic Status and Outlook of Religious Groups in America," *Information Service*, May 15, 1948.

DISTRIBUTION OF RELIGIOUS GROUPS BY CLASS

	Total	Upper	Middle	Lower
Nat'l Sample	100.0%	13.1%	30.7%	56.2%
Protestants	69.0	13.8	32.6	53.6
Catholics	19.9	8.7	24.7	66.6
Jews	4.5	21.8	32.0	46.2
Others	6.6			

4. Pope, "Religion and the Class Structure," *Annals*, p. 89. See also David W. Barry, "The Fellowship of Class," *The City Church*, Vol. VI, No. 1, January–February 1955.

5. DISTRIBUTION OF RELIGIOUS GROUPS BY EDUCATIONAL LEVEL

	Total	Part High School or Less	High School Graduate or More
Nat'l Sample	100.0%	51.9%	48.1%
Protestants	69.2	50.9	49.1
Catholics	19.9	57.0	43.0
Jews	4.4	36.9	63.1
Others	6.5		

(The considerable number of foreign-born still to be found among American Jews at the time the survey was made accounts in large part for those found to possess less than a high school education; to a somewhat smaller extent, this was also the case with the Catholics, among whom too there were many immigrants.) On the basis of a study made in 1947, Helen E. Davis found: (1) out of 10,063 high school seniors, male and female, there applied for college: national sample 35 per cent, Protestants 36 per cent, Catholics 25 per cent, Jews 68 per cent: (2) out of 5,564 *urban* high school seniors, there applied for college: national sample 42 per cent, Protestants 43 per cent, Catholics 26 per cent, Jews 64 per cent (*On Getting Into College* [Washington: American Council on Education, 1949], pp. 13, 20).

6. The differences here indicated would be even more strik-

ing had criteria relating to higher education been taken. As we have seen (above, chap. viii, p. 188), about three times as many Jews attend college in proportion to the general population; for Catholics, despite their high degree of urbanization, the proportion would seem to be below the general level. "The proportion of Protestants to Catholics rises as one moves up the educational scale. . . . Outside the South, the proportion of college graduates is almost twice as high for Protestants as for Catholics" (Pope, "Religion and the Class Structure," *Annals*, p. 86). See also "Who Belongs to What Church?", *The Catholic Digest*, January 1953, table for question 28a.

7. DISTRIBUTION OF RELIGIOUS GROUPS BY RESIDENCE, RURAL AND URBAN

	Total	Farm	Under 2,500	2,500-10,000	10,000-100,000	100,000-500,000	500,000 and Over
Nat'l Sample	100.0%	16.4%	8.9%	20.4%	20.8%	13.5%	20.0%
Protestants	69.3	19.9	10.5	23.7	20.4	12.5	13.0
Catholics	19.7	8.5	6.1	13.9	24.8	18.4	28.3
Jews	4.4	0.7	0.0	4.2	9.0	9.4	76.7
Others	6.6						

8. DISTRIBUTION OF RELIGIOUS GROUPS BY OCCUPATION

	Total	Profes.	Bus.	White-Collar	Serv.	Skilled, Semi-Sk.	Unsk.	Farmer
Nat'l Sample	100.0%	10.5%	8.5%	20.4%	11.2%	27.2%	5.5%	16.7%
Protestants	69.0	11.1	8.3	18.6	11.2	25.0	5.5	20.3
Catholics	20.0	7.1	6.6	23.0	13.6	35.3	5.8	8.6
Jews	4.4	14.4	21.7	36.5	4.3	22.3	0.2	0.6
Others	6.6							

(The relatively high figure, 22.3 per cent, for skilled and semi-skilled workers among Jews is largely the consequence of considerable numbers of first-generation immigrants still working in the shops, mostly in light manufacturing; their children and grandchildren, as we have seen, do not follow them into the factories.)

9. "While America in general became more markedly middle class in its occupational structure, Jews became even more so. . . . [The Jewish community today] consists largely of well-to-do professionals, merchants, and white-collar workers" (Glazer, "Social Characteristics of American Jews, 1654–1954," *American Jewish Year Book*, Vol. 56 [1955], pp. 20, 35). Not only has there been a shift from manufacturing to trade and professions among American Jews, but "no less significant is the fact

that the proportion of Jewish factory workers to manufacturers
has decreased. 96.5 per cent of the Jews from Russia in manufacturing were in 1900 employees and approximately only 63
per cent in the 1930s" (Nathan Goldberg, "Occupational Patterns of American Jews," *The Jewish Review*, Vol. III, No. 4,
January 1946). This tendency has, of course, become accentuated since the 1930s. For a closer view of the extraordinary
economic and occupational structure of American Jewry, see
Nathan Reich, "Economic Trends," in Oscar I. Janowsky, ed.,
The American Jew: A Composite Portrait (Harper, 1942), pp.
161–82; and Eli E. Cohen, "Economic and Occupational Structure," *The American Jewish Year Book*, Vol. 51 (1950), pp.
53–70.

10. The question was: "Are you (or is your husband) a member of a labor union?"

11. See Pope, "Religion and the Class Structure," *Annals*, p.
87, note 6. Twelve per cent of the AFL leaders and 6 per cent
of the CIO leaders reported no religious affiliation. The CIO
figure is about average for the American people. May we explain the anomalously high AFL figure by the fact that the AFL
leadership still includes some old-time "radicals," who have long
abandoned their social radicalism but not yet their "non-
religion," while the CIO leaders, generally younger men, reflect
latter-day trends more truly?

12. Pope, "Religion and the Class Structure," *Annals*, p. 84.

13. See Pope, "Religion and the Class Structure," *Annals*, p.
86. Pope compares the 1945–46 materials with data gathered
in 1939–40 by the same agency (Office of Public Opinion Research, Princeton) and by the same methods, and finds a very
considerable increase in the proportion of the lower class among
both Catholics and Protestants at the later date (Catholics 66.6
per cent as against 41 per cent, Protestants 53.6 per cent as
against 34 per cent). There seems to be considerable doubt in
interpreting the data. It does appear to be true, however, that
religious affiliation is weakest among the most "disadvantaged"
classes, who are less given to "joining" than other strata of the
population.

14. In earlier times "denominational" differences in social-
class and occupational structure were to be noted among American Jews as well—the "German" Jews (usually Reform) being
very largely upper and middle class, engaged in business,
finance, and the professions, and better educated; the "Russian" Jews (usually Orthodox or secular, to some extent Conservative) being largely lower and middle class, engaged in
manufacturing (mostly workers) or in low-prestige business, just
beginning to acquire an education. But Jewish mobility was so
high that by the 1920s these differences were pretty well wiped

out. Today, whatever social-class, cultural, or occupational differences remain are related rather to stage of acculturation (first, second, or third generation) than to "denominational" lines.

15. Walter R. Goldschmidt, "Class Denominationalism in Rural California Churches," _The American Journal of Sociology_, Vol. XLIX, No. 4, January 1944. All quotations are from this article.

16. "Though all of these major [Protestant] denominations have adherents from the lower classes, the religious expression of the latter has increasingly taken place in the last quarter-century through the new Pentecostal and holiness sects" (Pope, "Religion and the Class Structure," _Annals_, p. 89).

17. "Of the 51 recent immigrant white workers interviewed, 25 had been members in their former residence of churches such as Methodist and Baptist—churches which in this [California] community serve the nuclear group. Of these 25, only one still attends such a church, while 12 have joined or are attending the outsider denominations, and 12 report no attendance whatsoever. There are no shifts in the opposite direction" (Goldschmidt, "Class Denominationalism in Rural California Churches," _The American Journal of Sociology_, Vol. XLIX, No. 4, January 1944).

18. "Perhaps a majority of the younger generation [of American Jews] is now composed of businessmen and professional men. This community of businessmen and professional men is a better educated and wealthier element of the population—probably as well educated and as wealthy as some of the oldest and longest established elements in the United States" (Glazer, "Social Characteristics of American Jews, 1654–1954," _American Jewish Year Book_, Vol. 56 [1955], p. 26). "From a review of the data [of a nation-wide poll conducted in 1948 by the Office of Public Opinion Research], it becomes apparent that the class structure of American Jewry is closest to that of the following religious groups: Presbyterians, Congregationalists, and particularly Episcopalians. These denominations have high status because of the class levels of their adherents. The preponderant majority of their membership is 'old American.' Jews outrank the Catholics, a denomination which includes many ethnics who came here contemporaneously with the Jews. Even Protestant groups like the Lutherans, composed of ethnics most of whom arrived in the United States before the Jews, have occupations which rank them lower than the Jews. Results of community studies are in agreement with poll data. The one done in 'Yankee City,' for example, shows that Jews occupy the highest position among all ethnic groups in the community. Such rapid mobility has been characteristic of an entire segment of

the Jewish population, a larger middle class was created here than in any comparable ethnic group" (Marshall Sklare, *Conservative Judaism: An American Religious Movement* [Free Press, 1955], p. 27). The "Yankee City" reference is to W. Lloyd Warner and Leo Srole, *The Social System of American Ethnic Groups* (Yale, 1945).

19. The survey conducted by Ben Gaffin and Associates and published in installments in *The Catholic Digest;* see above, chap. iv, note 2. These differences in religiousness, even more sharply accentuated, are to be found among Catholic, Protestant, and Jewish college graduates (see Ernest Havemann and Patricia Salter West, *They Went to College: The College Graduate in America Today* [Harcourt, Brace, 1952], pp. 104–7). All Gallup poll surveys on religion indicate the same differential ranking in religiousness.

20. See "Do Americans Believe in God?", *The Catholic Digest,* November 1952.

21. See "Do Americans Go to Church?", *The Catholic Digest,* December 1952. These figures agree generally with the data of other polls and surveys. Thus, a survey reported by the National Opinion Research Center in 1945 shows that only 6 per cent of those who identified themselves as Catholics stated that they seldom or never attended church, 19 per cent of Protestants, and 32 per cent of Jews. Of Catholics, 69 per cent said they attended services once a week or more; of Protestants, 36 per cent; of Jews, 9 per cent. At least once a month: Catholics 81 per cent, Protestants 62 per cent, Jews 24 per cent (*Opinion News,* December 25, 1945). An American Institute of Public Opinion (Gallup) poll in 1954 showed that 55 per cent of Americans claimed they had attended church the previous week: 78 per cent of the Catholics, 48 per cent of the Protestants, and 31 per cent of the Jews (*Public Opinion News Service,* July 21, 1954).

22. See "How Important Religion Is to Americans," *The Catholic Digest,* February 1953.

23. See "What Do Americans Think of the Bible?", *The Catholic Digest,* May 1954.

24. Most of the polls and surveys here referred to give breakdowns according to class, education, age, urbanization, occupation, etc., from which rough correlations may be drawn.

25. See "Do Americans Want Their Children to Receive Religious Instruction?", *The Catholic Digest,* September 1953. The poll showed that 98 per cent of the American people wanted their children to receive a religious education, but only 25 per cent chose the religious or parochial school as the instrument of such education—more preferred the Sunday school or instruction at home. Of Catholics, 74 per cent preferred the religious or

parochial school; of Protestants, only 9 per cent; but of Jews, fully 40 per cent. (Jews also were strong for the Sunday school and for home instruction.) It is interesting that Protestants and Jews were about equal in their belief that children should be raised as church members rather than be brought up "free to make up their own minds": 67 per cent of the Protestants and 67 per cent of the Jews affirmed themselves in favor, as against 72 per cent of the national sample and 91 per cent of the Catholics ("How Important Religion Is to Americans," *The Catholic Digest*, February 1953). Here the sub-average deviation of the Jews is much reduced.

26. See "Personal Happiness and the 'Mixed' Marriage," *The Catholic Digest*, April 1954. The American Institute of Public Opinion (Gallup) has made public similar data, but without a breakdown for Jews (*Public Opinion News Service*, December 28, 1951).

X. *The Three Religious Communities: Unity and Tension*

The basic unity of American religion is something that goes deeper than the similarities and differences of social pattern we have been examining. The basic unity of American religion is rooted in the underlying presuppositions, values, and ideals that together constitute the American Way of Life on its "spiritual" side. It is the American Way of Life that is the shared possession of all Americans and that defines the American's convictions on those matters that count most. Just as the three great religious communities are the basic subdivisions of the American people, so are the three great "communions" (as they are often called) felt to be the recognized expressions of the "spiritual" aspect of the American Way of Life. This underlying unity not only supplies the common content of the three communions; it also sets the limits within which their conflicts and tensions may operate and beyond which they cannot go.

I

For the fundamental unity of American religion, rooted in the American Way of Life, does not preclude conflict and tension; rather, in a way, it stimulates and accentuates it. Since each of the three communities recognizes itself as fitting into a tripartite scheme, each feels itself to be a minority, even the Protestants who in actual fact constitute a large majority of the American people. In this sense, as in so many others, America is pre-eminently a land of minorities.

The communal tensions in American society are of major

importance in the life of the nation. So much attention is usually focused, properly, of course, on political and economic conflicts that we are only too prone to overlook or underestimate tensions on other levels of social life, particularly the religious, since religion is generally felt to be a matter that must be kept free of "controversy." Yet the religious tensions are real and significant; they have, moreover, become considerably accentuated in recent years in connection with a number of issues that have emerged into public life, centering on the problem of church and state. Such is the peculiar structure of American religious institutionalism under the constitutional doctrine of "separation" that every tension between religious communities, however deep and complex it may actually be, tends to express itself as a conflict over church-state relations. This approach is perhaps as useful a way as any of focusing the religio-communal tensions in American life.

American Catholics still labor under the heavy weight of the bitter memory of non-acceptance in a society overwhelmingly and self-consciously Protestant. Hardly a century has passed since Catholics in America were brutally attacked by mobs, excluded from more desirable employment, and made to feel in every way that they were unwanted aliens. Despised as foreigners of low-grade stock, detested and denounced as "minions of Rome," they early developed the minority defensiveness that led them to withdraw into their own "ghetto" with a rankling sense of grievance and to divide the world into "we" and "they." This was, for a time, the case even with the Irish, who of all Catholic immigrants found their place in American society soonest. Thomas Sugrue recalls from his childhood: "I began to hear what came to be familiar phrases: 'those people,' 'the Prods,' 'our own kind,' 'they don't want us.' I became aware that we did not live in a community of friendly neighbors, but that as Catholics we were camped instead in the middle of warlike Protestants, who didn't want us and wouldn't let us 'get ahead.' . . . When I was twelve, a Protestant boy invited me to join the Boy Scouts . . . I asked my mother, and she said no. 'They don't want you,' she added, 'they're all Protestants.' . . . About this time, too, I began to hear the phrase, 'They have everything.' The Protestants, of course, were 'they.'"[1]

These feelings of rejection, exclusion, and grievance, though they no longer correspond to the facts of American life, and though they are deplored by more thoughtful Catholics, are still a real force among the great mass of Catholic people in this country. It takes a long time for such wounds to heal.

Partly in the interest of corporate survival in a hostile world, though basically in line with the demands and teachings of the church, Catholics in America have built up a vast and complex system of parallel institutions, the most important and pervasive of which are the church schools operating at every academic level. Though initiated under other circumstances, these parallel institutions soon fell in rather neatly with the emerging religio-communal pattern of American life. At the same time, the development of these institutions no doubt helped accentuate that tradition of Catholic "separatism" which has recently come under the criticism of Catholics themselves.[2]

American Catholics generally seem to feel that their Catholic educational institutions, particularly the parochial schools, are much misunderstood and regarded with undue hostility by non-Catholics.[3] They also feel themselves unjustly dealt with since they are taxed for the maintenance of "neutral" public schools they cannot in conscience use, but are denied adequate support for the Catholic schools so many of their children attend and which in actuality form part of the nation's educational system.[4] This issue—about which no clear-cut decision is possible, since religious schools are in fact granted certain types of government assistance but are denied others—has become exacerbated in recent years and has served to bring the larger question of church-state relations into the area of bitter controversy as the focus of religio-communal conflict in present-day America.[5]

Minority defensiveness breeds aggressiveness, intensifies separatism, and accentuates prejudice. Many Catholics still, as in earlier days, attempt to sustain their corporate self-esteem by an attitude that makes Protestant almost equivalent to unbeliever, or in more modern terminology, to "secularist." But authoritative Catholic opinion is increasingly taking another line of ideological defense—that Catholicism is, in fact, a true expression of Americanism and that the genuine Catholic position on church and state is fully in line with American tradition and experience. The extensive system of Catholic institutions is interpreted in terms of the emerging community structure of American society, involving no more separatism than any other aspect of community organization. By and large, American Catholicism has succeeded in shifting the ground of self-understanding and self-justification from the earlier negative defensiveness to a more positive affirmation of its legitimate place in the tripartite America of today. The Catholic attitude is increasingly that of a substantial minority with a strong sense of self-assurance.[6]

Protestantism in America today presents the anomaly of a strong majority group with a growing minority consciousness. "The psychological basis of much of American Protestantism," *Social Action* (Congregational) somewhat ruefully pointed out in 1952, "lies in a negative rejection of Roman Catholicism. . . . The one emotional loyalty that of a certainty binds us [Protestants] together . . . is the battle against Rome."[7] The fear of "Rome" is indeed the most powerful cement of Protestant community consciousness, and it seems to loom larger today than it has for some time. Discussion of Protestant communal affairs moves increasingly under the shadow of the "Catholic problem," and Protestant attitudes tend more and more to be defined in terms of confrontation with a self-assured and aggressive Catholicism.[8] The tension here has become really acute.

The fear of Catholic domination of the United States would seem to be hardly borne out by statistics. In the period from 1926 to 1950 church membership in this country increased 59.8 per cent, as against a 28.6 per cent increase in population. The Catholic Church grew 53.9 per cent, but in the same period Protestantism increased 63.7 per cent. Moreover, Protestant proselytism seemed to be more intensive and successful than Catholic. Most of the Protestant margin of increase, however, was accounted for by the expansion of the Baptists, especially the Southern Baptists. The churches affiliated with the National Council grew only 47 per cent, falling short of the total increase as well as of the comparable Roman Catholic growth.[9] In those parts of the country where Protestants and Catholics come into more direct contact, particularly in the urban centers, the Catholic Church has been making considerable headway.

But it is not this numerical growth, such as it is, that so deeply disquiets the Protestant consciousness, for, after all, the Protestant-Catholic balance has remained pretty steady in the past thirty years.[10] Neither is it entirely the mounting intellectual prestige that American Catholicism has been acquiring from the work of a number of artists, philosophers, and writers, mostly European. What seems to be really disturbing many American Protestants is the sudden realization that Protestantism is no longer identical with America, that Protestantism has, in fact, become merely one of three communions (or communities) with equal status and equal legitimacy in the American scheme of things. This sudden realization, shocking enough when one considers the historical origins of American life and culture, appears to have driven Protestantism into an essentially defensive posture, in which it feels itself a mere minority threatened with Catholic domination.[11]

This minority-group defensiveness has contributed greatly toward turning an important segment of American Protestantism into a vehement champion of an extreme doctrine of the separation of church and state, of religion and education, despite a disturbed awareness of the growing "religious illiteracy" of the American people. This minority-group defensiveness and fear of "Rome" have tended to drive American Protestantism into a strange alliance with the militant secularist anti-Catholicism that is associated with the recent work of Paul Blanshard.[12] It would seem to be of some significance that the contemporary Protestant case against Catholicism is not primarily religious or theological, as it was in previous centuries, but is characteristically secular: Catholicism, we are told, is un-American, undemocratic, alien to American ways, and prone to place loyalty to church above loyalty to state and nation. Particularly shocking to many Protestants is the Catholic insistence on by-passing the public schools and educating their children in their own religious institutions. The "neutral" public school, inculcating a common national ideology above religious "divisiveness," has in fact become to large numbers of Protestants the symbol of their cause in the face of dreaded Catholic encroachment.

This argument of Catholic "divisiveness" seems to loom largest in the American Protestant mind. It has been given persuasive expression in a much-noted editorial in *The Christian Century*, entitled "Pluralism—National Menace."[13] "The threat of a plural society based on religious differences" confronts the nation, the editorial asserts, and the prime promoters of this threat are the Catholics. Pluralism, which is defined in J. S. Furnivall's formulation as a society "comprising two or more elements which live side by side, yet without mingling, in one political unit," is said to have become the deliberate and conscious policy of American Catholicism in recent years. "The proliferation of Catholic parochial schools, Catholic labor unions, Catholic civic clubs, Catholic veterans' organizations, Catholic political lobbies," the editorial concludes, "has more than religious significance to American society. It means that a conscious and well-planned large-scale attempt is being made to separate Catholics from other Americans in almost every area of social life. It means that an effort is under way to create a separate social order which will exist side by side with the rest of American society in the same political unit, but will as far as possible limit its contact with that society to the market place."

The radical evil of a plural society, we are told, is that "it can have no common will; it makes for national instability; it puts an undue emphasis on material things; [and] it nullifies the unifying function of education." The last point, which seems most basic, again raises the question of the "divisive" parochial school. "A plural society," it is alleged, "nullifies the unifying function of education by splitting up among its constituent units the responsibility for providing education, rather than allowing the state to provide a common education for all children." In a most curious way, the authoritarian doctrine of *l'état enseignant* (the "teaching state," the state as the molder of the ideology of its citizens) has become part of the creed of a large segment of American Protestantism.[14]

Pluralism in Furnivall's sense would indeed be a serious matter for a society such as ours. But there would seem to be little danger of it in contemporary America. Indeed, *The Christian Century* appears to have discovered the menace precisely at a time when, due to advanced acculturation and increasing mobility, American Catholics are becoming increasingly integrated into the general community rather than the reverse. But this integration is taking place in a new and characteristic fashion, in and through the religious community as one of the three "pools" in the "triple melting pot" that is America. This *The Christian Century* writer apparently does not see, yet his outburst of alarm is not unrelated to the sociological process.

American Protestantism is so apprehensive at the development of religio-communal pluralism in part at least because in this kind of pluralistic situation it would seem to be at a serious disadvantage. It has been so long identified with America as a whole that it has neither the background nor the conviction necessary to build up its own Protestant community institutions in the same way that Jews and Catholics have built up theirs. Jews and Catholics have their own war veterans' associations, but it would probably appear strange and unwholesome to Protestants to establish a Protestant war veterans' organization; aren't the "general" war veterans' organizations sufficiently Protestant? Once they were, just as until the last quarter of the nineteenth century the public schools were virtually Protestant "parochial" schools, but they are no longer such today. Protestants, particularly the old-line Protestant leadership, cannot seem to reconcile themselves to this primary fact. Nor do they seem capable of overcoming, in many cases even of mitigating, the fragmentation of denominationalism, which places Protestantism at another disadvantage

in the face of an ecclesiastically united Catholicism. All
this contributes to the Protestant distaste for "pluralism"
and adds fuel to Protestant defensive resentment against
"Rome."

It would be gravely misleading, however, to leave the
impression that this attitude is universal among Protestants
or that there are no Protestant voices urging other counsels.
There is, in the first place, a striking difference in outlook
between the older and the younger generations of Protestants in America. The older generation, still thinking of
America as the Protestant nation of their youth, cannot
help feeling bitter and resentful at what must appear to
them to be menacing encroachments of Catholics in American life; the younger generation, accustomed to America
as a three-religion country, cannot understand what the excitement is all about: "After all, we're all Americans . . ."
On the other side, theologically concerned Protestants find
it difficult to go along with the kind of negative "anti-
Romanism" current in many Protestant circles; they find
it both too sterile and too secularist, too reminiscent of
cultural totalism, for their taste. Reinhold Niebuhr, John
C. Bennett, Robert McAfee Brown, Angus Dun, Liston
Pope, Henry P. Van Dusen, and other Protestant theologians, while criticizing what they regard as erroneous views
and abuses of power among Catholics, have been particularly insistent on the necessity of a new Protestant orientation more in conformity with the facts of American life and
more faithful to its own religious tradition.[15]

Minority consciousness is, of course, particularly strong
among American Jews, and it is among American Jews that
the "philosophy" and strategy of minority-group defensiveness has been most elaborately developed. "Defense" activities play a major part in American Jewish community
life: the "defense" is against "defamation" (anti-Semitism)
on the one hand, and against the intrusion of the "church"
into education and public life on the other. Spokesmen of
American Jewish institutions and agencies—no one, of
course, can speak for American Jewry as a whole—have
almost always displayed an attitude on matters of church

and state, religion and public affairs, more extreme even than that of the Protestant champions of the "wall of separation." Their alliance with secularism is even closer; perhaps it would be more accurate to say that they have themselves taken over the entire secularist ideology on church-state relations to serve as defensive strategy.

It is not difficult to understand why an extreme secularism and "separationism" should appeal to so many American Jews as a defensive necessity. At bottom, this attitude may be traced to the conviction, widely held though rarely articulated, that because the Western Jew achieved emancipation with the secularization of society, he can preserve his free and equal status only so long as culture and society remains secular. Let but religion gain a significant place in the everyday life of the community, and the Jew, because he is outside the bounds of the dominant religion, will once again be relegated to the margins of society, displaced, disfranchised culturally if not politically, shorn of rights and opportunities. The intrusion of religion into education and public life, the weakening of the "wall of separation" between religion and the state, is feared as only too likely to result in situations in which Jews would find themselves at a disadvantage—greater isolation, higher "visibility," an accentuation of minority status. The most elementary defensive strategy would thus seem to dictate keeping religion out of education and public life at all costs; hence the passionate attachment of so many American Jews to the secularist-Protestant interpretation of the principle of "separation" and to the general "Blanshardite" position.

The defensive necessities of Jewish minority interests do not, in the case of most Jews, seem to imply any particular tension with Protestants, especially the more "liberal" Protestants in the big cities where Jews are to be found; suspicion and tension emerge, however, more obviously in Jewish-Catholic relations. A recent survey indicated that more than three times as many Jews felt themselves "interfered with" by Catholics as by Protestants, almost twice as many Jews felt they were "looked down upon" by Catholics as by Protestants, and three times as many Jews confessed to harboring "ill feeling" toward Catholics as toward

Protestants.[16] Catholicism represents, to many Jews, a much more aggressive form of religion than Protestantism (most Jews never come into contact with the militant fundamentalism of rural and small-town America); deep down, it is the Catholic Church that is suspected of untoward designs and Catholic domination that is feared.

The precarious minority position of the American Jew in a non-Jewish world also impels him to strenuous, and what to some might seem extravagant, efforts at corporate self-validation. The extensive building programs that are being feverishly pursued by Jewish communities throughout the land are not merely the reflection of unparalleled prosperity and a rising level of synagogue affiliation; these programs serve a public relations function which is never entirely unconscious. Indeed, public relations seems to be more anxiously, and skillfully, cultivated by American Jewry than by either the Catholics or the Protestants; nothing that any Jewish community agency does, whatever may be its intrinsic nature or value, is ever without its public relations angle. A curious manifestation of this concern with corporate self-validation in the face of the "outside" world is the extraordinarily high salaries Jewish rabbis receive in comparison with those received by Protestant ministers of equal status and service.[17] The salary and style of life of the rabbi is, to a Jewish community outside the very big cities, a significant form of vicariously defining and enhancing its corporate status in the larger society. It is felt to be humiliating to the entire Jewish community if the rabbi cannot maintain a manner of life that would make him at home in the upper strata—something that would never occur to the average Protestant community, which hardly expects its minister to achieve equal standing with the social elite. Considerations of minority-group validation and defense thus enter into every phase and aspect of Jewish life in America.

Religio-communal tensions have grown in recent years, particularly Protestant-Catholic tensions in most parts of the country. Because of these tensions, which are in some sense inherent in the situation in which we find ourselves as we undergo the transition from a "Protestant nation" to a "three-religion country," the religious community has tended to be turned into a self-enclosed defensive institution. Catholicism maintains its communal solidarity through a strong emphasis on a common faith and tradition, and through a pervasive system of ecclesiastical control. The unity of American Jewry is not the unity of religious affiliation, but rather an impalpable unity of history and destiny expressed through common institutions of philanthropy, public relations, and communal welfare; such denominationalism as exists is, therefore, without real divisive effect. American Protestantism, however, possesses neither a common tradition, nor an ecclesiastical machinery, nor an armature of community institutions. It is therefore at a grave disadvantage in the struggle for security and status that characterizes religious community life in America today.

Yet *The Christian Century* editorialist had little reason to despair, either for Protestantism or the nation. The structure of American society being what it is, no large-scale defections from Protestantism to Catholicism seem probable in the foreseeable future. The American Protestant may, on occasion, move from one denomination to another as convenience and association dictate, but under normal circumstances (barring intermarriage, and much more rarely, conversion) he will not leave the Protestant fold, for it is Protestantism that gives him his "brand name" in the bewildering complexity of American society, and "brand names" are not easily changed. American Protestantism will maintain itself and grow with the general growth of church membership and religious affiliation in this country. Whether it will prove able to recover the initiative and overcome the paralyzing negativism which burdens it today, whether it will once again become a dynamic religious movement with a new and creative word for America, only the future can tell.

Nor need we be unduly disturbed lest the growing religio-communal pluralism disrupt the unity and subvert the foundations of American society. However severe the tensions, however deep the suspicions, that divide Protes-

tant and Catholic and Jew, there are limits beyond which
they cannot go. In the last analysis, Protestant and Catholic
and Jew stand united through their common anchorage in,
and common allegiance to, the American Way of Life. The
"unifying" function of education is not annulled because
Catholics have their own schools and Jews attempt to in-
culcate their children with a loyalty to their "people." The
same basic values and ideals, the same underlying commitment to the American Way of Life, are promoted by
parochial school and public school, by Catholic, Protestant,
and Jew, despite the diversity of formal religious creed.
After all, are not Protestantism, Catholicism, and Judaism,
in their sociological actuality, alike "religions of democracy"? Are they not essentially, from this aspect at least,
variant expressions of the same "common religion" which,
as Williams insists, "every functioning society has to an
important degree" and which supplies "an overarching
sense of unity" even when that society is "riddled with conflicts"?[18] The unity of American life is a unity in multiplicity; it is a unity that is grounded in a "common faith"
and is therefore capable of being re-established, despite tension and conflict, on the level of "interfaith."[19]

II

The interfaith[20] movement, which has assumed considerable dimensions in recent years, emerged in its present form
in the early 1920s. In 1923, in order to counter the bigotry
that was spreading through the nation under the growing
influence of the Ku Klux Klan, the Federal Council of
Churches set up a Commission on Good Will Between Jews
and Christians. By 1928 it was deemed wiser to establish
the movement on its own foundations, and in that year
the National Conference of Christians and Jews[21] was
launched as a joint organization of "Protestants, Catholics,
and Jews" with the stated purpose "to promote justice,
amity, understanding, and co-operation among Protestants,
Catholics, and Jews."[22]

The activities of the N.C.C.J., largely educational in the
broad sense of the term, have been conducted on the fami-

liar tripartite basis; for example, speaking tours of teams comprising a Protestant minister, a Catholic priest, and a Jewish rabbi have been arranged, conferences on human relations have been set up, a widely syndicated news service and much pamphlet literature issued, all in line with the basic purposes of the movement. In furtherance of these purposes, moreover, a Brotherhood Week was launched in 1934 during the week of Washington's Birthday and has been observed ever since on a constantly expanding scale. The Conference has repeatedly insisted that its purpose is neither to sponsor nor to oppose "joint worship, exchange of pulpits, or common observance of holy days," but simply to "promote brotherhood in those ways which are acceptable to Protestants, Catholics, and Jews," and to serve as a "civic agency" for "affirmative co-operative action among Protestants, Catholics, and Jews in areas of common civic concern." From the beginning, "tolerance" and "co-operation" have been its most familiar watchwords.

But, of course, interfaith activities in this sense have not been limited to the program of the National Conference of Christians and Jews. On a local and national scale these activities have been growing steadily in widening areas. Most college campuses have interfaith organizations or committees. Thanksgiving is increasingly observed as an interfaith holiday.[23] New York and other cities have a special Interfaith Day with appropriate ceremonies.[24] The struggle against Communism is organized as an interfaith venture.[25] Conferences on alcoholism, juvenile delinquency, and other social problems are run on an interfaith basis.[26] In fact, virtually every civic enterprise possessing any moral, cultural, or spiritual aspect is today thought of, and where possible organized, along interfaith—that is, tripartite—lines. This is, in part, frequently a matter of "political" expediency, but the interfaith pattern has extended far beyond such necessity; the very notion of tripartite arrangement is something that increasingly commends itself to the American mind as intrinsically right and proper because it is so obviously American and so obviously all-inclusive of the total American community.

This is not to say that the tensions and anxieties that

divide American religious communities have not invaded
the field of interfaith. Quite the contrary; the familiar
themes of religio-communal suspicion reappear in this area
and are on occasion given overt expression. Thus, Catholics are constantly concerned that interfaith should not lead
to "interreligious worship" or "interreligious theological discussion,"[27] or to the notion that "one religion is as good as
another." Protestants and Jews seem perpetually disturbed
lest interfaith be subverted by Catholics into an instrument
of corporate aggrandizement.[28] But on the whole, each
recognizes a need and a responsibility that overrides, if it
does not dispel, all suspicions and doubts. The interfaith
movement has emerged as one of the most vigorous and
extensive enterprises on the American scene; above all, the
interfaith idea has become one of the accepted aspects of
the American Way of Life.

It is hardly accidental that the interfaith enterprise,
which flourishes so vigorously in the United States, has
never been able to make much headway in Britain, on the
European continent, or elsewhere in the world. Similar
organizations have been set up in various countries, beginning with a conference in London in November 1924,
but these have led a rather tenuous existence, with a very
limited scope of activities; much the same can be said of the
world organization launched at an international conference
held in Oxford in August 1946.[29] Most of these ventures
outside the United States have either been emergency
agencies to fight anti-Semitism, and have generally lapsed
with the waning of the danger, or they have been converted into vehicles of theological discussion. It is this latter
enterprise—the so-called "Jewish-Christian conversation"[30]
—that is characteristic of the "interfaith" idea on the continent, rather than the religio-communal co-operation familiar in this country.

The contrast is striking and significant. The American
kind of interfaith, operative at all levels of civic life, but
carefully steering clear of religious or theological discussion, makes little appeal to the European to whom the
tripartite system is strange and who feels that religiously

concerned people should be interested in mutual discussion of their theological positions. In this country, on the other hand, controversial discussion of religion in which each participant confesses and bears witness to his convictions is felt to be undesirable and "un-American," since it might tend to accentuate "ideological" differences rather than stress commitment to the shared values and ideals of the American Way of Life. One's particular religion is, of course, to be cherished and loyally adhered to, but it is not felt to be something that one "flaunts" in the face of people of other faiths. When at the Second Assembly of the World Council of Churches at Evanston, in August 1954, the proposal was made to include a special reference to Christian evangelical witness to the Jews in the message to the churches, Charles P. Taft, lay delegate of the Protestant Episcopal Church of the United States, "objected strongly to the reference. Insisting that his views had no political implications, he said that the reference would make for bad interfaith relations . . ."[31] The special reference to the Jews was deleted by a vote of 195 to 150.[32] In Europe, an omission of such reference to the Jews would very likely have been regarded as an outcropping of anti-Semitic prejudice, reminiscent of the Nazi exclusion of the Jews from the scope of the church; in the United States, to include such reference was felt by even earnest Christians to be somehow insulting to the Jews and an impairment of interfaith relations! It will be noted how big this American idea of "interfaith relations" is beginning to loom in church councils even on the highest level.

Interfaith in this country is the device that American experience has elaborated for bringing some measure of harmony among the religious communities and in some degree mitigating their tensions and suspicions. It is made possible by their common grounding in the American Way of Life and their feeling that despite all differences of creed "brotherhood" and "affirmative co-operative action" among Protestants, Catholics, and Jews is not only possible and desirable but is also in a sense mandatory if American democracy is to function properly.[33] Interfaith in the American sense is America's answer to the problem of religious divisiveness in a society structured along religio-communal lines.

III

The three great religious communities—Protestant, Catholic, and Jewish—constitute the three basic subdivisions of the American people in the American society that is emerging today. The three great religious communions—Protestantism, Catholicism, and Judaism—constitute the three great American religions, the "religions of democracy." We have now, at some length, examined the tripartite structure of American society in its impact on various aspects of American social life. But what can we say about the *religious* content and significance of these "religions of democracy" from the point of view of the faith from which these religions are historically derived and to which they profess to stand witness? Hitherto our inquiry has, broadly speaking, been sociological in character; now it must become theological, for what we are concerned with at this point is a theological interpretation and critique of religion in America today.

FOOTNOTES

1. Thomas Sugrue, *A Catholic Speaks His Mind on America's Religious Conflict* (Harper, 1951), pp. 47–48.

2. See, e.g., John J. Kane, "Catholic Separatism," in *Catholicism in America: A Series of Articles from The Commonweal* (Harcourt, Brace, 1953), pp. 47–57; also Joseph E. Cunneen, "Catholics and Education," pp. 143–63, in the same volume.

3. There is some indication that these fears may be exaggerated. An American Institute of Public Opinion (Gallup) survey in 1949, immediately after the controversy between Cardinal Spellman and Mrs. Roosevelt, found that some 41 per cent of the American people favored federal aid to parochial schools on the same basis as aid to public schools, 49 per cent were against, with 10 per cent of no opinion. Catholics, naturally, were overwhelmingly (79 per cent) in favor, but so were 31 per cent of the Protestants (59 per cent against, 10 per cent no opinion). "The greatest acceptance of the Catholic argument in favor

of federal aid to parochial institutions was to be found among young voters of all religions" (*Public Opinion News Service,* August 17, 1949).

4. For data as to Catholic schools, see "Catholic Schools in America," *Information Service* (Federal Council of Churches of Christ), December 16, 1950; Bertha Blair, "Church-Related Elementary and Secondary Schools in Continental United States," *Information Service,* January 3, 1959; *The 1959 National Catholic Almanac,* pp. 467–99.

5. The literature on the church-state problem, particularly as it relates to education, is vast and irreducibly controversial. For a moderately "separationist" Protestant view, see Anson Phelps Stokes, *Church and State in the United States,* 2 vols. (Harper, 1950); for an extreme "separationist" work written by a Jew, see Leo Pfeffer, *Church, State, and Freedom* (Beacon, 1953); the Catholic position is well stated in James M. O'Neill, *Religion and Education Under the Constitution* (Harper, 1949). See also Will Herberg, "The Sectarian Conflict Over Church and State," *Commentary,* Vol. XIV, No. 5, November 1952; and "Religion, Democracy, and Public Education," in John Cogley, ed., *Religion in America* (Meridian, 1958).

6. For an informed Catholic account of Protestant-Catholic tensions, see John J. Kane, *Catholic-Protestant Conflicts in America* (Regnery, 1955). Kenneth W. Underwood, *Protestant and Catholic: Religious and Social Interaction in an Industrial Community* (Beacon, 1957) provides a careful analysis of relations in an important New England community. An interesting discussion of current religio-social conflicts, from a very different standpoint, will be found in Leo Pfeffer, *Creeds in Competition* (Harper, 1958).

7. "Christian Faith and the Protestant Churches," *Social Action,* Vol. XVIII, No. 6, May 1952, p. 1.

8. The columns of *The Christian Century,* (especially in earlier years), as well as of other Protestant journals in this country, are full of evidences of the pervasive Protestant concern with Catholic aggression: e.g., "Christian Cooperation in Buffalo" (*The Christian Century,* June 13, 1951), a report of a special survey of Buffalo Protestantism; John F. Schaefer, "Needed: A Local Protestant Strategy" (*The Christian Century,* January 27, 1954), a call for united, militant Protestant action in Elgin, Illinois, which is 80 per cent Protestant; Reuben L. Speaks, "Will the Negro Remain Protestant?" (*The Christian Century,* June 2, 1954); Carl J. Scherzer, "More Protestant Hospitals!" (*The Christian Century,* July 21, 1954). In each of these cases, and the examples could be multiplied, the program or policy proposed is motivated in terms of resistance to Catholic aggression: "straightforward, uncompromising resistance to any efforts by

any group to subvert to ecclesiastical control a basically democratic way of life"; "the aggressive and comprehensive program of expansion promoted by the Roman Catholic Church"; "the rapid and increasing trend [of Negroes] toward Roman Catholicism"; "some Protestants are beginning to wonder about Roman Catholic expansion in the hospital field."

9. See "Trends of Church Membership in the Larger Religious Bodies," *Information Service*, March 8, 1952. For data on proselytizing activity, see "Are Catholics Winning the U.S.?" (*The Catholic Digest*, June 1953), the thirteenth installment of the Gaffin survey of religion in America. A special tabulation, covering the Catholic Church and 18 large Protestant bodies with about 65 per cent of all Protestant church members, indicated that: "In the period 1929–52, inclusive, 18 large Protestant bodies reported a gain in total membership from 24,641,243 persons to 35,160,482, or 42.7 per cent. During the same years, the officially reported Roman Catholic membership increased from 20,078,202 persons to 30,253,427, or 50.7 per cent. The membership of both the Protestant bodies and of the Roman Catholic Church increased more rapidly in the period 1942–52 than in earlier years" (*Information Service*, January 8, 1955).

10. See above, chap. vii, p. 160.

11. See, e.g., Harold Fey, "Can Catholicism Win America?", *The Christian Century*, November 29, December 6, December 13, December 20, December 27, 1944, January 3, January 10, January 17, 1945. Mr. Fey draws a picture of Roman Catholic advance on all fronts and concludes: "Until such [Protestant] unity appears, the answer to the question, Can Catholicism Win America? is—Yes." Ten years later, however, in an editorial headed, "Protestant, Be Yourself!", *The Christian Century* described this attitude as "Protestant paranoia," designating the corresponding Catholic attitude as "Catholic claustrophobia" (October 19, 1955). The editorial is a powerful plea for realism and understanding in Protestant-Catholic relations in this country.

12. Paul Blanshard, *American Freedom and Catholic Power* (Beacon, 1949); *Communism, Democracy, and Catholic Power* (Beacon, 1951); *The Irish and Catholic Power* (Beacon, 1953).

13. "Pluralism—National Menace," *The Christian Century*, June 13, 1951.

14. The phrase, *l'état enseignant*, emerged in seventeenth century France and became established French policy with the Revolution and Napoleon. American democratic doctrine is very different; it was laid down by the United States Supreme Court in two crucial opinions, in the Oregon case (1925) and in another case some two decades later (1944). The Oregon decision speaks of "the right of parents to direct the rearing and educa-

tion of their children free from any general power of the state to standardize children by forcing them to accept instruction from public school teachers only" (Pierce *v.* Society of Sisters, 1925). In 1944 the court stated: "It is cardinal with us that the custody, care, and nurture of the child reside first in the parents, whose primary function and freedom include preparation for obligations the state can neither supply nor hinder" (Prince *v.* Massachusetts, 1944).

15. This significant difference between the generations is clearly reflected in responses given to queries in recent public opinion polls on voting for a Catholic for President. Younger voters uniformly show a considerably higher percentage ready to vote for a Catholic than do older voters (*Public Opinion News Service*, June 24, 1956; October 26, 1958). In general, the figures show a long-term trend of decline in anti-Catholic attitudes on the Presidency. See also note 3, above pp. 246–47. For the newer theological attitudes among Protestants, see such publications as *Christianity and Crisis*, edited by Reinhold Niebuhr and John C. Bennett, and *Social Action*, edited in recent years successively by Liston Pope, Kenneth Underwood, and F. Ernest Johnson. See especially the "Statement on Church and State" signed by twenty-seven leading Protestant theologians, church leaders, and educators, *Christianity and Crisis*, Vol. VIII, No. 12, July 5, 1948, and the introductory editorial article, "Implications of the 'New Conception of "Separation," '" by J. C. B. (John C. Bennett). Note particularly Reinhold Niebuhr, "The Rising Catholic-Protestant Tension," *Christianity and Crisis*, August 8, 1949; "Catholics and Politics: Some Misconceptions," *Christianity and Crisis*, June 23, 1952; "Editorial Note," *Christianity and Crisis*, February 2, 1953; "Democracy, Secularism, and Christianity," *Christianity and Crisis*, March 2, 1953. In recent years, *Christianity and Crisis* has done outstanding service in initiating a fruitful Protestant-Catholic dialogue on a high level; see especially the issue for June 8, 1959, given over to articles by three Catholic thinkers (Gustave Weigel, S.J., Thomas F. O'Dea, and William Clancy), with editorial introduction and comment by J. C. B. There has been considerable response in *America* and *The Commonweal*. An authoritative presentation of the Protestant position on many of the social and political issues involved in the Protestant-Catholic discussion will be found in John C. Bennett, *Christians and the State* (Scribner's, 1958), especially "Part Three: Church and State"; also Reinhold Niebuhr, "A Protestant Looks at Catholics," in *Catholicism in America*, pp. 25–36. For a discussion of these and other "Issues Between Catholics and Protestants at Mid-century," see the articles by George H. Williams, Waldo Beach, and H. Richard Niebuhr in *Religion in Life*, Vol. XXIV, No. 2, Spring 1954.

16. See "What We Think of Each Other," *The Catholic Di-*

gest, February 1953, the sixth installment of the Gaffin survey. About 4 per cent of Jews felt themselves "interfered with" by Protestants, but 13 per cent by Catholics; 16 per cent of Jews felt "looked down upon" by Protestants, but 30 per cent by Catholics; 5 per cent of Jews confessed to having an "ill feeling" for Protestants but 15 per cent said they had such feelings for Catholics.

17. The median income reported by male clergymen for 1949 was $2,412. Nowhere, in no state or community reporting, did the median income reach $3,000 ("The Number and Incomes of Clergymen," *Information Service,* January 9, 1954). In 1954, Congregational ministers averaged $3,313, United Presbyterian ministers $3,709 (*Time,* September 20, 1954). According to a study conducted by F. Ernest Johnson for the National Council of Churches, Protestant clergymen's salaries averaged $4,432 in 1958 (*New York Times,* June 15, 1958). It is common knowledge that the *starting* salaries of Jewish rabbis are substantially higher than these medians and averages, with all due consideration given to the minister's "perquisites" beyond salary. These differences cannot be accounted for simply in terms of the market, regional factors, or the differing class structure of the Protestant and Jewish communities in this country.

18. Robin M. Williams, *American Society: A Sociological Interpretation* (Knopf, 1951), p. 312.

19. This is true despite the fact that anti-Semitism remains, and is bound to remain, an unresolved problem for American society; see Herberg, "Anti-Semitism Today," *The Commonweal,* July 16, 1954.

20. The term "interfaith" is hardly accurate; whatever may have been the original intentions, the movement has not developed as a movement of relations *between* the three faiths, but rather as a movement of co-operation *among* them for commonly accepted purposes. Indeed, the National Conference of Christians and Jews has on occasion denied that it is "an 'interfaith' organization in the sense in which that word is commonly understood." Of late, it has been suggested that the term "interfaith" be replaced by "tri-faith" as more accurate and descriptive.

21. Because of its origin as a commission of the Federal Council of Churches, the Conference bears the anomalous "theological" name of National Conference of *Christians and Jews,* rather than the more familiar "sociological" designation of National Conference of *Protestants, Catholics, and Jews.* All its publications and statements, however, use the tripartite designation, and some writers have referred to it that way: thus, Schneider speaks of "The National Council of Protestants, Catholics, and Jews" in obvious allusion to the N.C.C.J. (Herbert Wallace

Schneider, *Religion in 20th Century America* [Harvard, 1952], p. 32).

22. "Lighting Lamps: The Program of the National Conference of Christians and Jews." See also "One Nation Under God: Report of the National Conference of Christians and Jews, 1954"; Everett R. Clinchy, *The Growth of Good Will: A Sketch of Protestant-Catholic-Jewish Relations* (National Conference of Christians and Jews, 1953).

23. "New Yorkers settled back today after a day of good cheer and prayerful Thanksgiving. The 19th annual interfaith service was held yesterday at Christ Church Methodist . . . by members of that congregation, Central Synagogue, and Central Presbyterian Church" (*New York Post*, November 26, 1954). In such interfaith services, Catholics of course do not participate.

24. "Senator Irving M. Ives and Averell Harriman, Republican and Democratic candidates for Governor, will participate in Interfaith Day ceremonies in the metropolitan area tomorrow" (*New York Herald Tribune*, September 25, 1954).

25. "WASHINGTON, Nov. 10.—The interfaith leaders seeking a statement of common faith on which to fight Communism concluded a three-day conference here today" (*The New York Times*, November 11, 1954). The reference is to the National Conference on the Spiritual Foundations of Our Democracy.

26. "An interfaith seminar on alcoholism will be held on September 27 and 28 in North Conway, N.H." (*The New York Times*, September 18, 1954).

27. See, e.g., "Campus Cooperation Without Compromise," *America*, April 24, 1954. In some cases, caution has impelled Catholic authorities to forbid co-operation in certain interfaith ventures; thus Bishop Walter E. Foery of Syracuse forbade Catholic students at Utica College of Syracuse University to participate in interfaith programs, panels, or meetings in the college's annual Religious Emphasis Day (*The New York Times*, March 21, 1954). See also Albert S. Foley, "Catholic Participation in Intergroup Activities," in *The McAuley Lectures 1955* (West Hartford, Conn.: Saint Joseph College, 1956).

28. For an apprehensive Jewish view, see Judah Raby, "Interfaith—On What Terms?", *Congress Weekly*, December 13, 1954, in which an interfaith conference in defense of democracy against Communism is regarded with suspicion as possibly the instrument of a Catholic effort to subvert the separation of church and state. See also Morris N. Kertzer, "Interfaith Relations in the United States," *Judaism*, Vol. III, No. 4, Fall 1954. For a deeply suspicious Protestant view, see "Protestantism and Tolerance," *The Christian Century*, February 14, 1945: "[This] organization, representing all three faiths, has exploited the con-

cept of tolerance—or good will, or mutual respect—on the assumption that the tolerance generated in such an association would be evenly distributed among the three groups, inasmuch as they all pay pious respect to the principle. It does not, however, work out this way. The result produced by this associated propaganda is one-sided. And the relative status of the several groups being what it is, this is not surprising. The tolerance that is generated is chiefly Protestant tolerance. Whatever degree of tolerance (if any) is produced in the other groups is hardly more than academic and sentimental, because, being a minority, they have no concrete occasion to exercise it. Protestantism in the United States is in no danger of persecution or overt unfriendly action by Catholics—certainly not yet. And as for Jewry, its numerical inferiority (not to mention the limited application which it gives to its religious faith) makes any suggestion that it should tolerate Protestantism or Catholicism absurd."

29. For a brief survey of the interfaith movement in the United States and abroad, see William W. Simpson, "Cooperation Between Christians and Jews," in Göte Hedenquist, ed., *The Church and the Jewish People* (Edinburgh House Press, 1954), esp. pp. 123–34.

30. See Hans Joachim Schoeps, *Jüdisch-Christliches Religionsgespräch in 19 Jahrhunderten* (Atharva-Verlag, Frankfurt, 1949). These discussions continued in the twentieth century up to the time of Hitler, and were resumed, under very different circumstances, in 1947. There are signs of the beginnings of a theological "conversation" between Protestants and Catholics in this country, but none so far between Christians and Jews.

31. "Literalists Lose By Close Vote," *The Christian Century*, September 8, 1954.

32. This vote was made possible by the fact that "when the issue came to the floor for debate, the Coptic and Orthodox churches in the Middle East and Africa rallied to Mr. Taft's side. Their delegates took the position that the reference to the evangelization of the Jews would be a handicap to the work of their churches and would complicate the relation of their churches with the World Council" ("Literalists Lose By Close Vote," *The Christian Century*, September 8, 1954). The motivation here was obviously anti-Jewish, or at least an unwillingness to appear to give any special consideration to the Jews. Thus curiously was Mr. Taft's reluctance to impair interfaith relations by giving offense to American Jews made to prevail through the votes of Coptic and Orthodox delegates motivated by very different, even opposite, considerations.

33. Interfaith unity is today immensely enhanced by the growing sense of common cause in defense of democracy against Communism, the sworn enemy of both democracy and religion.

For an account of a recent effort to set up a religious front against Communism, and a discussion of some of the problems involved, see Herberg, "Communism, Democracy, and the Churches," *Commentary*, Vol. XIX, No. 4, April 1955.

XI. *Religion in America in the Perspective of Faith*

Jewish-Christian faith[1] is God-centered. All being finds its beginning and its end in God, and its unity, reality, and order in its ordination to Him. Jewish-Christian faith sees man's proper life, the life for which he was created and which corresponds to his "essential nature," as the life of responsive love of God and hence love of fellow man. But it also knows that man's actual life is corrupted by idolatrous self-love, which disrupts and perverts all human relations. We are always prone to idolize ourselves and our works, to attribute quite uncritically final significance to our interests, ideas, and institutions, to make of our achievements an instrument of pride, power, and self-aggrandizement. Such perverse egocentricity is not without its consequences. "Thus saith the Lord God: Because you count yourself wise as a god, behold I bring strangers against you. . . . Your heart was proud because of your beauty; you corrupted your wisdom by reason of your splendor. [Therefore] I cast you to the ground . . ." (Ezek. 28.6-7, 17). The prophets trace all the evils of life to this kind of human self-idolatrization, which is at the heart of what the theologians know as "original sin."

Sinful egocentricity invades all areas of life, including the religious. Man is *homo religiosus*, by "nature" religious: as much as he needs food to eat or air to breathe, he needs a faith for living. He is always striving to find a center of life beyond life, a larger whole transcending the self in which to ground the meaning and security of existence; he is always searching for some god and some way of salvation from the fears, futilities, and frustrations of life. But—and this is the challenging word of Jewish-Christian faith—so long as he pursues this search in self-sufficiency, relying on his own virtue, wisdom, or piety, it will not be God that he finds, but an idol—the self, or some aspect of the self, writ large, projected, objectified, and worshiped. The living God of Jewish-Christian faith is to be found not through self-sufficient "searching," but through "meeting" Him as He discloses Himself in the divine-human encounter of which Scripture and the tradition of the believing community are the witness. He is a God Who goes forth to "visit" man in the midst of life, and discloses Himself in the encounter.

The God of the Bible makes His unconditional demand upon men, calls them to total love and obedience, and therewith also judges them in their self-interest and self-aggrandizing pretensions. In Jewish-Christian faith, the word of redeeming grace comes only after the word of judgment has shattered all human claims to security and self-sufficiency. "I dwell in a high and holy place, saith the Lord, but also with him that is of a contrite and humble spirit" (Is. 57.15).

The word of judgment upon human self-sufficiency is also a word of judgment upon human religion, or the human element in religion. "There is nothing in the Bible to support the view that religion is necessarily a good thing. Scripture has no ax to grind for religion; on the contrary, it is highly suspicious of much that passes for religion."[2] "Religion qua religion," says Reinhold Niebuhr, "is naturally idolatrous, accentuating rather than diminishing the self-worship of men, [institutions] and nations by assuring them of an ultimate sanction for their dearest desires. . . . Religion per se and faith per se are not virtues, or a cause of virtue. The question is always what the object of worship is, and whether the worship tends to break the pride of the self so that a truer self may arise, either individually or collectively."[3] To the man of biblical faith, religion is not self-validating or self-justifying; it has to be tested, critically examined, and evaluated in terms of its authenticity in mediating the will, judgment, and redeeming grace of the God Who can be "met" only in repentance and the abandonment of all claims to human self-sufficiency.

The ambivalence of religion extends to the church. Biblical faith is defined by, and expressed through, community: the Jew or Christian finds access to his God from within the People of God. "The individual Israelite," Alan Richardson points out, "approached God in virtue of his membership in the holy people. . . . In the whole of the Bible, in the Old Testament as well as the New, there is no such thing as a private, personal relation between an individual and God apart from his membership in the covenant-folk."[4] Biblical faith is thus the faith of man-in-community, and both Judaism and Christianity place strong emphasis on the corporate dimension of the religious life. In this sense, the church—of which the equivalent in Judaism is the People Israel—is divine, with a divine vocation.

But in another sense, in the temporal, institutional sense, the church is, of course, human, and subject to all of the temptations and corruptions of human institutions. Indeed, precisely because in the church man confronts God in a quite unique way, the church may well become the "final battleground between God and man's self-esteem,"[5] where "the hostility of men against God is brought to a head."[6] Since there is nothing human that self-interest and irresponsibility may not attempt to exploit for its own purposes, the church too (in its human aspects, at least) stands under judgment.

Religion, then, is an ambiguous and doubtful thing, requiring careful scrutiny on the part of the man of faith. And what is true of religion in general is particularly true of religion in contemporary America, where the great and almost unprecedented upsurge of religiosity under way today stems from so many diverse sources and manifests itself in so many contradictory forms.

I

The outstanding feature of the religious situation in America today is the pervasiveness of religious self-identification along the tripartite scheme of Protestant, Catholic, Jew. From the "land of immigrants," America has, as we have seen, become the "triple melting pot," restructured in three great communities with religious labels, defining three great "communions" or "faiths." This transformation has been greatly furthered by what may be called the dialectic of "third generation interest": the third generation, coming into its own with the cessation of mass immigration, tries to recover its "heritage," so as to give itself some sort of "name," or context of self-identification and social location, in the larger society. "What the son wishes to forget"—so runs "Hansen's Law"—"the grandson wishes to remember." But what he can "remember" is obviously not his grandfather's foreign language, or even his grandfather's foreign culture; it is rather his grandfather's *religion*—America does not demand of him the abandonment of the ancestral religion as it does of the ancestral language and culture. This religion he now "remembers" in a form suitably "Americanized," and yet in a curious way also "retraditionalized." Within this comprehensive framework of basic sociological change operate those inner factors making for a "return to religion" which so many observers have noted in recent years—the collapse of all secular securities in the historical crisis of our time, the quest for a recovery of meaning in life, the new search for inwardness and personal authenticity amid the collectivistic heteronomies of the present-day world.

Self-identification in religious terms, almost universal in the America of today, obviously makes for religious belonging in a more directly institutional way. It engenders a sense of adherence to a church or denomination and impels one to institutional affiliation. These tendencies are reinforced by the pressures of other-directed adjustment to peer-group behavior, which today increasingly requires religious identification and association with some church. Thus a pattern of religious conformism develops, most pronounced, perhaps, among the younger, "modern-minded" inhabitants of Suburbia, but rapidly spreading to all sections of the American people.

The picture that emerges is one in which religion is accepted as a normal part of the American Way of Life. Not to be—that is, not to identify oneself and be identified as—either a Protestant, a Catholic, or a Jew is somehow not to be an American. It may imply being foreign, as is the case when one professes oneself a Buddhist, a Muslim, or anything but a Protestant, Catholic, or Jew, even when one's Americanness is otherwise beyond question. Or it may imply being obscurely "un-American," as is the case with those who declare themselves atheists, agnostics, or even "humanists." Sidney H. Scheuer, a leading Ethical Culturist, was expressing a genuine concern when he stated recently: "There is a tendency to regard all people who are not committed to one of the three great faiths as being disloyal to American principles and traditions."[7] Americanness today entails religious identification as Protestant, Catholic, or Jew in a way and to a degree quite unprecedented in our history. To be a Protestant, a Catholic, or a Jew are today the alternative ways of being an American.

This religious normality implies a certain religious unity in terms of a common "American religion" of which each of the three great religious communions is regarded as an equi-legitimate expression. America has emerged as a "three-religion country,"[8] in which the Protestant, the Catholic, and the Jew each finds his place. Insofar as America knows of a church in the Troeltschean sense—a form of religious belonging that goes along with being a member of the national community—it is this tripartite unity of Protestant-Catholic-Jew. Each on his part—the Protestant, the Catholic, the Jew—may regard his own "faith" as the best or even the truest, but unless he is a theologian or affected with a special theological interest, he will quite "naturally" look upon the other two as sharing with his communion a common "spiritual" foundation of basic "ideals and values"—the chief of these being religion itself. America thus has its underlying culture-religion—best understood as the religious aspect of the American Way of Life—of which the three conventional religions are somehow felt to be appropriate manifestations and expressions. Religion is integral to Americanism as currently understood. "Recognition of the Supreme Being," President Eisenhower declared early in 1955 in his address launching the American Legion's "Back to God" campaign, "is the first, the most basic, expression of Americanism. Without God, there could be no American form of government, nor an American way of life."[9] In uttering these words, Mr. Eisenhower was speaking for the great mass of American people and affording an important insight into one aspect of contemporary American religiosity.

The religious unity of American life implies an institutional and ideological pluralism. The American system is one of stable coexistence of three equi-legitimate religious communities grounded in the common culture-religion of America. Within this common framework there is persistent tension and conflict, reflecting the corporate anxieties and minority-group defensiveness of each of the three communities. To mitigate these tensions and prevent the conflicts from becoming too destructive, American experience has brought forth the characteristically American device of "interfaith," which, as idea and movement, has permeated broad areas of national life. Interfaith, as we have seen, is a religiously oriented civic co-operation of Protestants, Catholics, and Jews to bring about better mutual understanding and to promote enterprises and causes of common concern, despite all differences of "faith." The interfaith movement is not secularistic or indifferentist but in its own way quite religious, for it is conceived as a joint enterprise of representative men and women of the three religious communities dedicated to purposes of common interest felt to be worth while from the religious point of view. Interfaith is thus the highest expression of religious coexistence and co-operation within the American understanding of religion.

II

The ultimate ambiguity of the present religious situation in this country is obvious on the face of it. Every manifestation of contemporary American religion reveals diverse sides, of varying significance from the standpoint of Jewish-Christian faith. No realistic estimate of the present religious situation is possible unless this fundamental ambiguity is recognized.

The new status of religion as a basic form of American "belonging," along with other factors tending in the same direction, has led to the virtual disappearance of antireligious prejudice, once by no means uncommon in our national life. The old-time "village atheist" is a thing of the past, a folk curiosity like the town crier; Clarence Darrow, the last of the "village atheists" on a national scale, has left no successors. The present generation can hardly understand the vast excitement stirred up in their day by the "atheists" and "iconoclasts" who vied for public attention less than half a century ago, or imagine the brash militancy of the "rationalist" movements and publications now almost all extinct. Religion has become part of the ethos of American life to such a degree that overt anti-religion is all but inconceivable.

The same factors that have led to the virtual disappearance of overt anti-religion have also made for a new openness to religion and what religion might have to say about the urgent problems of life and thought. In many ways the contemporary mind is more ready to listen to the word of faith than Americans have been for decades.

Yet it is only too evident that the religiousness characteristic of America today is very often a religiousness without religion, a religiousness with almost any kind of content or none,[10] a way of sociability or "belonging" rather than a way of reorienting life to God. It is thus frequently a religiousness without serious commitment, without real inner conviction, without genuine existential decision. What should reach down to the core of existence, shattering and renewing, merely skims the surface of life, and yet succeeds in generating the sincere feeling of being religious. Religion thus becomes a kind of protection the self throws up against the radical demand of faith.

Where the other-directed adjustment of peer-group conformity operates, the discrepancy becomes even more obvious. The other-directed man or woman is eminently religious in the sense of being religiously identified and affiliated, since being religious and joining a church or synagogue is, under contemporary American conditions, a fundamental way of "adjusting" or "belonging." But what can the other-directed man or woman make of the prophets and the prophetic faith of the Bible, in which the religion of the church he joins is at least officially grounded? The very notion of being "singled out," of standing "over against" the world, is deeply repugnant to one for whom well-being means conformity and adjustment. Religion is valued as conferring a sense of sociability and "belonging," a sense of being really and truly *of* the world and society, a sense of reassurance; how can the other-directed man then help but feel acutely uncomfortable with a kind of religion—for that is what biblical faith is—which is a declaration of permanent resistance to the heteronomous claims of society, community, culture, and cult? The other-directed man generally protects himself against this profoundly disturbing aspect of biblical faith by refusing to understand it; indeed, insofar as he is other-directed, he really cannot understand it. The religion he avows is still formally the Christian or Jewish faith rooted in the prophetic tradition; it is, however, so transformed as it passes through the prism of the other-directed mind that it emerges as something quite different, in many ways, its opposite. The other-directed man, no matter how religious, simply cannot understand an Elijah or an Amos, a Jesus or an Isaiah; nor can he conceivably feel any warmth of admiration for these "zealots of the Lord." Zeal, nonconformity, uncompromising witness are so "unsociable," so terribly "unadjusted"! The very purpose of the other-directed man's built-in radar apparatus is to protect him against such perils;[11] it protects him so well that it makes the prophetic faith of the Bible almost unintelligible to him. The Christianity or Judaism he understands—and which he finds, or convinces himself that he finds, in church or synagogue—is something very different; it is an other-directed gospel of adjustment, sociability, and comfort, designed to give one a sense of "belonging," of being at home in the society and the universe. It is thus not too much of a paradox to assert that many of the inner-directed "unbelievers" of the nineteenth century in a sense stood closer to, or at least less distant from, authentic biblical faith than do so many of the religious people of our time, whose religion comes to them as an aspect of other-directed conformism and sociability.

Equally dubious from the standpoint of Jewish-Christian faith is that aspect of the present religious situation which makes religion in America so thoroughly American. On the one side this means that no taint of foreignness any longer adheres to the three great American "faiths." Catholics, Jews, Lutherans, and others, who remember how formidable an obstacle to the preservation and communication of their faith the taint of foreignness once was, will not be altogether ungrateful for this development. And all Americans may be thankful for the new spirit of freedom and tolerance in religious life that the emergence of the tripartite system of three great "religions of democracy" has engendered; it makes increasingly difficult the sinister fusion of religious prejudice with racist or nationalist chauvinism. But on the other side, the "Americanization" of religion has meant a distinct loss of the sense of religious uniqueness and universality: each of the three "faiths," insofar as the mass of its adherents are concerned, tends to regard itself as merely an alternative and variant form of being religious in the American way. This is true even of rank-and-file American Catholics, whose official theology places the strongest possible emphasis on the uniqueness and universality of the Roman Catholic Church as the "one true church"; this is true even of the vast majority of American Jews, who possess so pronounced a sense of worldwide Jewish kinship. The common ground between Judaism and Christianity, and on another level between Protestantism and Catholicism, is real and important, sufficiently real and important, indeed, to make it possible to speak significantly of Jewish-Christian faith in a way that no one could conceivably speak of Jewish-Buddhist or Christian-Hindu faith; yet the very existence of this common ground makes the unique and distinctive witness of each communion, even the advocacy of universal claims where such are felt to be justified, all the more necessary for the life of faith. Insofar as the "Americanness" of religion in America blunts this sense of uniqueness and universality, and converts the three religious communions into variant expressions of American spirituality (just as the three religious communities are understood to be three subdivisions of American society), the authentic character of Jewish-Christian faith is falsified, and the faith itself reduced to the status of an American culture-religion.[12]

This American culture-religion is the religious aspect of Americanism, conceived either as the common ground of the three "faiths" or as a kind of super-religion embracing them.[13] It will be recalled that President Eisenhower declared "recognition of the Supreme Being" to be "the first, the most basic expression," not of our historical religions, although undoubtedly Mr. Eisenhower would agree that it is, but of . . . *Americanism*. Americanism thus has its religious creed, evoking the appropriate religious emotions; it may, in fact, be taken as the civic religion of the American people.

But civic religion has always meant the sanctification of the society and culture of which it is the reflection, and that is one of the reasons why Jewish-Christian faith has always regarded such religion as incurably idolatrous. Civic religion is a religion which validates culture and society, without in any sense bringing them under judgment. It lends an ultimate sanction to culture and society by assuring them that they constitute an unequivocal expression of "spiritual ideals" and "religious values." Religion becomes, in effect, the cult of culture and society, in which the "right" social order and the received cultural values are divinized by being identified with the divine purpose. Any issue of *Christian Economics*, any pronouncement of such organizations as Spiritual Mobilization, will provide sufficient evidence of how Christian faith can be used to sustain the civic religion of "laissez-faire capitalism." Similar material from Catholic and Jewish sources comes easily to hand, from "liberal" quarters as well as from "conservative." On this level at least, the new religiosity pervading America seems to be very largely the religious validation of the social patterns and cultural values associated with the American Way of Life.

In a more directly political sense, this religiosity very easily comes to serve as a spiritual reinforcement of national self-righteousness and a spiritual authentication of national self-will. Americans possess a passionate awareness of their power and of the justice of the cause in which it is employed. The temptation is therefore particularly strong to identify the American cause with the cause of God, and to convert our immense and undeniable moral superiority over Communist tyranny into pretensions to unqualified wisdom and virtue. In these circumstances, it would seem to be the office of prophetic religion to raise a word of warning against inordinate national pride and self-righteousness as bound to lead to moral confusion, political irresponsibility, and the darkening of counsel. But the contemporary religious mood is very far indeed from such prophetic transcendence. Aside from occasional pronouncements by a few theologians or theologically-minded clergymen, religion in America seems to possess little capacity for rising above the relativities and ambiguities of the national consciousness and bringing to bear the judgment of God upon the nation and its ways.[14] The identification of religion with the national purpose is almost inevitable in a situation in which religion is so frequently felt to be a way of American "belonging." In its crudest form, this identification of religion with national purpose generates a kind of national messianism which sees it as the vocation of America to bring the American Way of Life, compounded almost equally of democracy and free enterprise, to every corner of the globe;[15] in more mitigated versions, it sees God as the champion of America, endorsing American purposes, and sustaining American might. "The God of judgment has died."[16]

Insensibly, this fusion of religion with national purpose passes over into the direct exploitation of religion for economic and political ends. A good deal of the official piety in Washington, it is charged, is of this kind,[17] and much of the new religiousness of businessmen and business interests throughout the country.[18] Certainly, when we find great corporations such as U. S. Steel distributing Norman Vincent Peale's *Guideposts* in huge quantities to their employees, when we find increasing numbers of industrial concerns placing "plant chaplains" on their staffs,[19] we are not altogether unjustified in suspecting that considerations of personnel policy have somehow entered into these good works of religion. On another level, there seems to be a concerted effort to turn President Eisenhower's deep and sincere religious feeling into a political asset. How otherwise are we to interpret the paragraph in the resolution officially adopted by the Republican National Committee on February 17, 1955, in which it is declared: "He [President Eisenhower], in every sense of the word, is not only the political leader, but the spiritual leader of our times"?[20] The fusion of political and spiritual leadership in the person of one national leader is in accord with neither the American democratic idea nor the tradition of Jewish-Christian faith; yet the statement of the Republican National Committee, making explicit the political exploitation of the "President's religon," seems to have aroused no comment in American religious circles. If indeed religion is the "spiritual" side of being an American, why should not the President of the United States be hailed as the "spiritual leader of our times"?

Religion is taken very seriously in present-day America, in a way that would have amazed and chagrined the "advanced" thinkers of half a century ago, who were so sure that the ancient superstition was bound to disappear very shortly in the face of the steady advance of science and reason. Religion has not disappeared; it is probably more pervasive today, and in many ways more influential, than it has been for generations. The only question is: What kind of religion is it? What is its content? What is it that Americans *believe in* when they are religious?

"The 'unknown God' of Americans seems to be faith itself."[21] What Americans believe in when they are religious is, as we have already had occasion to see,[22] religion itself. Of course, religious Americans speak of God and Christ, but what they seem to regard as really redemptive is primarily religion, the "positive" attitude of *believing*. It is this faith in faith, this religion that makes religion its own object, that is the outstanding characteristic of contemporary American religiosity. Daniel Poling's formula: "I began saying in the morning two words, 'I believe'—those two words *with nothing added* . . ."[23] (emphasis not in original) may be taken as the classic expression of this aspect of American faith.

On the social level, this faith in religion involves the conviction, quite universal among Americans today, that every decent and virtuous nation is religious, that religion is the true basis of national existence and therefore presumably the one sure resource for the solution of all national problems.[24] On the level of personal life, the American faith in religion implies not only that every right-minded citizen is religious, but also that religion (or faith) is a most efficacious device for getting what one wants in life.[25] "Jesus," the Rev. Irving E. Howard assures us, "recommended faith as a technique for getting results. . . . Jesus recommended faith as a way to heal the body and to remove any of the practical problems that loom up as mountains in a man's path."[26]

As one surveys the contemporary scene, it appears that the "results" Americans want to get out of faith are primarily "peace of mind," happiness, and success in worldly achievement. Religion is valued too as a means of cultural enrichment.

Prosperity, success, and advancement in business are the obvious ends for which religion, or rather the religious attitude of "believing," is held to be useful.[27] There is ordinarily no criticism of the ends themselves in terms of the ultimate loyalties of a God-centered faith, nor is there much concern about what the religion or the faith is all about, since it is not the content of the belief but the attitude of believing that is felt to be operative.

Almost as much as worldly success, religion is expected to produce a kind of spiritual euphoria, the comfortable feeling that one is all right with God. Roy Eckardt calls this the cult of "divine-human chumminess" in which God is envisioned as the "Man Upstairs," a "Friendly Neighbor," Who is always ready to give you the pat on the back you need when you happen to feel blue. "Fellowship with the Lord is, so to say, an extra emotional jag that keeps [us] happy. The 'gospel' makes [us] 'feel real good.' "[28] Again, all sense of the ambiguity and precariousness of human life, all sense of awe before the divine majesty, all sense of judgment before the divine holiness, is shut out; God is, in Jane Russell's inimitable phrase, a "livin' Doll." What relation has this kind of god to the biblical God Who confronts sinful man as an enemy before He comes out to meet repentant man as a Savior? Is this He of Whom we are told, "It is a fearful thing to fall into the hands of the living God" (Heb. 10.31)? The measure of how far contemporary American religiosity falls short of the authentic tradition of Jewish-Christian faith is to be found in the chasm that separates Jane Russell's "livin' Doll" from the living God of Scripture.

The cultural enrichment that is looked for in religion varies greatly with the community, the denomination, and the outlook and status of the church members. Liturgy is valued as aesthetically and emotionally "rewarding," sermons are praised as "interesting" and "enjoyable," discussions of the world relations of the church are welcomed as "educational," even theology is approved of as "thought provoking." On another level, the "old-time religion" is cherished by certain segments of the population because it so obviously enriches their cultural life.

But, in the last analysis, it is "peace of mind" that most Americans expect of religion. "Peace of mind" is today easily the most popular gospel that goes under the name of religion; in one way or another it invades and permeates all other forms of contemporary religiosity. It works in well with the drift toward other-direction characteristic of large sections of American society, since both see in adjustment the supreme good in life. What is desired, and what is promised, is the conquest of insecurity and anxiety, the overcoming of inner conflict, the shedding of guilt and fear, the translation of the self to the painless paradise of "normality" and "adjustment"! Religion, in short, is a spiritual anodyne designed to allay the pains and vexations of existence.

It is this most popular phase of contemporary American religiosity that has aroused the sharpest criticism in more sophisticated theological circles. The Most Rev. Patrick A. O'Boyle, Catholic archbishop of Washington, has warned that although "at first glance piety seems to be everywhere . . ." many persons appear to be "turning to religion as they would to a benign sedative to soothe their minds and settle their nerves."[29] Liston Pope emphasizes that the approach of the "peace of mind" school is not only "very dubious on psychological grounds," but its "identification

[with] the Christian religion . . . is of questionable validity."[30] Roy Eckardt describes it as "religious narcissism," in
which "the individual and his psycho-spiritual state occupy
the center of the religious stage" and piety is made to "con-
centrate on its own navel."[31] I have myself spoken of it as
a philosophy that would "dehumanize man and reduce his
life to the level of sub-human creation which knows neither
sin nor guilt."[32] It encourages moral insensitivity and social
irresponsibility, and cultivates an almost lascivious preoccupation with self. The church becomes a kind of emotional
service station to relieve us of our worries: "Go to church
—you'll feel better," "Bring your troubles to church and
leave them there" (slogans on subway posters urging
church attendance). On every ground, this type of religion
is poles apart from authentic Jewish-Christian spirituality
which, while it knows of the "peace that passeth understanding" as the gift of God, promotes a "divine discontent"[33] with things as they are and a "passionate thirst for
the future,"[34] in which all things will be renewed and restored to their right relation to God.[35]

The burden of this criticism of American religion from
the point of view of Jewish-Christian faith is that contemporary religion is so naively, so innocently *man-centered*.
Not God, but man—man in his individual and corporate
being—is the beginning and end of the spiritual system of
much of present-day American religiosity. In this kind of
religion there is no sense of transcendence, no sense of the
nothingness of man and his works before a holy God; in
this kind of religion the values of life, and life itself, are
not submitted to Almighty God to judge, to shatter, and to
reconstruct; on the contrary, life, and the values of life, are
given an ultimate sanction by being identified with the divine. In this kind of religion it is not man who serves God,
but God who is mobilized and made to serve man and his
purposes—whether these purposes be economic prosperity,
free enterprise, social reform, democracy, happiness, security, or "peace of mind." God is conceived as man's "omnip-
otent servant,"[36] faith as a sure-fire device to get what we
want. The American is a religious man, and in many cases

personally humble and conscientious. But religion as he understands it is not something that makes for humility or the uneasy conscience: it is something that reassures him about the essential rightness of everything American, his nation, his culture, and himself; something that validates his goals and his ideals instead of calling them into question; something that enhances his self-regard instead of challenging it; something that feeds his self-sufficiency instead of shattering it; something that offers him salvation on easy terms instead of demanding repentance and a "broken heart." Because it does all these things, his religion, however sincere and well-meant, is ultimately vitiated by a strong and pervasive idolatrous element.

III

Returning from a five-month visit to the United States, Bishop Eivind Berggrav, the eminent Norwegian Lutheran churchman, reported his impressions of religious life in America. He not only defended American churches against the charge of "materialism" and "activism," so often leveled against them by European observers; he also testified that "American Christianity is real, true, and personal." He found the American churches in a "period of youthful vigor," representing "a family rather than an individual Christianity," in which the congregation was a true "organism of fellowship." While he foresaw a future period of "crisis" for the American churches, he confessed himself much impressed by them and their genuine vitality.[37]

Similar testimonies may be noted in the comments of other European churchmen, Catholic as well as Protestant.[38] With all their criticism of American religion, they find in American religious life a vigor and a closeness to the people, a pervasive sense of the importance of religion, that is most impressive.

Yet this is the same American religion that, seen from another angle, we have found to be so empty and contentless, so conformist, so utilitarian, so sentimental, so individualistic, and so self-righteous. Each judgment has its validity and is necessary to correct and supplement the other. Both may be summed up by saying that Americans are "at one and the same time, one of the most religious and most secular of nations."[39]

Americans fill the houses of worship, but their conceptions, standards, and values, their institutions and loyalties, bear a strangely ambiguous relation to the teachings that the churches presumably stand for. The goals and values of life are apparently established autonomously, and religion is brought in to provide an enthusiastic mobilization of human resources for the promotion of the well-being of the individual and society. Of the very same Americans who so overwhelmingly affirm their belief in God and their membership in the historic churches, a majority also affirm, without any sense of incongruousness, that their religion has little to do with their politics or business affairs,[40] except to provide an additional sanction and drive. Most of the other activities of life—education, science, entertainment—could be added to the list; they too apparently operate under their own rules, with religion invoked as a "spiritual" embellishment and a useful sustaining force. This is not felt as in any sense a disparagement of religion; it is merely America's way of defining for itself the place of religion and the church in the total scheme of things. But this way of looking at things is precisely the way of secularism, for what is secularism but the practice of the absence of God in the affairs of life? The secularism characteristic of the American mind is implicit and is not felt to be at all inconsistent with the most sincere attachment to religion. It is, nevertheless, real and pervasive, and in this sense Handlin is certainly right in saying that America is growing more secularist, at the very time when in another sense, in the sense of affiliation and identification and of the importance attributed to religion, America is becoming increasingly more religious.[41]

So thoroughly secularist has American religion become that the familiar distinction between religion and secularism appears to be losing much of its meaning under present-day conditions. Both the "religionists" and the "secularists" cherish the same basic values and organize their lives on the same fundamental assumptions—values and assumptions defined by the American Way of Life. What really seems to distinguish one from the other is that the explicit secularism of the avowed secularists is suspicious of, sometimes even hostile to, institutional religion and its influence in public life, while the implicit secularism pervading American religion identifies itself wholeheartedly with the religious institutions of the nation. The tension between the two is no less sharp, though the issues that divide them are rather different than the simple distinction between religion and secularism would imply.[42]

The widespread secularism of American religion, in which religion is made to provide the sanctification and dynamic for goals and values otherwise established, is often difficult for Europeans to understand, since in Europe the confrontation between secularism and religion tends to be much more explicit and well defined. In the United States explicit secularism—hostility or demonstrative indifference to religion—is a minor and diminishing force; the secularism that permeates the American consciousness is to be found within the churches themselves and is expressed through men and women who are sincerely devoted to religion. The witness to authentic Jewish-Christian faith may well prove much more difficult under these conditions than when faith has to contend with overt and avowed unbelief.

The spirit of secularism has always been pervasive and powerful and has always had its effect on religious institutions. The unique feature of the present religious situation in America is that this secularism is being generated out of the very same conditions that are, in part at least, making for the contemporary religious revival. The sociological factors that underlie the new urge to religious identification and affiliation are also factors that enhance the secularization of the religiousness they engender. It is not secularism as such that is characteristic of the present religious situation in this country but secularism within a religious framework, the secularism of a religious people.

Yet we must not see the picture as all of one piece. Within the general framework of a secularized religion embracing the great mass of American people, there are signs of deeper and more authentic stirrings of faith. Duncan Norton-Taylor, in his comments on the new religiousness of businessmen, may not be altogether wrong in noting that "particularly among the younger men, there *is* a groping for a spiritual base."[43] Norman Thomas, though recognizing that the "return to religion," which is "one of the significant phenomena of our confused and troubled times," is a "phenomenon of many and contradictory aspects," nevertheless finds it, in part at least, "definitely characterized by an awareness of, or search after God."[44] Certainly among the younger people, particularly among the more sensitive young men and women on the campuses of this country, and in the suburban communities that are in so many ways really continuous with the campus, there are unmistakable indications of an interest in, and concern with, religion that goes far beyond the demands of mere social "belonging."[45] These stirrings are there; they are not always easily identified as religion on the one hand, or easily distinguishable from the more conventional types of religiousness on the other—but they constitute a force whose range and power should not be too readily dismissed. Only the future can tell what these deeper stirrings of faith amount to and what consequences they hold for the American religion of tomorrow.

But even the more conventional forms of American religion, for all their dubiousness, should not be simply written off by the man of faith. Even in this ambiguous structure there may be elements and aspects—not always those, incidentally, that seem most prepossessing to us today—which could in the longer view transform the inner character of American religion and bring it closer to the faith it professes. Nothing is too unpromising or refractory to serve the divine will. After all, the God Who is able to make the "wrath of man" to praise Him (Ps. 76.10) is surely capable of turning even the intractabilities and follies of religion into an instrument of His redemptive purpose.

FOOTNOTES

1. The theological critique and evaluation here undertaken is carried out in terms of "Jewish-Christian faith," by which is meant the basic theological outlook underlying both Judaism and Christianity as biblical religions. In this view, Judaism and Christianity are understood as two religions sharing a common faith. For a statement of this position, see Paul Tillich, "Is There a Judeo-Christian Tradition?", *Judaism*, Vol. I, No. 2, April 1952. In defining the unity of Judaism and Christianity, Tillich speaks of their "identity of structure at all points and identity of content in most." See also Will Herberg, "Judaism and Christianity: Their Unity and Difference," *The Journal of Bible and Religion*, Vol. XXI, No. 2, April 1953. For statements of biblical faith, see G. Ernest Wright, *The Challenge of Israel's Faith* (University of Chicago Press, 1944); Martin Buber, *The Prophetic Faith* (Macmillan, 1949); Paul Minear, *Eyes of Faith: A Study in the Biblical Point of View* (Westminster, 1946); J. Guillet, *Thèmes bibliques* (Aubier, Paris, 1950).

2. A. Roy Eckardt, "The New Look in American Piety," *The Christian Century*, November 17, 1954. See also the vivid account of "The Religion That Is No Religion" and "A Religion to End All Religion" in Alexander Miller, *The Renewal of Man* (Doubleday, 1955), chaps. ii and iii.

3. Reinhold Niebuhr, "The Peril of Complacency in Our Nation," *Christianity and Crisis*, Vol. XIV, No. 1, February 8, 1954; "Religiosity and the Christian Faith," *Christianity and Crisis*, Vol. XIV, No. 24, January 24, 1955.

4. Alan Richardson, "Instrument of God," *Interpretation*, Vol. III, No. 3, July 1949.

5. Reinhold Niebuhr, *The Nature and Destiny of Man*, 2 vols. (Scribner's, 1941, 1943), Vol. I, p. 200.

6. "In the Church, the hostility of men against God is brought to a head; for there human indifference, misunderstanding, and opposition attain their most sublime and also their most naive form" (Karl Barth, *The Epistle to the Romans*, tr. by Edwyn C. Hoskyns [Oxford, 1933], p. 418).

7. Sidney H. Scheuer, a vice president of the American Ethical Union, in an address to the annual assembly of that organization, St. Louis, April 1954; reported in *Information Service* (National Council of the Churches of Christ), October 30, 1954. Revealing of the universal American attitude is the outraged disapproval expressed by a ninth-grade girl at a suburban New Jersey junior high school in a composition entitled "Matilda": "Not the least bit patriotic, Matilda does not even go to church . . . !"

8. This illuminating term comes from an article, "A 3-Religion Country," by Max Lerner commenting on the original edition of this book (*New York Post*, November 6, 1955). References to the United States as a "Christian country," once so common, are now extremely rare. The appropriate designation today is contained in Justice Douglas' celebrated dictum, speaking for the Supreme Court, in the New York released-time case: "We are a religious people whose institutions presuppose a Supreme Being" (Zorach v. Clauson, 72 S. Ct. 679, 1952).

9. Associated Press dispatch from Washington, *New York Herald Tribune*, February 22, 1955. A well-known religious newsletter carries the following injunction in a box on its first page: "Boost the Best in American Life: Support Your Churches and Synagogues."

10. "What, then, are some of the *dangers* in the 'return to religion'? For one thing, religion can become a very convenient dodge word. It can mean almost anything the user wants it to. It has no cutting edge. It is very pliable. Sample definitions of religion in this new age of spiritual vitality might run, 'Oh, you know, values and all that sort of thing,' or perhaps, 'Being true to your own highest instincts,' or perhaps (more indignantly), 'Surely you believe there's Something Greater Than Ourselves, don't you?' It's all so intangible and so easy. I can make 'religion' or 'God' or 'spiritual values' mean pretty much what I want, with the result that I may not be talking about anything more than a high-minded humanism or a glorified Americanism" (Robert McAfee Brown, "The 'Return to Religion,' Liability and Opportunity," *Presbyterian Life*, Vol. VII, No. 25, December 25, 1954). This contentlessness of American religion is curiously illustrated by the confessions of faith of a hundred "thoughtful men and women in all walks of life," published in 1952 (by Simon and Schuster) in the volume *This I Believe*, edited by Edward P. Morgan. As one reads these statements, perplexity grows. The great majority of the hundred men and women who present their "philosophies of life" are unquestionably professed Christians or Jews, yet barely half of them found it necessary so much as to mention God, and only ten made reference to their formal religious beliefs. These eminent citizens proclaimed their faith in many and diverse things—in "brotherhood," "service," "idealism," and "spiritual values," in "life," "reason," and "tolerance," in "freedom," "self-reliance," "democracy," and, of course, in "faith"—but only incidentally, if at all, in God. Not that they did not believe in God; of course they did—between 95 and 98 per cent of the American people, as we have seen (see above, chap. v, note 1), cherish this belief. But somehow their belief in God, and the God they believed in, did not seem to be very central to whatever it was that they had in mind when they stood up to tell the world "This I Believe." The popularity of the

radio program conducted by Mr. Murrow, and the praise and applause it has received from all quarters, religious and secular, lay and clerical, would seem to indicate that this kind of religiousness is accepted as quite normal and proper by Americans concerned with religion. The Rev. John Sutherland Bonnell has severely criticized the "This I Believe" kind of faith as "often so vague and so completely lacking in basic Christian convictions that I have been impressed with the need for instruction on these lines." Dr. Bonnell expresses his confidence that, in contrast to the "confusion" of the "big name people" included in the "This I Believe" series, "the rank and file of people possess a firmer and more enduring faith" (*The New York Times*, February 21, 1955). The polls and surveys reported above in chap. v would not seem to bear this out.

11. For a description of the character mechanism of other-direction, see above, chap. iv, pp. 57–59; see also Herberg, "Faith and Character Structure," *Christianity and Crisis*, Vol. XII, No. 24, January 25, 1954.

12. "We have to ask ourselves: are we Catholics who happen to live in England or America, or are we English or Americans who happen to attend a Catholic church on Sundays?" (Christopher Dawson, "Problems of Christian Culture," *The Commonweal*, April 15, 1955). Somewhat differently formulated, the same question confronts the Protestant and the Jew in America.

13. "What the Deists hoped to achieve without a church has to a large degree come to pass in the land of many churches. Indeed, the idea that religion is a handmaiden to democracy has made such headway that American Catholicism, American Protestantism, and American Judaism appear like parallel shoots on a common stock" (Arthur Mann, "Charles Fleischer's Religion of Democracy," *Commentary*, June 1954).

14. "Another consequence of much of the 'religion' to which we have 'returned' is that it has no sense of judgment. It is genuinely alarming . . . to note how frequently our national obeisances to God are made in a self-congratulatory mood. The notion that we are a nation 'under God' *ought* to be a terrifying, not a smug notion. It is an idea which should inspire penitence rather than complacency. Instead of being the prelude to new paeans of praise for America, it should make us more deeply critical of ourselves than we have ever been before" (Brown, "The 'Return to Religion,' Liability and Opportunity," *Presbyterian Life*, Vol. VII, No. 25, December 25, 1954). D. W. Brogan, in his comments on contemporary American religion, notes that "a surprising amount of American political discussion is carried on in theological terms" ("God and the Juke Box," *The Manchester Guardian Weekly*, October 14, 1954). Thus it is *atheistic* Communism, rather than Communism or totalitarian-

ism as such, that is threatening the world; it is "lack of faith"
that is undermining democracy; and the like. The "theological
terms" in which the political discussion is carried on are generally such as to reinforce the American's good opinion of himself,
his purposes, and his institutions.

15. National messianism is nothing new in American history.
Over a century ago, in 1850, Herman Melville delivered himself
of the following impassioned outburst in *White Jacket:* "God
has predestined, mankind expects, great things for our race; and
great things we feel in our souls. The rest of the nations must
soon be in our rear. We are the pioneers of the world, the advance guard, sent on through the wilderness of untried things,
to break a new path in the New World that is ours. . . . Long
enough have we debated whether, indeed, the political Messiah
has come. But he has come in us. . . . And let us remember
that with ourselves, almost for the first time in history, national
selfishness is unbounded philanthropy, for we cannot do a good
to America but we give alms to the world." Nor is national messianism today limited to the chauvinists and "imperialists"; it
has its "liberal" version as well. "America," writes Hugh Miller,
"was not created to be supreme among the 'great powers.' It
was created to inaugurate the transition of human society to just
government. It is a missionary institution propagating a
gospel to all men" (*An Historical Introduction to Modern Philosophy* [Macmillan, 1948], p. 570). At the turn of the century,
the "liberal" rabbi, Charles Fleischer, proclaimed: "We of America are the 'peculiar people' consecrated to that 'mission' of re-
alizing Democracy [which] is potentially a universal spiritual
principle, aye, a religion" (quoted by Arthur Mann, "Charles
Fleischer's Religion of Democracy," *Commentary*, June 1954).

16. "It is just a short step from a god who is the Great Ad-
juster and/or the Friendly Neighbor to the god who fights on
the side of his chosen people, supporting their racial, economic,
or national interests. . . . The God of judgment has died"
(Eckardt, "The New Look in American Piety," *The Christian
Century*, November 17, 1954). How even the highest of national
purposes may be submitted to divine judgment without impair-
ing human responsibility or the will to resolute action may be
seen from the closing passages of Lincoln's Second Inaugural
(March 4, 1865). Lincoln, who had a strong sense of divine
providence in human affairs, declared: "Both [North and South]
read the same Bible, and pray to the same God; and each in-
vokes his aid against the other. It may seem strange that any
men should dare to ask a just God's assistance in wringing their
bread from the sweat of other men's faces; but let us not judge,
that we be not judged. The prayers of both could not be answered—that of neither has been answered fully. The Almighty
has his own purposes. . . . With malice toward none, with

charity for all, with firmness in the right, as God gives us to see the right, let us strive on to finish the work we are in . . ."

17. This is the main contention of William Lee Miller's critical analysis, "Piety Along the Potomac," *The Reporter*, August 17, 1954.

18. "The evangelizing in which some businessmen are now conspicuous has been described as at best superficial, and at worst arrogant and materialistic in its methods and motives. Are businessmen merely promoting religion as a useful tool and God as a good partner to have in the firm? Or are American businessmen, while putting their religion to daily 'practical' uses, also experiencing a spiritual awakening that is indeed genuine?" (Duncan Norton-Taylor, "Businessmen on Their Knees," *Fortune*, October 1953). Mr. Norton-Taylor records criticisms that "the movement lacked genuine spiritual underpinnings, that it was far too pragmatic, too 'practical' . . . to inspire real hope," but he believes that "particularly among the younger men, there *is* a groping for a spiritual base."

19. See the significant article on "bringing Christianity into business and industry" by Irving E. Howard, "The Spirit Stirs in Secular Society," *Christian Economics*, March 8, 1955.

20. *The New York Times*, February 18, 1955.

21. Reinhold Niebuhr, "Religiosity and the Christian Faith," *Christianity and Crisis*, Vol. XIV, No. 24, January 24, 1955.

22. See above, chap. v, pp. 84–85.

23. Daniel A. Poling, "A Running Start for Every Day," *Parade: The Sunday Picture Magazine*, September 19, 1954.

24. At the Conference on the Spiritual Foundations of Our Democracy, held in Washington, D.C. in November 1954, Monsignor George G. Higgins, director of the social action department of the National Catholic Welfare Conference, issued a sharp warning against the widespread notion that a "return to God" on the part of the American people was in itself sufficient to solve all national problems, without the necessity of resorting to responsible and informed thinking on the "secular" level, on the level of institutions and social strategies. His warning was echoed by others at the conference.

25. The top two sermon subjects in a preference poll conducted by *This Week* magazine were "Happier Families Through Religion" and "How Can Religion Eliminate Worry and Tension?" (Willard A. Pleuthner, "The Sermons America Wants to Hear." *This Week*, January 18, 1959). For a critique of this pragmatic conception of religion, see H. Richard Niebuhr, "Utilitarian Christianity," *Christianity and Crisis*, Vol. VI, No. 12, July 8, 1946.

26. Howard, "Random Reflections," *Christian Economics*, March 8, 1955.

27. This is the burden of the philosophy of "positive thinking" so effectively expounded by Norman Vincent Peale, and may be documented in any of Dr. Peale's many writings. For example: "How do you practice faith? First thing every morning, before you arise, say out loud, 'I believe,' three times" (*The Power of Positive Thinking* [Prentice-Hall, 1952], p. 154). Note also some of the titles of Dr. Peale's syndicated column, "Confident Living": "Have Faith in Faith," "Believe You Can and You Can," "Your Faith Makes Miracles" (*New York Herald Tribune*, July 31, 1955; September 25, 1955; August 4, 1956). For a sharp criticism of this philosophy, see Miller, "Some Negative Thinking About Norman Vincent Peale," *The Reporter*, January 13, 1955; see also Paul Hutchinson, "Have We a 'New' Religion?", *Life*, April 11, 1955, pp. 148–57; and A. Roy Eckardt, *The Surge of Piety in America* (Association Press, 1958). A penetrating critique of the Peale gospel of "positive thinking" by a Catholic theologian will be found in Gustave Weigel, "Protestantism As a Catholic Concern," *Theological Studies*, Vol. XVI, No. 2, June 1955. A Jewish version of the same cult of "faith in faith" may be found in Louis Binstock, *The Power of Faith* (Prentice-Hall, 1952). Declares Rabbi Binstock: "You, like everyone else, have access to a great storehouse of dynamic power on which you can draw. . . . That storehouse is *Faith*. Not religion. Not your immortal soul. Not this House of Worship. Not God. But—FAITH" (p. 4). For a critical review of this book, see Herberg, "Faith and Idolatry," *The Pastor*, Vol. XVI, No. 3, November 1952. One of the oldest and most respectable of Protestant denominations recently ran a newspaper advertisement in which the readers were told that "there are times in life when faith alone protects" and were urged to attend church because "regular church attendance helps you build your own personal reserve of faith." Neither God nor Christ was anywhere mentioned.

28. "The cult of the 'Man Upstairs.' A rhapsodic inquiry greets us from the TV screen and the radio: 'Have you talked to the Man Upstairs?' God is a friendly neighbor who dwells in the apartment just above. Call on him any time, especially if you are feeling a little blue. He does not get upset over your little faults. He understands. . . . Thus is the citizenry guided to divine-human chumminess. . . . Fellowship with the Lord is, so to say, an extra emotional jag that keeps him [the individual] happy. The 'gospel' makes him 'feel real good' " (Eckardt, "The New Look in American Piety," *The Christian Century*, November 17, 1954). A strong strain of this "divine-human chumminess" is to be found in certain aspects of American revivalistic religion; there, too, the gospel makes you "feel real good." "What

today's cult of reassurance most lacks—and indeed disavows—is a sense of life's inevitable failures. Here is the point at which it stands in starkest contrast to the teaching of America's most searching contemporary theologian, Reinhold Niebuhr . . . There is one central idea in his writing which . . . is validated by universal experience. This is his contention that all human effort, however noble, however achieving, contains within it an element of failure. Perhaps one reason Americans say they cannot understand Niebuhr is because their minds simply will not harbor this fact that all success is dogged by failure" (Hutchinson, "Have We a 'New' Religion?", *Life*, April 11, 1955, p. 148).

29. Address at the forty-first annual meeting of the Association of American Colleges, held in Washington, January 1955, as reported in *New York Herald Tribune,* January 12, 1955.

30. Address at the dinner meeting of the broadcasting and film commission of the National Council of Churches, New York City, March 1, 1955 (unpublished). See also Hutchinson, "Have We a 'New' Religion?", *Life*, April 11, 1955, pp. 147–48; Hutchinson calls it the "cult of reassurance."

31. Eckardt, "The New Look in American Piety," *The Christian Century*, November 17, 1954.

32. Herberg, *Judaism and Modern Man: An Interpretation of Jewish Religion* (Farrar, Straus, and Young, 1951), p. 29.

33. "I most emphatically prefer a divine discontent to peace of mind. . . . Are you satisfied with the state of the world? Are you content with the behavior of modern man? Have you reached the point where soporific relaxation is the real goal, where more than anything else you want rest and quiet and protection from stimulation? . . . If that's what you want, count me out. . . . God pity me on the day when I have lost my restlessness! God forgive me on the day when I am satisfied! God rouse me up if ever I am so dull, insensitive, lazy, complacent, phlegmatic, and apathetic as to be at peace!" (Warren Weaver, "Peace of Mind," *The Saturday Review*, December 11, 1954). Mr. Weaver is director of the division of natural sciences of the Rockefeller Foundation.

34. Ernst Renan is reported to have described the "true Israelite" as a man "torn with discontent and possessed with a passionate thirst for the future."

35. "We are undoubtedly in the midst of a widespread and powerful revival of religion. There is, however, a real danger of this spiritual current running up against a steep wall of compulsive escapism and becoming a giant pool of stagnation and futility, instead of a vital tide of constructive energy and new creative work" (Charles W. Lowry, co-chairman of the Foundation for Religious Action, Washington, D.C., in a press release of the Foundation, issued June 10, 1954).

36. The phrase is from Jules H. Masserman, "Faith and Delusion in Psychotherapy: The Ur-Defenses of Man," *The American Journal of Psychiatry*, Vol. 110, No. 5, November 1953. For a critique of the theological aspects of Masserman's thesis, see Herberg, "Biblical Faith and Natural Religion," *Theology Today*, Vol. XI, No. 4, January 1955.

37. See "Bishop Berggrav Praises American Church Life," *The Christian Century*, January 19, 1955; see also Bishop Berggrav's letter, "Contact-Club-Christ," *Christianity and Crisis*, Vol. XV, No. 2, February 21, 1955.

38. See, e.g., "U. S. Catholics Through Spanish Eyes," *America*, March 27, 1954, reporting the impressions of Francisco de Luis on the condition of American Catholicism. (De Luis, general manager of Editorial Católica, a Madrid publishing house, had visited the United States to study mass communications.) "Señor Luis found the 'happy, optimistic' U. S. priests, who are 'pleased with their people, proud of them,' a striking contrast to European priests, who radiate no such confidence. In Chicago . . . he found himself at a weekday mass in a crowded downtown church, marveling at the people thronging the altar rails. The coverage given by even the secular press to Lenten religious services convinced him that the 'materialism' of the United States has been much exaggerated in European eyes. Our observance of Sunday as a day of rest and prayer bettered that of some European countries." See also H. R. Weber, "A Greenhorn's Impressions of the People of God in North America," *The Ecumenical Review*, Vol. IX, No. 3, April 1957; Cecil Northcott, "America as a Religious Country," *The Listener*, September 26, 1957. The comments of the "English theologian, well acquainted with the American religious scene," whom H. Richard Niebuhr quotes, are worth noting (H. Richard Niebuhr, *The Purpose of the Church and Its Ministry* [Harper, 1956], p. 7).

39. Reinhold Niebuhr, "Prayer and Politics," *Christianity and Crisis*, October 27, 1952.

40. See above, chap. v, pp. 73–74.

41. "The trend toward secularism in ideas was not [at midtwentieth century] reversed" (Oscar Handlin, *The American People in the Twentieth Century* [Harvard, 1954], p. 222). "Too many of us wave our church and synagogue cards to camouflage our basically irreligious character" (Label A. Katz, chairman of the B'nai B'rith youth commission, *Indianapolis Times*, November 12, 1956).

42. For variant views on the nature and implications of secularism in present-day American life, see: J. Richard Spann, ed., *The Christian Faith and Secularism* (Abingdon-Cokesbury, 1948); Georgia Harkness, *The Modern Rival of Christian Faith: An Analysis of Secularism* (Abingdon-Cokesbury, 1952); Ed-

win E. Aubrey, *Secularism a Myth: Spiritual Values in Secular Culture* (Harper, 1954); Horace M. Kallen, *Secularism Is the Will of God* (Twayne, 1954). See also Reinhold Niebuhr, "The Relationship of Our Faith and the World of the Christian Church to Secularism," in *For a Christian World* (Home Missions Council of North America, New York, 1950).

43. Norton-Taylor, "Businessmen on Their Knees," *Fortune*, October 1953; see above, note 18.

44. Norman Thomas, "Religion and Civilization," *The Atlantic Monthly*, August 1947.

45. Herberg, "The Religious Stirring on the Campus," *Commentary*, Vol. XIII, No. 2, March 1952.

Chief Works Cited or Referred To

Abel, Theodore, *Protestant Home Missions to Catholic Immigrants*. Institute of Social and Religious Research, New York, 1933.

Abell, Aaron Ignatius, "The Catholic Church and the American Social Question," in Waldemar Gurian and M. A. Fitzsimons, eds., *The Catholic Church in World Affairs*. Notre Dame, 1954.

——, *The Urban Impact on American Protestantism, 1865–1900*. Harvard, 1943.

Abrams, Ray H., ed., "Organized Religion in the United States," *The Annals of the American Academy of Political and Social Science*, Vol. 256, March 1948.

Agee, James, and Others, *Religion and the Intellectuals: A Symposium*. Partisan Review, 1950.

Agus, Jacob B., *Guideposts in Modern Judaism: An Analysis of Current Trends*. Bloch, 1954.

Arzt, Max, "The Synagogue and the Center in Contemporary Jewish Life," *Judaism*, Vol. III, No. 4, Fall 1954.

Aubrey, Edwin E., *Secularism a Myth: Spiritual Values in Secular Culture*. Harper, 1954.

Bach, Marcus, *They Have Found a Faith*. Bobbs-Merrill, 1946.

Bailey, Wilfrid C., "The Sacred and the Profane Worlds of Jonesville," in W. Lloyd Warner and Associates, *Democracy in Jonesville*. Harper, 1949.

Barnett, Lincoln, "God and the American People," *Ladies' Home Journal*, November 1948.

Barron, Milton L., *People Who Intermarry*. Syracuse, 1946.

Barry, Coleman J., *The Catholic Church and German Americans*. Bruce, 1953.

Barry, David W., "The Fellowship of Class," *The City Church*, Vol. VI, No. 1, January–February 1955.

Beach, Waldo, George H. Williams, and H. Richard Niebuhr, "Issues Between Catholics and Protestants at Mid-century," *Religion in Life*, Vol. XXIII, No. 2, Spring 1954.

Bender, Irving E., "Changes in Religious Interest: A Retest After 15 Years," *The Journal of Abnormal and Social Psychology*, Vol. 57, No. 1, July 1958.

Bennett, John C., "New Conceptions of 'Separation,'" *Christianity and Crisis*, Vol. VIII, No. 12, July 5, 1948.

——, *Christians and the State*. Scribner's, 1958.

Bentwich, Norman, *Solomon Schechter*. Jewish Publication Society, 1938.

Berggrav, Eivind, "Contact-Club-Christ," *Christianity and Crisis*, Vol. XV, No. 2, February 21, 1955.

Bernstein, Philip, "Jewish Chaplains in World War II," *American Jewish Year Book*, Vol. 47. American Jewish Committee, 1946.

Bigman, Stanley K., *The Jewish Population of Greater Washington in 1956*. Jewish Community Council of Greater Washington, 1957.

Billington, Ray Allen, *The Protestant Crusade, 1800–1860*. Macmillan, 1938.

Binstock, Louis, *The Power of Faith*. Prentice-Hall, 1952.

Blair, Bertha, "Church-Related Elementary and Secondary Schools in Continental United States," *Information Service*, January 3, 1959.

Blanshard, Paul, *American Freedom and Catholic Power*. Beacon, 1949.

——, *Communism, Democracy, and Catholic Power*. Beacon, 1951.

——, *The Irish and Catholic Power*. Beacon, 1953.

Blau, Joseph L., "The Spiritual Life of American Jewry, 1654–1954," *American Jewish Year Book*, Vol. 56. American Jewish Committee, 1955.

Bogue, Donald J., *The Population of the United States*. Free Press, 1959.

Braden, Charles S., *They Also Believe*. Macmillan, 1949.

——, "The Sects," *The Annals of the American Academy of Political and Social Science*, Vol. 256, March 1948.

Brauer, Jerald C., *Protestantism in America*. Westminster, 1953.

Brogan, D. W., "God and the Juke Box," *The Manchester Guardian Weekly*, October 14, 1954.

Brown, Robert McAfee, "The 'Return to Religion,' Liability and Opportunity," *Presbyterian Life*, Vol. VII, No. 25, December 25, 1954.

Brynes, Asher, "Religion More or Less," *The Freeman*, October 30, 1950.

Buber, Martin, *The Prophetic Faith*. Macmillan, 1949.

Burke, Thomas J. M., "Did Four Million Catholics Become Protestants?", *America*, April 10, 1954.

Carter, Paul A., *The Decline and Revival of the Social Gospel.* Cornell, 1954.

Chenkin, Alvin, and Ben B. Seligman, "Jewish Population in the United States, 1958," *American Jewish Year Book*, Vol. 60. American Jewish Committee, 1959.

Child, Irwin L., *Italian or American?* Yale, 1943.

Chipkin, Israel S., "Census of Jewish School Enrollment (1953–1954)," *JEC Bulletin*, No. 92, December 1954.

Clancy, William P., and Others, *Catholicism in America: A Series of Articles from the Commonweal.* Harcourt, Brace, 1953.

Clark, Elmer T., *Small Sects in America.* Abingdon-Cokesbury, 1949.

Clark, Walter H., *The Oxford Group: Its History and Significance.* Bookman Associates, 1951.

Clinchy, Everett R., *The Growth of Good Will: A Sketch of Protestant-Catholic-Jewish Relations.* National Conference of Christians and Jews, 1953.

Cohen, Eli E., "Economic and Occupational Structure," *American Jewish Year Book*, Vol. 51. American Jewish Committee, 1950.

Cohen, Elliot E., ed., *Commentary on the American Scene: Portraits of Jewish Life in America.* Knopf, 1953.

Cohon, Samuel S., "The Contemporary Mood in Reform Judaism," *The Journal of Bible and Religion*, Vol. XVIII, No. 3, July 1950.

Commission on Research, *Reform Judaism in the Large Cities: A Survey.* Union of American Hebrew Congregations, 1931.

Cook, Clair M., "A New Industrial Chaplaincy," *The Christian Century*, September 1, 1954.

Corrigan, Raymond, *The Church and the Nineteenth Century.* Bruce, 1938.

Crèvecoeur, J. Hector de, *Letters from an American Farmer.* 1782; 1904 ed., Fox Duffield.

Cross, Robert D., *The Emergence of Liberal Catholicism in America.* Harvard, 1957.

Cunneen, Joseph E., "Catholics and Education," in *Catholics in America: A Series of Articles from the Commonweal.* Harcourt, Brace, 1953.

Davis, Helen E., *On Getting into College.* Washington: American Council on Education, 1949.

Davis, Moshe, "Jewish Religious Life and Institutions in America," in Louis Finkelstein, ed., *The Jews: Their History, Culture, and Religion.* Jewish Publication Society, 1949.

Davis, Moshe, *The Shaping of American Judaism* (in Hebrew). Jewish Theological Seminary, New York, 1951.

Davison, Elmer E., ed., *The American Style: Essays in Value and Performance.* Harper, 1958.

Dawson, Christopher, "Problems of Christian Culture," *The Commonweal,* April 15, 1955.

Delmirani, Mario, "Church and State: Positions in the Controversy," *The Theologian,* Vol. VIII, No. 2, Spring 1953.

Dignan, Patrick J., *History of the Legal Incorporation of Catholic Church Property in the United States.* Catholic University, 1953.

Dobriner, William, ed., *The Suburban Community.* Putnam, 1958.

Douglass, H. Paul, *Church Unity Movements in the United States.* Institute of Social and Religious Research, New York, 1934.

——, "Religion, the Protestant Faiths," in Harold E. Stearns, ed., *America Now: An Inquiry into Civilization in the United States.* Scribner's, 1938.

——, *The Springfield Church Survey.* Doran, 1926.

——, and Edmund deS. Brunner, *The Protestant Church as a Social Institution.* Harper, 1935.

Duker, Abraham G., "Emerging Culture Patterns in American Jewish Life," *Publications of the American Jewish Historical Society,* No. XXXIX, Part 4, June 1950.

——, "On Religious Trends in American Jewish Life," *Yivo Annual of Jewish Social Science,* Vol. IV, 1949.

——, "Structure of the Jewish Community," in Oscar I. Janowsky, ed., *The American Jew: A Composite Portrait.* Harper, 1942.

Dushkin, Alexander, and Uriah Z. Engelman, *Jewish Education in the United States: Report of the Commission for the Study of Jewish Education in the United States,* Vol. I. American Association for Jewish Education, 1959.

Dwyer, Robert J., "The American Laity," *The Commonweal,* August 27, 1954.

Eckardt, A. Roy, "The New Look in American Piety," *The Christian Century,* November 17, 1954.

——, *The Surge in American Piety.* Association, 1958.

Ellis, John Tracy, *American Catholicism.* Chicago, 1956.

——, *The Life of James Cardinal Gibbons,* 2 vols. Bruce, 1952.

Engelman, Uriah Zevi, "Jewish School Enrollment," *American Jewish Year Book,* Vol. 56. American Jewish Committee, 1955.

Epstein, Melech, *Jewish Labor in the U.S.A.*, 2 vols. Trade Union Sponsoring Committee, New York, 1950, 1953.

Escoulin, Georges, "Le Catholicisme aux États-Unis," *Le Monde* (Paris), January 10, 11, 12, 1950.

Fauset, A. H., *Black Gods of the Metropolis*. University of Pennsylvania, 1944.

Fennell, Desmond, "Continental and Oceanic Catholicism," *America*, March 26, 1955.

Fey, Harold E., "Can Catholics Win America?", *The Christian Century*, November 29, December 6, 13, 20, 27, 1944; January 3, 10, 17, 1945.

——, "Lutherans Centralize," *The Christian Century*, October 27, 1954.

Fichter, Joseph H., *Parochial School: A Sociological Study*. Notre Dame, 1959.

——, *Social Relations in the Urban Parish*. University of Chicago, 1954.

——, *Southern Parish: The Dynamics of a City Church*. University of Chicago, 1951.

Finkelstein, Louis, ed., *The Jews: Their History, Culture, and Religion*, 4 vols. Jewish Publication Society, 1949.

——, J. Elliot Ross, and William Adams Brown, *The Religions of Democracy: Judaism, Catholicism, and Protestantism in Creed and Life*. Devin-Adair, 1946.

Fisher, Dorothy Canfield, *Vermont Tradition*. Little, Brown, 1953.

Foley, Albert S., "Catholic Participation in Intergroup Activities," in *The McAuley Lectures 1955*. West Hartford, Conn.: Saint Joseph College, 1956.

Friedman, Theodore, and Robert Gordis, eds., *Jewish Life in America*. Horizon, 1955.

Fry, C. Luther, *The U.S. Looks at Its Churches*. Institute of Social and Religious Research, New York, 1930.

Garrison, Winfred E., "Characteristics of American Organized Religion," *The Annals of the American Academy of Political and Social Science*, Vol. 256, March 1948.

——, *Religion Follows the Frontier*. Harper, 1931.

Gaustad, Edwin Scott, *The Great Awakening in New England*. Harper, 1959.

Gersh, Harry, "The New Suburbanites of the 50's," *Commentary*, Vol. XVII, No. 3, March 1954.

Gibbons, James Cardinal, *Retrospect of Fifty Years*, 2 vols. John Murphy, Baltimore, 1916.

Gilkey, Charles W., "Religion in Our College Generations," *Christianity and Crisis*, Vol. IX, No. 19. November 14, 1949.

Ginzberg, Eli, *Agenda for American Jews*. King's Crown, 1950.

Glanz, Rudolf, "Jews in Relation to the Cultural Milieu of the Germans in American Life up to the Eighteen Eighties" (in Yiddish), *Yivo Bleter*, Vol. XXV, Nos. 1 and 2, 1945.

Glatzer, Nahum N., *Franz Rosenzweig: His Life and Thought*. Schocken, 1953.

Glazer, Nathan, "America's Ethnic Pattern," *Perspectives*, No. 9, Autumn 1954.

——, *American Judaism*. Chicago, 1957.

——, "The Jewish Revival in America," *Commentary*, December 1955, January 1956.

——, "Social Characteristics of American Jews, 1654–1954," *American Jewish Year Book*, Vol. 56. American Jewish Committee, 1955.

——, "What Sociology Knows About American Jews," *Commentary*, Vol. IX, No. 3, March 1950.

Goldberg, Nathan, "The Jewish Population of the United States," *The Jewish People, Past and Present*. Central Yiddish Culture Organization, New York, 1948.

——, "Occupational Patterns of American Jews," *The Jewish Review*, Vol. III, No. 4, January 1946.

Goldschmidt, Walter R., "Class Denominationalism in Rural California Churches," *The American Journal of Sociology*, Vol. XLIX, No. 4, January 1944.

Gordon, Albert I., *Jews in Transition*. University of Minnesota, 1949.

——, *Jews in Suburbia*, Beacon, 1959.

Graeber, Isacque, Steuart Henderson Britt, and Others, *Jews in a Gentile World*. Macmillan, 1941.

Griffin, Martin I. J., *Documents Relating to the History of the Catholic Church in the United States*. American Catholic Historical Society, n.d.

Guilday, Peter K., *The Life and Times of John Carroll*, 2 vols. Encyclopedia Press, 1922.

——, *The Life and Times of John England*, 2 vols. America Press, 1927.

——, *Trusteeism*. American Catholic Historical Society, 1928.

Guillet, J., *Thèmes bibliques*. Aubier, Paris, 1950.

Gurian, Waldemar, and M. A. Fitzsimons, eds., *The Catholic Church in World Affairs*. Notre Dame, 1954.

Hales, E. E. Y., *The Catholic Church in the Modern World*. Hanover House, 1958.

Handlin, Oscar, *Adventure in Freedom: Three Hundred Years of Jewish Life in America.* McGraw-Hill, 1954.

——, *The American People in the Twentieth Century.* Harvard, 1954.

——, "Group Life Within the American Pattern," *Commentary,* Vol. VIII, No. 5, November 1949.

——, *Race and Nationality in American Life.* Little, Brown, 1957.

——, *The Uprooted: The Epic Story of the Great Migrations That Made the American People.* Little, Brown, 1951.

——, and Mary F. Handlin, "The Acquisition of Political and Social Rights by Jews in the United States," *American Jewish Year Book,* Vol. 56. American Jewish Committee, 1955.

——, and Mary F. Handlin, "A Century of Jewish Immigration to the United States," *American Jewish Year Book,* Vol. 50. American Jewish Committee, 1949.

——, and Jacob R. Marcus, "The Goals of Survival: What Will U.S. Jewry Look Like in 2000?—Two Views," *The National Jewish Monthly,* May 1957.

Handy, Robert T., "From 'Social Ideals' to 'Norms for Guidance,'" *Christianity and Crisis,* Vol. XIV, No. 24, January 24, 1955.

——, "The Protestant Quest for a Christian America," *Church History,* Vol. XXII, No. 1, March 1953.

Hansen, Marcus Lee, *The Immigrant in American History.* Harvard, 1940.

——, *The Problem of the Third Generation Immigrant.* Augustana Historical Society, Rock Island, Ill., 1938.

Harkness, Georgia, *The Modern Rival of Christian Faith: An Analysis of Secularism.* Abingdon-Cokesbury, 1952.

Haynes, Leonard L., *The Negro Community Within American Protestantism.* Boston: Christopher Publishing House, 1953.

Hedenquist, Göte, ed., *The Church and the Jewish People.* Edinburgh House, 1954.

Herberg, Will, "Anti-Semitism Today," *The Commonweal,* July 16, 1954.

——, "Biblical Faith and Natural Religion," *Theology Today,* Vol. XI, No. 4, January 1955.

——, "Communism, Democracy, and the Churches," *Commentary,* Vol. XIX, No. 4, April 1955.

——, "Faith and Character Structure," *Christianity and Crisis,* Vol. XIII, No. 24, January 25, 1954.

——, "Faith and Idolatry," *The Pastor,* Vol. XVI, No. 3, November 1952.

Herberg, Will, "A Jew Looks at Catholics," in *Catholicism in America: A Series of Articles from the Commonweal.* Harcourt, Brace, 1953.

——, "The Jewish Labor Movement in the United States," *American Jewish Year Book,* Vol. 53. American Jewish Committee, 1952.

——, "Judaism and Christianity: Their Unity and Difference," *The Journal of Bible and Religion,* Vol. XXI, No. 2, April 1953.

——, *Judaism and Modern Man: An Interpretation of Jewish Religion.* Farrar, Straus & Young, 1951.

——, "The Postwar Revival of the Synagogue," *Commentary,* Vol. IX, No. 4, April 1950.

——, "Religion, Democracy, and Public Education," in John Cogley, ed., *Religion in America.* Meridian, 1958.

——, "Religious Communities in Present-Day America," *The Review of Politics,* Vol. XVI, No. 2, April 1954.

——, "The Religious Stirring on the Campus," *Commentary,* Vol. XIII, No. 2, March 1952.

——, "Religious Trends in American Jewry," *Judaism,* Vol. III, No. 3, Summer 1954.

——, "The Sectarian Conflict Over Church and State," *Commentary,* Vol. XIV, No. 5, November 1952.

Hertling, Ludwig, *Geschichte der katholischen Kirche in den Vereinigten Staaten.* Morus, Berlin, 1953.

Heschel, Abraham J., *God in Search of Man: A Philosophy of Judaism.* Farrar, Straus & Cudahy, 1955.

——, *Man Is Not Alone: A Philosophy of Religion.* Farrar, Straus & Young, 1951.

——, *Man's Quest for God: Studies in Prayer and Symbolism.* Scribner's, 1954.

Hollingshead, August B., "Cultural Factors in the Selection of Marriage Mates," *American Sociological Review,* Vol. XVI, No. 1, October 1950.

Hopkins, Charles H., *The Rise of the Social Gospel in American Protestantism, 1865–1915.* Yale, 1940.

Houtart, François, "A Sociological Study of the Evolution of American Catholics," *Social Compass* (The Hague), Vol. 2, No. 5/6.

Howard, Irving E., "Random Reflections," *Christian Economics,* March 8, 1955.

——, "The Spirit Stirs in Secular Society," *Christian Economics,* March 8, 1955.

Hughes, H. Stuart, "On Social Salvation," *Saturday Review of Literature*, March 3, 1951.

Hughley, Neal, *Trends in Protestant Social Idealism*. King's Crown, 1948.

Hurley, Neil P., "The Church in Suburbia," *America*, November 16, 1957.

——, "Suburbanism and the Church," *Worship*, January 1959.

Hutchinson, Paul, "Have We a 'New' Religion?", *Life*, April 11, 1955.

——, "The President's Religious Faith," *The Christian Century*, March 24, 1954.

Jacob, Philip E., *Changing Values in College*. Harper, 1957.

Janowsky, Oscar I., ed., *The American Jew: A Composite Portrait*. Harper, 1942.

——, *The JWB Survey*. Dial, 1948.

Jenkins, Daniel, *Europe and America: Their Contributions to the World Church*. Westminster, 1951.

Johnson, Chas. A., *The Frontier Camp Meeting: Religion's Harvest Time*. Southern Methodist University Press, 1955.

Johnston, Ruby Fundess, *The Religion of Negro Protestants*. Philosophical Library, 1956.

Kallen, Horace M., "Democracy's True Religion," *Saturday Review of Literature*, July 28, 1951.

——, *Secularism Is the Will of God*. Twayne, 1954.

Kane, John J., *Catholic-Protestant Conflicts in America*. Regnery, 1955.

——, "Catholic Separatism," in *Catholicism in America: A Series of Articles from the Commonweal*. Harcourt, Brace, 1953.

——, "The Social Structure of American Catholics," *The American Catholic Sociological Review*, Vol. XVI, No. 1, March 1955.

Keenan, Charles, ed., *Pope Pius XII on the World Community*, with commentaries by Edward A. Conway and Gustave Weigel. America Press, 1954.

Kennedy, Ruby Jo Reeves, "Single or Triple Melting Pot? Intermarriage Trends in New Haven, 1870–1940," *The American Journal of Sociology*, Vol. XLIX, No. 4, January 1944.

Kertzer, Morris N., "Interfaith Relations in the United States," *Judaism*, Vol. III, No. 4, Fall 1954.

Klein, Isaac, "Experience of a Jewish Chaplain" (in Yiddish), *Yivo Bleter*, Vol. XXVII, 1946.

Kohs, Samuel C., "The Jewish Community," in Louis Finkel-

stein, ed., *The Jews: Their History, Culture, and Religion.*
Jewish Publication Society, 1949.

Kuehnelt-Leddihn, Erik von, "American Catholics Revisited,"
The Tablet (London), April 22, 1950.

Latourette, Kenneth Scott, *A History of the Expansion of Christianity,* 7 vols. Harper, 1937–45.

Lazaron, Morris S., "Reform Judaism in Europe and in the
U.S.A.," *Jewish Newsletter,* Vol. XI, No. 11, May 30, 1955.

Learsi, Rufus, *The Jews in America: A History.* World, 1954.

Lerner, Max, *America as a Civilization: Life and Thought in the
United States Today.* Simon and Schuster, 1957.

Levinger, Lee J., *History of the Jews in the United States.* Union
of American Hebrew Congregations, 1932.

Lewis, Fred, "Concerning a National Orthodox Council of
America," *St. Vladimir's Seminary Quarterly,* Vol. II, No. 4,
Summer 1954.

Lewisohn, Ludwig, *The American Jew: Character and Destiny.*
Farrar, Straus & Young, 1950.

——, *What Is This Jewish Heritage?* B'nai B'rith Hillel Foundations, 1954.

Liebman, Joshua Loth, *Peace of Mind.* Simon and Schuster,
1946.

Lipset, Seymour M., "Religion in America: What Religious Revival?", *Columbia University Forum,* Vol. II, No. 2, Winter
1959.

——, *et al., Union Democracy.* Free Press, 1956.

Livneh, Eliezer, *State and Diaspora.* Jewish Agency, Jerusalem,
1953.

Loeb, James Jr., "Liberals and Catholics," *The Commonweal,*
June 16, 1950.

Loescher, Frank, *The Protestant Church and the Negro.* Association, 1948.

Lopez, Lino M., "Spanish Americans in Colorado," *America,*
September 18, 1954.

Lubell, Samuel, *The Future of American Politics.* Harper, 1951.

Luthin, Reinhard, *American Demagogues, Twentieth Century.*
Beacon, 1954.

Lynn, Robert, Kenneth Underwood, and Others, "Christian
Faith and the Protestant Churches," *Social Action,* Vol.
XVIII, No. 6, May 1952.

MacIver, Robert M., *Report on the Jewish Community Relations
Agencies.* National Community Relations Advisory Council,
1951.

McAvoy, Thomas T., "The Catholic Church in the United States," in Waldemar Gurian and M. A. Fitzsimons, eds., *The Catholic Church in World Affairs*. Notre Dame, 1954.

———, "The Formation of the Catholic Minority in the United States, 1820–1860," *The Review of Politics*, Vol. X, No. 1, January 1948.

———, *The Great Crisis in American Catholic History, 1895–1900*. Regnery, 1957.

McLoughlin, William G., *Modern Revivalism: Charles Grandison Finney to Billy Graham*. Ronald, 1959.

Mann, Arthur, "Charles Fleischer's Religion of Democracy," *Commentary*, June 1954.

Marcus, Jacob R., and Oscar Handlin, "The Goals of Survival: What Will U.S. Jewry Be Like in 2000?—Two Views," *The National Jewish Monthly*, May 1957.

Marden, Charles F., *Minorities in American Society*. American Book Company, 1952.

Marty, Martin E., *The New Shape of American Religion*. Harper, 1959.

Masserman, Jules H., "Faith and Delusion in Psychotherapy: The Ur-Defenses of Man," *The American Journal of Psychiatry*, Vol. 110, No. 5, November 1953.

May, Henry F., *Protestant Churches and Industrial America*. Harper, 1949.

May, Max B., *Isaac Mayer Wise, Founder of American Judaism: A Biography*. Putnam, 1916.

Mayer, F. E., *The Religious Bodies of America*. Concordia, 1954.

Maynard, Theodore, *The Story of American Catholicism*. Macmillan, 1941.

Mead, Frank S., *Handbook of Denominations in the United States*. Abingdon-Cokesbury, 1951.

Mead, Sidney E., "American Protestantism Since the Civil War: From Denominationalism to Americanism," *The Journal of Religion*, Vol. XXXVI, No. 1, January 1956.

———, "Denominationalism: The Shape of Protestantism in America," *Church History*, Vol. XXIII, No. 4, December 1954.

———, "From Coercion to Persuasion: Another Look at the Rise of Religious Liberty and the Emergence of Denominationalism," *Church History*, Vol. XXV, No. 4, December 1956.

Miller, Alexander, *The Renewal of Man*. Doubleday, 1955.

Miller, Hugh, *An Historical Introduction to Modern Philosophy*. Macmillan, 1948.

Miller, Perry, *Errand into the Wilderness*. Harvard, 1956.

Miller, Perry, "The Location of American Religious Freedom," in *Religion and Freedom of Thought*. Doubleday, 1954.

Miller, William Lee, "Piety Along the Potomac," *The Reporter*, August 17, 1954.

——, "Religion and the American Way of Life," in *Religion and the Free Society*. Fund for the Republic, 1958.

——, "Some Negative Thinking About Norman Vincent Peale," *The Reporter*, January 13, 1955.

Mills, C. Wright, Clarence Senior, and Rose Kohn Goldsen, *The Puerto Rican Journey*. Harper, 1950.

Minear, Paul, *Eyes of Faith: A Study in the Biblical Point of View*. Westminster, 1946.

Moehlman, Conrad, *School and Church: The American Way*. Harper, 1944.

Morgan, Edward P., ed., *This I Believe*. Simon and Schuster, 1952.

Morison, Elting E., ed., *The American Style: Essays in Value and Performance*. Harper, 1958.

Moynihan, James H., *The Life of Archbishop John Ireland*. Harper, 1953.

Murray, Florence, ed., *The Negro Handbook*. Macmillan, 1949.

Murray, John Courtney, "On the Structure of the Church-State Problem," in Waldemar Gurian and M. A. Fitzsimons, eds., *The Catholic Church in World Affairs*. Notre Dame, 1954.

——, "The Problem of Pluralism in America," *Thought*, Vol. XXIX, No. 113, Summer 1954.

——, "Reflections on the Religiously Pluralist Society: Selected Articles and Addresses," *Catholic Mind*, Vol. LVII, No. 1143. May–June 1959.

Nichols, James Hastings, *Democracy and the Churches*. Westminster, 1951.

——, "For a State Religion?", *The Christian Century*, September 3, 1952.

Nichols, Roy F., *Religion and American Democracy*. Louisiana State University Press, 1959.

Nicholson, J. W., *The Negro's Church*. Institute of Social and Religious Research, New York, 1933.

Niebuhr, H. Richard, *The Kingdom of God in America*. Willett, Clark, 1937.

——, "On Our Conservative Youth," in *Seventy-Five*, Yale Daily News, 1953.

——, *The Purpose of the Church and Its Ministry*. Harper, 1956.

Niebuhr, H. Richard, *The Social Sources of Denominationalism.* Holt, 1929.

———, "Utilitarian Christianity," *Christianity and Crisis,* Vol. VI, No. 12, July 8, 1946.

———, George H. Williams, and Waldo Beach, "Issues Between Catholics and Protestants at Midcentury," *Religion in Life,* Vol. XXIII, No. 2, Spring 1954.

Niebuhr, Reinhold, "Catholics and Politics: Some Misconceptions," *Christianity and Crisis,* Vol. XII, No. 11, June 23, 1952.

———, "Democracy, Secularism, and Christianity," *Christianity and Crisis,* Vol. XIII, No. 3, March 2, 1953.

———, "Editorial Note," *Christianity and Crisis,* Vol. XIII, No. 1, February 2, 1953.

———, "The Impact of Protestantism Today," *The Atlantic Monthly,* February 1948.

———, *The Irony of American History.* Scribner's, 1952.

———, "Is There a Revival of Religion?", *The New York Times Magazine,* November 19, 1950.

———, *The Nature and Destiny of Man,* 2 vols. Scribner's, 1941, 1943.

———, "The Peril of Complacency in Our Nation," *Christianity and Crisis,* Vol. XIV, No. 1, February 8, 1954.

———, "Prayer and Politics," *Christianity and Crisis,* Vol. XII, No. 18, October 27, 1952.

———, "A Protestant Looks at Catholics," in *Catholicism in America: A Series of Articles from the Commonweal,* Harcourt, Brace, 1953.

———, "The Relationship of Our Faith and the World of the Christian Church to Secularism," in *For a Christian World.* Home Missions Council of North America, 1950.

———, "Religiosity and the Christian Faith," *Christianity and Crisis,* Vol. XIV, No. 24, January 24, 1955.

———, "The Rising Catholic-Protestant Tension," *Christianity and Crisis,* Vol. IX, No. 14, August 8, 1949.

———, "Varieties of Religious Revival," *New Republic,* June 6, 1955.

Northcott, Cecil, "America as a Religious Country," *The Listener,* September 26, 1957.

Norton-Taylor, Duncan, "Businessmen on Their Knees," *Fortune,* October 1953.

Nuesse, C. J., and T. S. Harte, eds., *Sociology of the Parish.* Bruce, 1951.

O'Brien, John A., *You Too Can Win Souls.* Macmillan, 1955.

O'Dea, Thomas F., *American Catholic Dilemma: An Inquiry into the Intellectual Life.* Sheed and Ward, 1958.

———, "The Catholic Immigrant and the American Scene," *Thought*, Vol. XXXI, No. 121, Summer 1956.

O'Neill, James M., *Catholicism and American Freedom*, Harper, 1952.

———, *Religion and Education Under the Constitution.* Harper, 1949.

Ong, Walter J., "American Catholicism and America," *Thought*, Vol. XXVII, No. 107, Winter 1952–53.

———, *Frontiers in American Catholicism.* Macmillan, 1957.

Parker, E. C., *et al., The Radio-Television Audience and Religion.* Harper, 1955.

Parzen, Herbert, "Religion," *American Jewish Year Book*, Vol. 52. American Jewish Committee, 1951.

Peale, Norman Vincent, "Norman Vincent Peale Answers Your Questions," *Look*, August 10, 1954.

———, *The Power of Positive Thinking.* Prentice-Hall, 1952.

Perry, Ralph Barton, *Characteristically American.* Knopf, 1949.

Pfeffer, Leo, *Church, State, and Freedom.* Beacon, 1953.

———, *Creeds in Competition.* Harper, 1958.

Pius XII, "Apostolic Adhortation *Menti Nostrae*," *Catholic Mind*, Vol. XLIX, No. 1057, January 1951.

Poling, Daniel A., "A Running Start for Every Day," *Parade: The Sunday Picture Magazine*, September 19, 1954.

Pope, Liston, "Broadcasting Religion—A Partnership," unpublished address.

———, *Millhands and Preachers.* Yale, 1942.

———, "Religion and the Class Structure," *The Annals of the American Academy of Political and Social Science*, Vol. 256, March 1948.

Putz, Louis J., ed., *The Catholic Church U.S.A.* Fides, 1956.

Raby, Judah, "Interfaith—On What Terms?", *Congress Weekly*, December 13, 1954.

Ramsay, Paul, "A Theology of Social Action," *Social Action*, Vol. XII, No. 8, October 15, 1948.

Rauschenbusch, Walter, *Christianity and the Social Crisis.* Macmillan, 1907.

———, *A Theology for the Social Gospel.* Macmillan, 1917.

Reich, Nathan, "Economic Trends," in Oscar I. Janowsky, ed., *The American Jew; A Composite Portrait.* Harper, 1942.

———, "The Economic Structure of Modern Jewry," in Louis

Finkelstein, ed., *The Jews: Their History, Culture, and Religion.* Jewish Publication Society, 1949.

Richardson, Alan, "Instrument of God," *Interpretation*, Vol. III, No. 3, July 1949.

Riesman, David, *Faces in the Crowd.* Yale, 1952.

——, *Individualism Reconsidered.* Free Press, 1954.

——, *The Lonely Crowd.* Yale, 1950.

Rischin, Moses, *An Inventory of American Jewish History.* Harvard, 1954.

Robertson, D. B., *Reinhold Niebuhr's Works: A Bibliography.* Berea College, 1954.

Robison, Sophia M., "How Many Jews in America?", *Commentary*, Vol. VIII, No. 2, August 1949.

Roemer, Theodore, *The Catholic Church in the United States.* Herder, 1950.

Rosenthal, Eric, "Five Million American Jews: Progress in Demography," *Commentary*, December 1958.

Ross, Roy G., and Roswell P. Barnes, "Notes on the State of the Churches," *Information Service*, December 25, 1954.

Ruff, G. Elson, *The Dilemma of Church and State.* Muhlenberg, 1954.

Ryan, John A., and Francis J. Boland, *Catholic Principles of Politics: The State and the Church.* Macmillan, 1940.

——, and Moorhouse F. X. Millar, *The State and the Church.* Macmillan, 1922.

Sanderson, Ross W., *The Church Serves the Changing City.* Harper, 1955.

Schaefer, John F., "Needed: A Local Protestant Strategy," *The Christian Century*, January 27, 1954.

Scherzer, Carl J., "More Protestant Hospitals," *The Christian Century*, July 21, 1954.

Schneider, Herbert Wallace, *Religion in 20th Century America.* Harvard, 1952.

Schneider, Louis, and Sanford M. Dornbusch, *Popular Religion: Inspirational Books in America.* Chicago, 1958.

Schoeps, Hans Joachim, *Jüdisch-Christliches Religionsgespräch in 19 Jahrhunderten.* Atharva-Verlag, Frankfurt, 1949.

Scotford, John R., *Within These Borders: Spanish-Speaking Peoples in the U.S.A.* Friendship Press, 1953.

Scott, Marshal, "The Industrial Chaplain," *The City Church*, Vol. 5, No. 2, March–April 1954.

Seligman, Ben B., "The American Jew: Some Demographic Features," *American Jewish Year Book*, Vol. 51. American Jewish Committee, 1950.

Shanks, Hershel, "Jewish-Gentile Intermarriage: Facts and Trends," *Commentary*, Vol. XVI, No. 4, October 1953.

Shaughnessy, Gerald, *Has the Immigrant Kept the Faith*. Macmillan, 1925.

Shea, John Gilmary, *History of the Catholic Church in the United States*, 4 vols. Privately printed, New York, 1886–92.

Shearer, Donald, *Pontificia Americana: A Documentary History of the Catholic Church in the United States, 1784–1884*. Catholic University, 1933.

Sherman, C. Bezalel, *Jews and Other Ethnic Groups in the United States* (in Yiddish). Ferlag Unzer Veg, 1945.

——, "Jewish Economic Adjustment in the U.S.A.," *The Reconstructionist*, December 18, 1953.

——, "Three Generations," *Jewish Frontier*, Vol. XXI, No. 7 (229), July 1954.

Shippey, Frederick A., *Church Work in the City*. Abingdon, 1952.

Shosteck, Robert, "Jewish Students in American Universities," *American Jewish Year Book*, Vol. 50. American Jewish Committee, 1949.

Siegfried, André, *America Comes of Age*. Harcourt, Brace, 1927.

Silcox, Claris E., and Galen M. Fisher, *Catholics, Jews, and Protestants: A Study of Relationships in the U.S. and Canada*. Harper, 1934.

Simpson, George Eaton, and J. Milton Yinger, *Racial and Cultural Minorities: An Analysis of Prejudice and Discrimination*. Harper, 1953.

Simpson, William W., "Cooperation Between Christians and Jews," in Göte Hedenquist, *The Church and the Jewish People*. Edinburgh House Press, 1954.

Sklare, Marshall, *Conservative Judaism: An American Religious Movement*. Free Press, 1955.

——, "Forms and Expressions of Jewish Identification," unpublished report presented at the Tercentenary Conference on American Jewish Sociology, New York, November 27–28, 1954.

——, ed., *The Jews: Social Patterns of an American Group*. Free Press, 1958.

——, and Mark Vosk, *The Riverton Study: How Jews Look at Themselves and Their Neighbors*. American Jewish Committee, 1957.

Smith, W. S., *Americans in the Making*. Appleton-Century, 1939.

Southey, Robert, *Life of Wesley and the Rise and Progress of Methodism*. 1820; 2nd American edition, Harper, 1847.

Spann, J. Richard, ed., *The Christian Faith and Secularism.* Abingdon-Cokesbury, 1952.

Speaks, Reuben L., "Will the Negro Remain Protestant?", *The Christian Century,* June 2, 1954.

Sperry, Willard L., *Religion in America.* Macmillan, 1946.

Stearns, Harold E., ed., *America Now: An Inquiry into Civilization in the United States.* Scribner's, 1938.

Stewart, George R., *American Ways of Life.* Doubleday, 1954.

Stokes, Anson Phelps, *Church and State in the United States,* 2 vols. Harper, 1950.

Sugrue, Thomas, *A Catholic Speaks His Mind on America's Religious Conflict.* Harper, 1951.

Sweet, William W., *The American Churches: An Interpretation.* Abingdon-Cokesbury, 1948.

——, "The Protestant Churches," in *The Annals of the American Academy of Political and Social Science,* Vol. 256, March 1948.

——, *Religion on the American Frontier,* 4 vols. University of Chicago, 1931, 1936, 1939, 1946.

——, *Revivalism in America: Its Origin, Growth, and Decline.* Harper, 1944.

——, *The Story of Religion in America,* rev. ed. Harper, 1939.

Thomas, John L., *The Catholic Family.* Prentice-Hall, 1956.

——, "The Factor of Religion in the Selection of Marriage Mates," *American Sociological Review,* Vol. XVI, No. 4, August 1951.

——, "Mixed Marriages—So What?", *Social Order,* Vol. II, No. 4, April 1952.

Thomas, Norman, "Religion and Civilization," *The Atlantic Monthly,* August 1947.

Tillich, Paul, "Is There a Judeo-Christian Tradition?", *Judaism,* Vol. I, No. 2, April 1952.

Toynbee, Arnold J., *A Study of History,* abridgment of Volumes I-VI by D. C. Somervell. Oxford, 1947.

Troeltsch, Ernst, *The Social Thinking of the Christian Churches.* 1911; tr. by Olive Wyon, Macmillan, 1931.

Trimble, Glenn, "Two Worlds of Church Life in the United States," *Information Serivce,* March 28, 1958.

Underwood, Kenneth W., *Protestant and Catholic: Religious and Social Interaction in an Industrial Community.* Beacon, 1957.

Van Dusen, Henry P., "Caribbean Holiday," *The Christian Century,* August 17, 1955.

Van Dusen, Henry P., "[The Third] Force's Lesson for Others," *Life*, June 9, 1958.

Vivas, Gustavo E., "Our Spanish-Speaking U.S. Catholics," *America*, May 15, 1954.

Wach, Joachim, *Sociology of Religion*. University of Chicago, 1944.

——, *Types of Religious Experience*. Routledge and Kegan Paul, 1951.

Ward, Barbara, "Report to Europe on America," *The New York Times Magazine*, June 20, 1954.

Warner, W. Lloyd, and Leo Srole, *The Social Systems of American Ethnic Groups*. Yale, 1945.

——, *Structure of American Life*. Edinburgh, 1952.

Waugh, Evelyn, "The American Epoch in the Catholic Church," *Life*, September 19, 1949.

Weaver, Warren, "Peace of Mind," *The Saturday Review*, December 11, 1954.

Weber, H. R., "A Greenhorn's Impressions of the People of God in North America," *The Ecumenical Review*, Vol. IX, No. 3, April 1957.

Weigel, Gustave, "The Church and the Democratic State," *Thought*, Vol. XXVII, No. 105, Summer 1952.

——, *Faith and Understanding in America*. Macmillan, 1959.

——, "An Introduction to American Catholicism," in Louis J. Putz, ed., *The Catholic Church U.S.A.* Fides, 1956.

——, "Protestantism as a Catholic Concern," *Theological Studies*, Vol. XVI, No. 2, June 1955.

Weiner, Herbert, "The Lubovitcher Movement," *Commentary*, March, April 1957.

Weisberger, Bernard A., *They Gathered at the River: The Story of the Great Revivalists and Their Impact upon Religion in America*. Little, Brown, 1958.

Weiss-Rosmarin, Trude, "From a Lecturer's Notebook," *Jewish Spectator*, April 1945.

Wessell, B. B., *An Ethnic Survey of Woonsocket, Rhode Island*. University of Chicago, 1931.

Whyte, William H., Jr., *The Organization Man*. Simon and Schuster, 1956.

Wiernick, Peter, *History of the Jews in America*. Jewish History Publishing Company, 1912.

Wiese, Leopold von, *Systematic Sociology*, adapted and amplified by Howard Becker. Wiley, 1932.

Will, Allen S., *Life of Cardinal Gibbons*, 2 vols. Dutton, 1922.

Williams, George H., Waldo Beach, and H. Richard Niebuhr, "Issues Between Catholics and Protestants at Midcentury," *Religion in Life*, Vol. XXIII, No. 2, Spring 1954.

Williams, J. Paul, *What Americans Believe and How They Worship*. Harper, 1952.

Williams, Robin M., Jr., *American Society: A Sociological Interpretation*. Knopf, 1951.

Winter, Gibson, "The Church in Suburban Captivity," *The Christian Century*, September 28, 1955.

Wood, Robert C., *Suburbia: The People and Their Politics*. Houghton Mifflin, 1959.

Wright, G. Ernest, *The Challenge of Israel's Faith*. University of Chicago, 1944.

Wynne, John J., *The Great Encyclical Letters of Pope Leo XIII*. Benziger, 1903.

Yale, William Harlan, "Going Down This Street, Lord . . .", *The Reporter*, January 13, 1955.

Yanitelli, Victor R., "A Church-State Anthology: The Work of Father Murray," *Thought*, Vol. XXVII, No. 104, Spring 1952.

Yinger, J. Milton, *Religion in the Struggle for Power*. Duke, 1946.

Zwierlein, Fred J., *The Life and Letters of Bishop McQuaid*, 3 vols. Art Print Shop, Rochester, N.Y., 1925–27.

American Jewish Year Book, ed. by Morris Fine, issued annually by the American Jewish Committee, New York.

Bureau of Research and Survey, *Churches and Church Membership in the United States: An Enumeration and Analysis by Counties, States, and Regions*. Office of Publications and Distribution, National Council of Churches of Christ, 1956–58.

The National Catholic Almanac, ed. by Felician A. Foy, issued annually by St. Anthony's Guild, Paterson, N.J.; distributed by Doubleday and Company.

Official Catholic Directory, published annually by P. J. Kenedy and Sons, New York.

Yearbook of American Churches, ed. by Benson Y. Landis, issued annually by the National Council of the Churches of Christ in the United States of America, New York.

The Catholic Digest, reports of the public opinion survey on religion conducted by Ben Gaffin and Associates.

November 1952: "Do Americans Believe in God?"
December 1952: "Do Americans Go to Church?"

January 1953: "Who Belongs to What Church?"
February 1953: "How Important Religion Is to Americans"
    "What We Think of Each Other"
March 1953: "What Do Americans Think of Heaven and
    Hell?"
May 1953: "What the U.S. Thinks of Life Here and Here-
    after"
June 1953: "Are Catholics Winning the U.S.?"
July 1953: "How Many in the U.S. Believe in the Trinity?"
August 1953: "What We Americans Think of Our Lord"
September 1953: "Do Americans Want Their Children to Re-
    ceive Religious Instruction?"
November 1953: "Americans and Prayer"
December 1953: "How Understanding Are Clergymen?"
February 1954: "The Religious Press"
March 1954: "Is the Church Too Much Concerned About
    Money?"
April 1954: "Personal Happiness and the 'Mixed' Marriage"
May 1954: "What Do Americans Think of the Bible?"

Information Service, issued by the Federal Council of the
    Churches of Christ in America; since 1951, by the National
    Council of the Churches of Christ in the United States of
    America.

May 15, 1948: "Christianity and the Economic Order, No.
    10: Social-Economic Status and Outlook of Religious
    Groups in America"
January 21, 1950: "Some Protestant Churches in Urban
    America"
February 4, 1950: "Some Protestant Churches in Rural
    America"
December 16, 1950: "Catholic Schools in America"
January 13, 1951: "Religious Education Statistics"
March 8, 1952: "Trends of Church Membership in the Larger
    Religious Bodies"
December 20, 1952: "New Church Buildings"
December 27, 1952: "Religious Affiliations of Senators"
    "Basic Religious Beliefs in Great Britain and U.S."
October 24, 1953: "'Businessmen on Their Knees'"
    "Our Children and Religion"
January 9, 1954: "The Number and Incomes of Clergymen"
April 3, 1954: "A New Trust in Religious Leaders"
May 8, 1954: "Religious Books Are Best Sellers"
    "Construction of 'Religious' Buildings"
September 4, 1954: "Chapels and Chaplains in Industry"
October 2, 1954: "Trends in Giving to 14 Religious Bodies"
October 30, 1954: "Observations Concerning 'Religious Con-
    formity'"

December 25, 1954: "Notes on the State of the Churches"

January 8, 1955: "Membership of 19 Religious Bodies, 1929–1952"

April 9, 1955: "Trends in Church Membership, 1916–1952"

December 24, 1955: "Eastern Orthodox Churches in the United States"

January 7, 1956: "The Roman Catholic Church in the U.S."

February 11, 1956: "Jewish Religious Life in America"

November 30, 1957: "Report on American Rabbis"

June 14, 1958: "Social Class and the Churches"

January 3, 1959: "Church-Related Elementary and Secondary Schools in Continental United States"

March 28, 1958: "Two Worlds of Church Life in the United States"

Index